Cause Related Marketing

D1462224

This book is dedicated to David Adkins, my husband, who has humoured me all this time, and to my parents, all my family, godchildren, adopted godchildren and friends. I also dedicate this book to my absent family and friends who are so often in my thoughts. Finally, this book is also dedicated to Nina and Catherine and my colleagues at Business in the Community and to all those people out there who are trying to do something to make the world a better place.

Cause Related Marketing

Who Cares Wins

Sue Adkins

OXFORD AUCKLAND BOSTON JOHANNESBURG MELBOURNE NEW DELHI

Butterworth-Heinemann
Linacre House, Jordan Hill, Oxford OX2 8DP
225 Wildwood Avenue, Woburn, MA 01801-2041
A division of Reed Educational and Professional Publishing Ltd

ℛ A member of the Reed Elsevier plc group

First published 1999

British Library Cataloguing in Publication Data
Adkins, Sue
Cause Related Marketing: Who Cares Wins
1. Marketing – Management
I. Title
658.8

ISBN 0 7506 4481 8

Author's note:
The findings, interpretations and conclusions expressed in this book are entirely
those of the author and should not be attributed in any manner to Business in the
Community.

The author has used all reasonable care to ensure that all statements presented in the
works as facts are true and accurate at the time of going to press and that the work
contains no advice or instruction and nothing should be interpreted as such.

All the royalties after tax and a proportion of the publisher's revenues from the sales
of the first 3000 copies of this book will be donated to Business in the Community.

Composition by Genesis Typesetting, Rochester, Kent
Printed and bound in Great Britain by Biddles Ltd, Guildford and King's Lynn

FOR EVERY TITLE THAT WE PUBLISH, BUTTERWORTH-HEINEMANN
WILL PAY FOR BTCV TO PLANT AND CARE FOR A TREE.

Contents

Foreword by
Sir Dominic Cadbury

In 1995 Business in the Community established the Cause Related Marketing Campaign, founded by Cadbury Schweppes plc and led by Sue Adkins. It was supported by a number of key companies including BT, Cadbury Ltd, Countrywide Porter Novelli, Lever Brothers Ltd, NatWest, Research International (UK) Ltd, TESCO PLC and The Marketing Society, each represented by senior executives. Since then Countrywide Porter Novelli and NatWest have moved on from the campaign, and Barclays Plc, Centrica plc, DIAGEO, GWR Group plc and SmithKline Beecham plc have joined the campaign leadership team.

The objective of the Business in the Community Campaign is to generate awareness and understanding of Cause Related Marketing, promoting a greater quality, extent and excellence of programmes. This clearly reflects the wider mission of Business in the Community to 'inspire business to increase the quality and extent of their contribution to social and economic regeneration by making corporate social responsibility an essential part of business excellence'.

In the first four years the focus has been on defining and scoping Cause Related Marketing; developing the awareness and understanding and beginning to establish Cause Related Marketing as a legitimate part of the marketing, corporate affairs, community affairs and corporate fundraising mix.

It is clear through case study and research evidence that Cause Related Marketing is an effective way of enhancing corporate image, differentiating product and increasing both sales and loyalty.

What we mean by Cause Related Marketing is really nothing more than another aspect of enlightened self-interest whereby we promote our products in conjunction with a good cause, raising money or value for the good cause while at the same time enlisting consumer loyalty and purchase for our own products. As consumer businesses we are all competing for a share of consumers' minds. That competition is becoming more frantic and expensive due to media inflation, audience fragmentation, zapping of commercial breaks and the ever-increasing noise and clutter bearing down on the consumer. We are all therefore looking for new routes to gain consumers' attention.

It is my belief that Cause Related Marketing allows you to contribute to the community while at the same time promoting your own products. I feel that it is increasingly becoming an established part of the marketing programme and marketing activity because the company as a totality understands that it has got to be a positive corporate citizen. But it is very important for companies that are engaged in Cause Related Marketing that they can measure for themselves that benefit because none of this works if you can't measure the benefit for the company as well as the cause.

Cause Related Marketing is an under-utilized strategy which can achieve both business and cause objectives. Get it right and everyone stands to benefit. There is no doubt the opportunity is there. The challenge is to release this potential for the benefit of everyone.

Cause Related Marketing should become a natural part of successful business practice because it is an effective way of enhancing corporate image, differentiating product and increasing both customer loyalty and sales. The challenge is for business, charities and causes to identify the appropriate partnerships, and then plan, implement and communicate them well. Cause Related Marketing is a potentially potent force that can provide benefits for all.

Almost four years ago when we founded the Business in the Community Cause Related Marketing Campaign relatively little was known about Cause Related Marketing. There was no clear definition, poor appreciation and little if any research or evidence as to its potential. Sue Adkins with the support of Business in the Community and the Cause Related Marketing leadership team has in my view been responsible for redressing this situation. She has defined Cause Related Marketing in the UK. She has built the business case for Cause Related Marketing for the benefit of both business and the wider community and has in fact been the leading campaigner in establishing Cause Related Marketing as a legitimate part of the marketing mix. I recommend this book to you and urge you to consider how the potential of Cause Related Marketing can be released for the benefit of your organization and the wider community.

Sir Dominic Cadbury
Chairman, Cadbury Schweppes

Foreword by Tim Mason

Cause Related Marketing is a very effective marketing tool. It is also becoming an increasingly significant contributor in addressing social issues and the needs of charities and causes. Cause Related Marketing works by integrating the core trading objectives and activities of a business with the needs of a particular cause or charity. Indeed, when done well, Cause Related Marketing provides a win for the charity or cause, a win for the consumer and other stakeholders and a win for the business.

Cause Related Marketing makes commercial sense. It can deliver greater benefits per pounds spent than almost anything else a company can do and can achieve a wide range of business, marketing, fundraising and social benefits. These include enhancing reputation and profile; building relationships and loyalty; adding value; demonstrating the organization's values; supporting existing programmes and providing resources. Cause Related Marketing also has the potential to increase sales, volume and income. In addition to these benefits differentiation can be provided as well as the opportunity to engage customers and other stakeholders, internally and externally, not only rationally but also emotionally. But Cause Related Marketing needs to be planned as part of the overall marketing mix if it is to deliver maximum returns.

From a business point of view, organizations need to be clear about the objectives and identify an appropriate cause. The balance of benefits, the communication message and the mechanics of the programme need to be thought through carefully, and for the maximum impact they need to be economically sustainable. Cause Related Marketing is most effective and its potential is more likely to be realized when it is based on a long term strategy and commitment. If it is not, support from the business is likely to fluctuate with business performance. This is clearly precarious for both the business and the cause, and risks failing to achieve the maximum returns for all parties.

An excellent example presented at one of the Business in the Community Cause Related Marketing conferences is the Kellogg's Kids Help Line in Australia. The Kids Help Line was so badly under-funded it was unable to answer the majority of calls. The charity put a proposal to Kellogg's. Its sponsorship provided the funding and, equally importantly, the profile that enabled the Kids Help Line not only to improve its service but also to enlist further support. The impact of this partnership cannot be understated either for the cause or the business. By linking itself with the cause clearly, helping it to be successful in achieving its goal, Kellogg's added layers to its brand.

Another very successful example of Cause Related Marketing is the TESCO Computers for Schools programme. Customers shop with TESCO PLC, collect vouchers, give them to schools, and the schools then choose and receive computers and related equipment. This programme has had a major impact on both sales and image for TESCO PLC. So much so that it has run for eight consecutive years and has led to further involvement in education by TESCO PLC, including teacher training on IT and TESCO SchoolNet 2000. The fusing of corporate and charitable objectives has proven to be both economically sustainable and enormously beneficial for everyone involved.

When TESCO PLC started Computers for Schools, no supermarket retailer in the UK had done anything like it before. Almost without exception, stakeholders from school teachers, government, customers and employees approved and supported the concept. TESCO Computers for Schools had a visibly beneficial effect on the company's corporate profile, has reinforced the philosophy of 'Every Little Helps' and over the long term has positioned TESCO PLC as having a special interest and a care for education.

The philosophy of 'Every Little Helps' on which TESCO PLC is based, is all about extras or added value, for consumers. TESCO Computers for Schools is exactly one such extra. By working hard at 'the little things' that make up supermarket shopping, TESCO PLC can provide a more pleasurable, more efficient customer experience and provide additional benefits to the local community through schools. This is important to retain customer loyalty in a highly competitive retail environment where accurately targeted marketing is crucial.

The marketing spend required to deliver a company's strategic priorities is tightly controlled and can be substantial. Measuring and attributing results for Cause Related Marketing presents the same challenges as most marketing or advertising activities but likewise has the same solutions. Cause Related Marketing is an additional corporate, marketing and community investment tool to be used appropriately. It is not a replacement for corporate charitable giving, for donating time or sponsoring publications. It unleashes new marketing budgets and delivers additional returns. The increasing importance of building customer loyalty, enhancing the brand and providing added value as a differentiator and the benefit that can be gained through Cause Related Marketing, increasingly validates Cause Related Marketing as a core part of the marketing mix.

The benefits of Cause Related Marketing are manifold and extend beyond external perceptions of corporate and brand image and the bottom line of the parties involved. Internally, Cause Related Marketing can deliver staff motivation, team building and business skills development. From the business point of view, support of a charity or cause allows all concerned to develop different relationships with each other and to learn from the partnership. TESCO Computers for Schools, for example, causes and promotes the link between parents, children, schools and stores. It is a very healthy development of the communities in which retailers such as TESCO PLC operate.

The future for Cause Related Marketing is bright. It is a proven part of the marketing mix; it is an effective part of the community investment strategy; it can build the corporate or brand image and bring business values to life; it can motivate employees and build teams. Cause Related Marketing can achieve all this for the business while providing huge benefits for the community and society as a whole. Cause Related Marketing is increasingly being seen as an integral part of marketing and fundraising for business, charities and causes. The challenge is to encourage more organizations to become involved and to ensure that the growth in this area continues to be underpinned by the strong ethical principles necessary for its success. With sound planning and preparation, based on the Business in the Community Cause Related Marketing Guidelines, all of us, as businesses, charities, causes and as individuals, have much to gain from Cause Related Marketing.

Sue Adkins is a great expert in Cause Related Marketing and I commend her book to you. Her enthusiasm for the subject is contagious and with her wonderful team at Business in the Community she has done more to define, identify and expose the benefits of Cause Related Marketing to businesses and causes in the UK than anyone else.

Cause Related Marketing can be a very potent tool for achieving your marketing objectives. It is important that marketing people understand as much about it as sponsorship, advertising, sales promotion, etc., so that they use Cause Related Marketing at the appropriate time.

Tim Mason
Director, TESCO PLC

Endorsements

'Sue Adkins with the support of Business in the Community and the Cause Related Marketing Leadership Team has in my view been responsible for redressing this situation. She has defined Cause Related Marketing in the UK. She has built the business case for Cause Related Marketing for the benefit of both business and the wider community and has in fact been the leading campaigner in establishing Cause Related Marketing as a legitimate part of the marketing mix. I recommend this book to you and urge you to consider how the potential of Cause Related Marketing can be released for the benefit of your organization and the wider community.'

Sir Dominic Cadbury, Chairman, Cadbury Schweppes plc

'Sue Adkins is a great expert of Cause Related Marketing and I commend her book to you. Her enthusiasm for the subject is contagious and with her wonderful team at Business in the Community she has done more to define, identify and expose the benefits of Cause Related Marketing to businesses and causes in the UK than anyone else.'

Tim Mason, Director, TESCO PLC

'This publication is a major contribution to the development of business excellence through Cause Related Marketing. It illustrates the way in which a company can maximise the impact of their marketing strategies, also build the value of their brand whilst at the same time making a positive contribution to the communities on which they depend.'

Julia Cleverdon CBE, Chief Executive, Business in the Community

'This book is essential reading for anyone thinking of undertaking Cause Related Marketing but also for marketers in general who want to keep up with developments in the marketing profession – whether you work for a company or a not-for-profits.'

Sally Shire, Head of Brand Management, Barclays Plc

'Anyone who knows Business in the Community and Sue Adkins in particular will know the enthusiasm and verve they bring to the causes they are promoting. What is also apparent from the book is the huge amount of research they have done and knowledge they have drawn on. Anyone who is interested in how companies and brands market themselves and can build up their affinity and brand equity, and anyone on the charity side who is looking to convince marketers of the benefits of Cause Related Marketing to them, should read the book. It certainly will be on my personal Booker list for next year!'
Ruth McNeil, Deputy Managing Director, Research International (UK) Ltd

'If you care about people and causes, and would like to understand how you (your business) can win by adding something back into the community, this excellent book is a must read.'
Mark Smith, Marketing Director, Cadbury Ltd

'Consumers have changed, they are still promiscuous, picky and petty but now they care. If you want to understand how to develop effective Cause Related Marketing partnerships, read this book.'
Chris McDowall, Director General, Public Relations Consultants Association

'Building, reinforcing and projecting values will be key to the future of brand development and Cause Related Marketing clearly provides a potent force in this. It will be at the heart of marketing strategies of the future. This book, from the leading expert in the field, is a must read for anyone who is considering Cause Related Marketing as a strategic part of their marketing mix.'
John Stubbs, Chief Executive, The Marketing Council and The Chartered Institute of Marketing

'In an environment where there is increased demand for consumer attention and loyalty, Cause Related Marketing provides a powerful option. Not only can Cause Related Marketing build the brand and enhance reputation, but it can make a significant impact on society. Cause Related Marketing is about mutual benefit. This book provides essential information on how to develop sound and sustainable Cause Related Marketing partnerships.'
Stephen Woodward, Chairman External Affairs, The Marketing Society

'Advertising agencies seek to add value to brand communcation on behalf of their clients. There is growing awareness that Cause Related Marketing can contribute effectively to company brand value. This book provides valuable insight and practical examples to enable those considering such a strategy to develop it appropriately and with integrity.'
Nick Phillips, Director General, IPA

About Business in the Community

Business in the Community, set up in 1982, represents over 600 companies who through their membership demonstrate a commitment to continually improving the quality of life in the communities in which they operate.

They are committed to developing their business excellence through making corporate social responsibility a key part of their mainstream business practice. These companies, who are concerned with measuring and reporting their impact on society, in terms of how they recruit, train, purchase and market, know that these are key indicators of the competitiveness of the business – building corporate reputation, developing morale and loyalty within their people and investing in communities in order that business and communities can be successful.

This publication is a major contribution to the development of business excellence through Cause Related Marketing. It illustrates the way in which a company can maximize the impact of their marketing strategies, also build the value of their brand whilst at the same time making a positive contribution to the communities on which they depend.

Julia Cleverdon CBE
Chief Executive, Business in the Community

A definition of Cause Related Marketing

Cause Related Marketing is about using marketing money, techniques and strategies to support worthwhile causes whilst at the same time building the business. It is defined by Business in the Community as 'a commercial activity by which businesses and charities or causes form a partnership with each other to market an image, product or service for mutual benefit'.

It is no more than enlightened self interest. A company promotes its image, product and services in conjunction with a good cause, raising money for the cause whilst at the same time enhancing its reputation, demonstrating its values, enlisting consumer loyalty and purchase of its own products and services.

Acknowledgements

I would like to acknowledge and thank a number of people without whom this book would not have been possible:

- to Sir Dominic Cadbury for his vision, support, wise-counsel, belief in me and excellent chocolate;
- to Julia Cleverdon for her inspiration, energy and commitment;
- to Tim Mason for his drive, enthusiasm, leadership and support.

To Sally Shire, Barclays Plc; Elizabeth Palmer, BT; Neil Makin, Alan Palmer, Lynne Todd and Mark Smith, Cadbury Ltd; Simon Henderson and Simon Waugh, Centrica plc; Gary Haigh, Guinness Great Britain; Simon Cooper, GWR Group plc; John Ballington and Helen Fenwick, Lever Brothers Ltd; Stephen Woodward, The Marketing Society; Peter Hayes, Ruth McNeil and Vicky Mirfin, Research International (UK) Ltd; Graham Neale, SmithKline Beecham plc; Fiona Archer, TESCO PLC; and Jerry Wright, Unilever, for their invaluable support.

To Richard Steckel and Carol Cone who, as experts in the field, have encouraged and supported me from the beginning.

To David Grayson, David Logan, Alan Mitchell, MORI, Jane Nelson, Bob Thacker, Tomorrows Company, and to all those individuals at businesses and charities who have shared their case studies and experience so generously.

To Roger Beale and *The Financial Times* for their kind permission to reproduce the cartoon on the back page.

To Catherine Sermon, whose tireless support, fantastic commitment, good humour and friendship have seen us both through some very long days and nights.

To Nina Kowalska whose wonderful humour, friendship and commitment have kept me going.

To Elaine for giving up so much time to proof read this book.

To Rugg, Oliver, Byrne and Richard for being there.

To my husband David who has contributed so much to me, my life, my work and this book.

Thank you.

Part One

Cause Related Marketing in Context

Chapter 1

Introduction

The 21st century company will be different. Many of Britain's best known companies are already redefining traditional perceptions of the role of the corporation. They are recognising that every customer is part of a community, and that social responsibility is not an optional extra.

The Rt Hon. Tony Blair MP, Prime Minister, 24 February 1998

What do TESCO PLC, Cadbury Schweppes plc, Barclays Plc, BT, Centrica plc, DIAGEO, Lever Brothers Ltd and others all have in common? Answer: they have understood the benefits and have been involved in leading Cause Related Marketing programmes that have reaped benefits for themselves whilst making a significant positive impact on the wider community. They have demonstrated and benefited from the essential win:win:win of Cause Related Marketing.

The proposition I intend to explore is this: if the role of the business is to provide shareholder value added and society value added – in other words stakeholder value added – then as part of this it must have a good corporate reputation. A good corporate reputation influences the price and purchase of stock, and the sale of products and/or services, which therefore enable the business to thrive.

Like building a brand, the building of the corporate reputation is based on the consistent delivery of quality and service over time, but where 'quality' extends to include the values and core ideology of a business.

Reputation is built on the fundamental benefits of a business, product or service and the affinity and perceptions stakeholders hold towards them.

Equally importantly corporate reputation is also founded on stakeholder appreciation of the values and vision on which the business is based. Part of building and reflecting those values and vision will be based on the corporate behaviour or responsibility of the organization in all the markets in which they operate.

In building understanding of and communicating this social responsibility, Cause Related Marketing has a clear and vital role to play. Cause Related Marketing is a highly effective way to build the brand, to reinforce, demonstrate and bring life to corporate values and to make corporate social responsibility and corporate community investment visible. But who cares?

Through the course of the text I will build the case for how Cause Related Marketing contributes to the overall development and enhancement of corporate reputation and illustrate who cares and why. Through guidelines and case studies I illustrate how Cause Related Marketing has or can be adopted as part of the corporate, marketing, community affairs, indeed overall business strategy. I will illustrate how Cause Related Marketing has enabled organizations to win.

In June 1995 when the Cause Related Marketing Campaign at Business in the Community was founded under Sir Dominic Cadbury with me as director, I had a fabulous brief. It was to define Cause Related Marketing, build the business case and to put it on the map in the UK. This interest was based on the idea that Cause Related Marketing could potentially help address the social and economic regeneration of communities whilst at the same time building the business. At the time examples of businesses linking with charities and causes included programmes like the TESCO Computer for Schools programme. In this case, consumers were encouraged to purchase products from TESCO PLC and for every £25 spent customers would receive a voucher which could be collected by participating schools and redeemed for computers and related equipment. This achieved great results for TESCO PLC in terms of sales, customer traffic, brand enhancement and customer loyalty whilst at the same time providing much needed valuable resources for the schools.

Cadbury Strollerthon, one of the events linked to Cadbury Ltd's long-term relationship with Save the Children, was another example of the use of the power of partnerships between business and brands, and a cause. In this case the programme each year motivated on average between 18,000 and 20,000 consumers to action on one day to participate in a sponsored stroll around London to raise funds for Save the Children. Not only were the values of Cadbury Ltd and Cadbury Schweppes plc reinforced, not only was significant PR and excitement generated, not only were tens of thousands of products sampled but in addition an average of over £400,000 was raised for Save the Children and One Small Step each year the event took place.

The question was to understand what was going on, why, what the benefits were to the parties concerned, whether it really did have potential to benefit businesses and charities or causes. If yes, then the challenge and opportunity was to define and scope it, create a focus and to generate awareness and understanding of it, to create a centre of knowledge, advice and information and to promote a greater quality and extent of programmes. Indeed the challenge was to establish Cause Related Marketing as a legitimate marketing, corporate, community investment and fundraising strategy in the UK. This quest fits well into Business in the Community's overall mission which is to 'inspire business to increase the quality and extent of their contribution to social and economic regeneration by making corporate social responsibility an essential part of business excellence'. Clearly one of the many ways in which business can make a contribution to social and economic regeneration is by leveraging all parts of its business, including marketing in support not only of the business but also of the community in which it operates.

Four years on having formed the Cause Related Marketing Campaign at Business in the Community, led by a vital leadership team, Business in the Community has provided the research on the subject in the UK with the *pro bono* support of Research International (UK) Ltd. We have concentrated on building the business case and on encouraging other businesses to consider Cause Related Marketing as a strategic part of their marketing mix. Clearly with Cause Related Marketing being worth 8 per cent of the estimated $7.6 billion sponsorship market in the USA[1], the potential for growth and benefit both for business and the wider community in the UK is significant. But it is essential that Cause Related Marketing is clearly understood, appreciated and developed with the integrity, transparency, sincerity, mutual respect, partnership and mutual benefit it requires.

To protect the integrity of the concept and at the same time to provide guidance on the way towards developing effective Cause Related Marketing, under the auspices of the Business in the Community Cause Related Marketing Campaign, I wrote the first ever Cause Related Marketing Guidelines. These were developed following an intense period of discussion and consultation with consumers, charity and business practitioners, agencies and representative bodies. These Business in the Community Cause Related Marketing Guidelines, together with the Business in the Community original research, contribute much to the framework of this book.

Cause Related Marketing knows no boundaries in terms of industry, market or cause sector, in terms of continent or cultures; Cause Related Marketing has proven itself to have a valid and important part to play in the development of business and in the contribution towards the wider community in addressing key social issues, be it through specific charities or causes.

Before going into the detail of what Cause Related Marketing is, how it works, why it works, what the opportunities and threats are and what the future might hold, it is important to set Cause Related Marketing in context.

Cause Related Marketing is not the panacea for all ills, nor is it a fig leaf to hide the inadequacies of a product, brand, service or organization; it is not the cure all. Neither do I believe that Cause Related Marketing is the threat to traditional forms of philanthropy that some consider it might be. Cause Related Marketing is a concept whose time has come. Cause Related Marketing provides an additional tool for marketing, corporate and community affairs and fundraisers alike, in partnership, to achieve their mutual objectives for the benefit of all.

In the last few years the interest in the concept of corporate social responsibility has grown and received increasing attention, with leading companies developing sophisticated approaches. At the same time marketing techniques have been refined and new concepts developed whilst corporate community investment and Cause Related Marketing have also developed. Cause Related Marketing demonstrates and indeed enhances corporate values and reputation and much more besides, and this is increasingly being appreciated by the chief executive, corporate affairs, marketing and fundraising departments.

In the marketing and fundraising world there has been a quest for new and more effective ways of engaging the various target audiences or stakeholders. Consumers are increasingly sophisticated and cynical and have growing expectations of business. They expect compliance, honesty and ethical trading standards.

> People in the UK trust a baked bean manufacturer more than the police, have greater faith in the makers of corn flakes than in the Church, and more confidence in a high street retailer than in Parliament[2].

Consumers also expect more individualized messages from the organizations with which they do business, from whom they purchase goods and services and to whom they donate their time, money and effort. This has precipitated the growth and focus on relationship marketing, on building loyalty and sustainable relationships with stakeholders. Price of media and reliability of audiences has further fuelled the trend towards one to one marketing where connecting with the whole person and not just the 'consumer' part is key; hence lifestyle marketing and the importance of understanding individuals' many and varied interests.

In line with these trends and expectations and with the creation and development of new and increasingly targeted marketing and fundraising techniques, interest and incidence of Cause Related Marketing programmes both in the UK, USA and elsewhere has developed.

The social, political and economic changes evident around the world with the universal drawing back of the state in its ability to fund welfare for all, demands increasing responsibility, flexibility, speed, and innovation from business. This is led by growing consumer expectations of business generally. It is also fuelled by consumers' expectations of more personalized messages and understanding of their needs; and indeed with what could be termed increased consumer compassion.

Through the course of this text, I hope to illustrate why I believe the time has come for Cause Related Marketing; how it fits into our current world of the global village, downsizing and re-engineering. A world in which the customer is king and is looking beyond the issues of price and quality. Price, parity and quality are increasingly taken for granted, and therefore there is an ever growing tendency for consumers to expect more and to want to understand the values behind the corporate brand or product .

In today's environment where the vast majority of consumers have access to information at the touch of a button, to take action against a company or organization which the consumer feels is behaving in an unacceptable way, is increasingly acceptable and seen as appropriate for people of all ages; not just the 18–35 year olds but the 60 plus too. I hope to illustrate why and how, given this background, Cause Related Marketing fits, provided of course it is planned, developed, implemented and communicated appropriately.

Drawing on the Business in the Community Cause Related Marketing research conducted by Research International (UK) Ltd and on other evidence, I will illustrate not only the different perspectives of the business, the charity or cause and the consumer but also highlight the key issues in terms of programme development, balance, implementation, communication and evaluation, illustrating many of the points through case studies.

Finally I will provide my thoughts on what the future might hold for Cause Related Marketing, for business, for charity and causes and for the wider community, supported by views from practitioners and opinion formers from around the world representing many different stakeholder groups.

There is simply not space in the remit of this book to discuss the global implications of Cause Related Marketing. If Nambarrie, a 35 person tea company in Northern Ireland, can have such a dramatic impact on the community, then simple multiplication demonstrates that multi-billion pound multi-national corporations could quite literally change the world.

Imagine what a continent wide education campaign communicated on the packaging of everyday consumables could do to address the causes of avoidable human catastrophes such as the horrifically high infant mortality rates in some of the developing countries. Cause Related Marketing would not have such a clear body of evidence or profile in the UK were it not for the vision of Julia Cleverdon CBE, Chief Executive at Business in the Community, or Sir Dominic Cadbury, Chairman of Cadbury Schweppes plc, together with TESCO PLC and BT, Barclays Plc, Cadbury Ltd, Centrica plc, DIAGEO, Lever Brothers Ltd, Research International (UK) Ltd, The Marketing Society, SmithKline Beecham plc, and GWR Group plc who together represent the Business in the Community Cause Related Marketing leadership team of the campaign.

Were it not for this group of individuals and businesses and indeed others who have supported our work and shared their insights and experience, we would not be on the brink of seeing some fantastic new Cause Related Marketing partnerships nor be in the position where they were being discussed or considered. Indeed individual consultants, new agencies and divisions of agencies would not have the level of research and information nor perhaps the confidence to establish a Cause Related Marketing focus were it not for the work of Business in the Community and its Cause Related Marketing Campaign. Charities, causes and the wider community perhaps would not be on the edge of a new dawn of constructing creative, positive and exciting partnerships of this type with business for the benefit of all, were it not for this group. We all therefore owe a debt of gratitude for their vision and commitment.

Throughout the book key themes and principles recur. When considering Cause Related Marketing, the key principles that should be considered at all times are integrity, transparency, sincerity, mutual respect, partnership and mutual benefit. Keeping these principles in the forefront of development of Cause Related Marketing partnerships, it is likely that these relationships will tend towards excellent partnerships.

As HRH the Prince of Wales wrote in the foreword of the Business in the Community Cause Related Marketing Guidelines:

> Business in partnership with charities and causes can play a vital role in the regeneration of communities. Cause Related Marketing is an exciting concept where both business and good causes can benefit. It also attracts new sources of funds, resources and support. I am sure that it will be one of the key developments in marketing for organisations in the future . . . I do hope, if you have not already done so, that you will consider what part Cause Related Marketing could play within your overall marketing and fundraising strategies.
>
> **HRH The Prince of Wales, July 1998[3]**

Notes

1 IEG Sponsorship Report (December 1998).
2 Henley Centre, 'Planning for Social Change' (1997/8).
3 The Cause Related Marketing Guidelines – Towards Excellence (1998), Business in the Community.

Chapter 2

Cause Related Marketing defined

The concept of a business linking with a charity or cause for the benefit of itself as well as addressing a particular social issue, is not a new idea.

In the 1890s for instance, William Hesketh Lever introduced gift schemes from America. The first time the programme was run, it was adapted so that it was more than a simple promotion. A £2000 prize was on offer, but it was not won by consumers participating in the scheme themselves, but instead participants were asked to vote for charities by sending in tokens from Sunlight cartons. The money was then distributed amongst these charities in proportion to the consumers' votes. Not only did the charities gain additional funds and the business benefit, but the consumer also benefited from the halo effect in participating in such a worthy scheme and through being eligible for minor prizes too.

An article in the 19 October 1889 edition of *The Illustrated London News* highlights another early example of a commercial link between a business, namely Sunlight soap, and a cause, The Royal National Lifeboat Institution. A sea rescue was reported by Sunlight Number 1, a life boat which was a gift to the RNLI as a result of a Sunlight soap competition in 1887.

Although this was not referred to as Cause Related Marketing at this time, these early examples demonstrated the commercial link between a charity and a business for mutual benefit. They also illustrate core components of today's effective Cause Related Marketing programmes, namely a win for the business, a win for the cause or charity and a win for the consumer.

Cause Related Marketing has been and is referred to by many names. These include social marketing, charity marketing, corporate and or strategic philanthropy, social investment, social marketing, responsible marketing, affinity marketing, public purpose marketing, passion marketing^{SM}, passion branding, cause branding, sponsorship, sales promotion, PR and indeed simply marketing.

Cause Related Marketing is just that. Marketing to its full extent including advertising, sales promotion, public relations, direct marketing, sponsorship, etc., related to a cause. 'Causes' include good causes, charities and other not for profit organizations. Together they cover a whole wealth of issues encompassing anything from, for example, health, homelessness, diversity and environmental issues through to animal welfare, the arts and education with every good cause in between. The range of causes and charities is vast; the strategies, techniques and activities that fall within the scope of marketing are enormous, therefore the types and methods of Cause Related Marketing are equally potentially extensive.

Some interpretations of Cause Related Marketing emphasize a transaction based donation to a non-profit organization, that is a sales promotion type approach where a percentage of the product price is donated to a cause or charity when triggered by a purchase. In my view this type of interpretation is too narrow. It focuses only on one aspect of Cause Related Marketing; it is equivalent to describing marketing as only sales promotion. Sponsorship, advertising, direct mail and all the other aspects of the marketing mix potentially constitute a form or component part of Cause Related Marketing; Cause Related Marketing is not constrained to purely sales promotion. Despite the many definitions of Cause Related Marketing, however, there are common threads: each describes a commercial relationship between a business and a charity or cause, where each partner has something clear to gain from the relationship. What seems to differ in the interpretation is the immediacy of the impact on the bottom line. In a sales promotion type approach which tends to be tactical, the benefit is faster to see than for instance using Cause Related Marketing strategically for brand building. Ultimately both approaches however fall within the marketing spectrum; both ultimately have an impact on the bottom line and when linked to a cause, both are examples of Cause Related Marketing.

Chapter 3

How Cause Related Marketing has developed

In 1995, at the start of the Cause Related Marketing Campaign at Business in the Community, I defined Cause Related Marketing as 'a commercial activity by which a business with a product, service or image to market builds a relationship with a cause or a number of causes for mutual benefit'. This definition has been taken up and widely used in the UK and abroad.

One of the challenges in understanding Cause Related Marketing is to appreciate that Cause Related Marketing is neither the unique tool or property of either the business nor the charity or cause. Cause Related Marketing is a tool equally available to both; it can be initiated by either and is about partnership and mutual benefit. To give this mutuality and joint ownership of the opportunity greater emphasis, we have refined the original Business in the Community definition. The definition of Cause Related Marketing we now use is that Cause Related Marketing is 'a commercial activity by which businesses and charities or causes form a partnership with each other to market an image, product or service for mutual benefit'.

The critical words within the definition are **commercial, partnership** or relationship and **mutual benefit**. Whatever Cause Related Marketing is, it is certainly not philanthropy nor is it altruism. Parties, be they business, charities or causes, enter a Cause Related Marketing relationship in order to meet their objectives and to receive a return on their investment, where that investment may be in cash, time or other resource or combination of all three (see Figure 3.1).

Cause Related Marketing provides commercial advantage for all parties involved, where commercial applies equally to a charity, cause or business. It is a key reason why partners come together from the outset. All partners have

Figure 3.1 Cause Related Marketing: The Continuum

objectives they wish to achieve whether they concern brand or image enhancement, increased customer traffic or PR or whether they be about increasing income and resources. Each of these objectives are of course equally relevant to a charity, cause or business. Cause Related Marketing is about a win:win:win scenario where the charity or cause and business win and indeed where the benefits also extend to consumers and other stakeholders.

Cause Related Marketing programmes are based on partnership, that is a relationship of equal balance over time where each side appreciates the contribution, strengths and weaknesses of the other. Neither side has greater weight, value or importance in the equation and integrity, sincerity, transparency, mutual respect, partnership and mutual benefit form the foundation[1].

Mutual benefit is the essence of the partnership and the ultimate goal or objective of Cause Related Marketing relationship. That is all parties involved strive to achieve their mutually agreed objectives with neither party gaining at the expense of the other.

Whatever Cause Related Marketing is, it is certainly not philanthropy nor altruism: it's good business, and it's good business for charities and businesses. As already mentioned, parties enter a Cause Related Marketing relationship in order to meet their objectives and receive a return on their investment. The objectives may not be directly linked to sales and/or financial gain in the short term, but ultimately there will be an impact on the bottom line.

There should be no question that in the end, the Cause Related Marketing relationship is entered into because both parties have something to gain. These gains can take a number of forms including making the organization, brand, product or service better known, stronger, healthier and more successful. Some organizations have raised the question of whether or not it is exploitative or manipulative to have very clear focused objectives for a Cause Related Marketing relationship. The research amongst consumers clearly indicates that this is not the case and is clearly demonstrated by, amongst other studies, the results of Business in the Community's Game Plan research published in 1997.

Key findings of the Business in the Community Game Plan[2] research indicated that consumers continue to view Cause Related Marketing as a positive approach which offers another means by which business and consumers can support charities or causes. The Game Plan findings also provide a word of caution however:

> Although able to appreciate that Cause Related Marketing works for the mutual benefit of both business and the charity or cause, consumers are quick to criticize any perceived imbalance in the relationship.[2]

Cause Related Marketing can take many forms. As has been indicated it is often associated with sales promotion techniques where product purchase leads to a donation to a charity or cause, but this is just one of many types of Cause Related Marketing. Cause Related Marketing has been and can be demonstrated in many other ways. This can include business supported charity or cause advertising, sponsorship, PR and direct marketing. Marketing is the operative word. Where the link with the charity or cause has been inspired in order to support the marketing of the business, whilst at the same time benefiting the charity or cause, this is Cause Related Marketing.

> The future lies not in using Cause Related Marketing to sell more product through a link with a cause but in social marketing – using the power of marketing to tackle social issues directly.

Mike Tuffrey, Editor, *Community Affairs Briefing*

The definition and appreciation of what Cause Related Marketing is, centres on understanding the objective and promotion of the activity or programme. Whether or not Cause Related Marketing programmes develop out of the marketing, community affairs or the corporate affairs department, indeed the technical services department, or in a charity's case from the covenants and legacies divisions for instance, is irrelevant. It is not where the inspiration, development or management originates that matters, but rather what the programme or partnership aims to achieve that counts, both fundamentally and in terms of definition.

This may sound trite but it describes exactly what Cause Related Marketing is about. It is surprising and somewhat depressing when one hears from organizations that a particular programme is not Cause Related Marketing because it does not come from or is not led by the marketing department, despite the fact that the activity has been developed to market an image, product or service for the mutual benefit of a charity or cause and business. Cause Related Marketing is not about where you are coming from, it's about where you are going to. Frankly of course it is irrelevant what you call it, what matters is that the ultimate result provides mutual benefit to the business, charity or cause and makes a real positive difference to the wider community.

History of Cause Related Marketing

Cause Related Marketing has been in existence for decades, indeed centuries, as the early Lever example indicates. The recent interest in Cause Related Marketing is generally argued to stem from American Express, who apparently coined the phrase in 1983.

Following various pilot schemes in 1981[3], American Express developed a campaign which donated funds to a number of different non-profit organizations as part of the San Francisco Arts Festival. Essentially every time someone used an American Express Card in the area, a 2 cent donation was triggered and each time new members applied for a card a larger contribution was made.

The marketing goals that American Express had for this programme were apparently exceeded. Card usage was reported as having increased significantly and relationships between American Express and their merchants also improved as a result of the promotion. From the charity's point of view, despite being a short-term campaign, $108,000 was raised, making a significant contribution to their work.

Jerry Welsh, a senior vice president of the company at the time, who masterminded these campaigns, was reported to have explained that the campaign was designed to encourage use of the card not just for business and holidays, but also for more day to day living. 'By giving people a local cause to rally around ... we hoped to spark cardmembers into using the Card for local purchases. We're giving away money, but we're doing it in a way that builds business.'[3]

American Express saw the potential of this form of marketing for achieving their commercial objectives whilst at the same time meeting the objectives of the non-profit or community partner, and they continued to use this approach. Between 1981 and 1984 American Express supported more than 45 causes. From this relatively modest but positive beginning, American Express finally applied the concept nationally in 1983 using it as the mechanic to raise funds to support the Restoration of the Statue of Liberty project. This is generally regarded as the start of the recent interest in what has become known as Cause Related Marketing.

> At American Express we were looking for new ways to help, particularly given the cutbacks in both private and public funding. The use of marketing dollars to both support worthwhile causes and build business could provide worthy non-profit organizations with a much needed source of funding in the future.
>
> **James D. Robinson III, Chairman, American Express**

> Two years ago when we first tested Cause Related Marketing we weren't sure if it would be a way to help business or just an interesting formula for giving money away.

It's both. After successful promotions for more than 30 worthy causes, we now know we can 'do well by doing good'.

Louis V. Gerstner Jr
Chairman, American Express Travel Related Services[4]

As with their previous programmes, the concept and the link with the Restoration of the Statue of Liberty project was straightforward, supported by approximately $4 million spend in support of the campaign including print, radio and TV advertising. Existing customers were encouraged to use their American Express card. Each time they did so, a 1 cent donation was made to the Restoration of the Statue of Liberty fund. New customers were encouraged to apply for an American Express card and participate. For every new American Express card account approved, a $1 donation would be made to the fund. American Express also made donations on purchases of American Express Travellers Cheques and on travel packages, excluding airfares made at an American Express vacation store.

In the course of this three month promotion, from September to December 1983, it was reported that over $1.7 million was raised for the Restoration of the Statue of Liberty; use of American Express cards rose by 28 per cent in just the first month of the promotion compared to the previous year and new card applications increased by 45 per cent[5].

Since then, American Express has run over 90 programmes in 17 different countries with one of its most recent programmes being Charge Against Hunger. Charge Against Hunger is a partnership with Share Our Strength (SOS), a charity which focuses on relieving hunger in the USA. This relationship began in 1988 and developed from the sponsorship of Taste of the Nation, the biggest food and wine tasting event in the USA, where the proceeds went to SOS, and saw the creation of the Charge Against Hunger Campaign. Using a variety mechanics, including a donation being triggered through the use or application of an American Express card, American Express in partnership with their existing and potential card users, customers, chefs and restaurateurs raised over $21 million for the cause between 1993 and 1996[6].

This has made a significant financial contribution to Share Our Strength, together with the benefits of awareness of Share Our Strength's name and mission through significant advertising, and promotional and employee support. As Bill Shore, Founder of Share Our Strength, wrote[7]:

American Express and Charge Against Hunger transformed Share Our Strength . . . Their contacts in the corporate world continue to help us expand in new directions. What began as a simple event sponsorship grew into an unprecedented national commitment that ultimately enabled Share Our Strength to build relationships with new partners ranging from Universal Studios and Northwest Airlines to K-Mart and This end up.

For American Express the benefits have been similarly multi-faceted.

Not only did American Express see benefits in terms of card usage and new card applications, but relationships with the chefs and restaurateurs who represent a vital link in the market chain developed, as did employee motivation. This relationship has therefore seen a win for the business, a win for employees, a win for the charity and cause, a win for the customers and restaurateurs, all of whom are also heroes.

Notes

1 The Cause Related Marketing Guidelines – Towards Excellence (1998), Business in the Community.
2 The Game Plan (1997), Business in the Community qualitative consumer research into Cause Related Marketing conducted by Research International (UK) Ltd.
3 Mescon, T.S. and Tilson, D.J. (1987) Corporate Philanthropy: A Strategic Approach to the Bottom-Line, *California Management Review,* **XXIX**, Number 2, Winter.
4 American Express Press Release, 5 October 1983.
5 Kotler, P. and Andreasen, A (1996) *Marketing for Non Profit Organisations,* Prentice Hall.
6 Share Our Strength Website, 1 July 1999.
7 Shore, B. (1995) *Revolution of the Heart,* Riverhead Books, New York.

Chapter 4

Cause Related Marketing in the context of corporate social responsibility

As the welfare state retreats . . . brands migrate into areas once reserved solely for public provision . . .others loom large in our lives simply because, like governments, they have the power, resources or technologies to shape our collective destinies[1].

Alan Mitchell, Freelance Journalist

Corporate social responsibility is defined as 'recognizing that companies have a responsibility to a range of stakeholder groups which include; customers, employees, suppliers, shareholders, the political arena, the broader community, the environment'. Corporate social responsibility is also referred to as corporate citizenship which is not just community involvement and corporate philanthropy, but 'is the totality of a company's impact on society at home and abroad through stakeholders such as employees, investors and business partners.'[2]

Since the collapse of the Soviet Union, the process of deregulation, trade liberalization and the internationalizing of markets has been rapid. With the drawing back of government funding which can be seen around the world, a gap is developing between society's needs and the government or state's ability to provide and fund them. In such an environment, companies have become an increasingly powerful force within society. With global mergers and acquisitions this economic power is enormous. The revenue of some companies far exceeds the GDP of many nations. As Charles Handy wrote:

'Draw up a list of the world's largest economies in 1997 and 50 will turn out to be corporations. General Motors' sales revenues will roughly equal the combined GNP of Tanzania, Ethiopia, Nepal, Nigeria, Kenya and Pakistan. In another list of the world's totalitarian and centrally managed economies, Cuba, in 73rd place, will find 71 corporations above it.'[3]

As David Logan argued[4] 'Multinational companies bestride the globe, their power and reach increased as never before in this post-communist era of economic and cultural globalization. Meanwhile the power of the nation state has suffered a relative decline.'

With such incredible economic power and influence in society, business has a profound influence on the lives of individuals and communities around the world. With this role comes responsibilities. The appreciation and fusion of these roles and responsibilities can have significant benefits to the business as well as the wider community. It is or can be a virtuous circle.

As Jerry Wright, Senior Strategist, Unilever argues:

Large corporations play an ever increasing role in the global economy and so have a greater impact on global society. People in their dual role as consumers and citizens will expect companies to use their power and influence wisely and to meet their needs more effectively.

Cause Related Marketing is one part of the portfolio of ways that companies can use/respond to these demands, enabling the companies to contribute to the development of the societies in which they operate, as well as enabling them to build long-term benefits for brands.

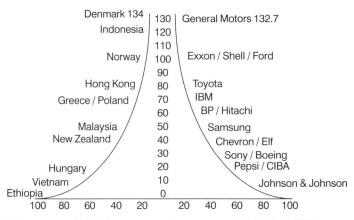

Figure 4.1 The power of global companies (countries ranked by GDP ($b), companies by revenue ($b)). GDP figures: *World in Figures 1995*, The Economist; company revenues: *Fortune* magazine, 26 July 1996. *Source:* David Logan, The Corporate Citizenship Company

Business and the wider community are interdependent. The strength or weakness of the one fundamentally effects the other. Put simply, 'you can't have a healthy high street without a healthy back street'; business and the wider community are locked together in a shared destiny. This is the core philosophy of Business in the Community and is a concept that many others support and promote. It was a key plank of the Royal Society for the Encouragement of Arts Manufacturers and Commerce (RSA) Inquiry which published a report in 1995 following two years of research into 'Tomorrow's Company'.[5] This report develops the idea of an 'inclusive' approach to business, believing that it is only by giving due weight to the interests of all key stakeholders, that shareholders' continuing value can be assured.

> The nature of competition is changing as the interdependence increases between companies and the community. In order to be internationally competitive the company requires a supportive operating environment. The responsibility for maintaining this is shared between business, government and other partners who therefore need to develop a shared vision and a common agenda. Failure to do so will have a serious effect on the competitiveness of companies.[5]

The idea that business is about **either** satisfying the shareholders **or** alternatively these stakeholders, misses the point. The fates of both are intertwined and therefore policies and strategies should and will be increasingly **inclusive** of customers, suppliers, employees, investors an the community, rather than exclusive. As concluded by the Tomorrow's Company report, to focus exclusively on any one stakeholder will not lead to sustainable competitive performance.

> The companies which will sustain competitive success in the future are those which focus less exclusively on shareholders and on financial measures of success – and instead include all their stakeholder relationships, and a broader range of measurements, in the way they think and talk about their purpose and performance.[5]

Mark Goyder, Director of Tomorrow's Company report team, illustrates these points well through a story he tells regarding a presentation by Polaroid to a group of American investors and managers. The presentation described the systematic way in which Polaroid had set about cleaning up the pollution of Boston Sound, ahead of the deadlines set by the regulatory authorities. One or two of the investors present were amazed that the company could justify spending shareholders' money on doing something over and above the legally required minimum. This precipitated a lively debate about the significance for shareholders of the company's licence to operate. As Mark Goyder says, two years later it was interesting to note that Polaroid was one of the highest scoring companies in a survey by ICF Kaiser. The study looked at 327 of the largest US public companies and concluded that the introduction of environmental programmes, and their communication to the investment community, reduced share price volatility and could make their shareholders up to 5 per cent better off as a result.

The notion of interdependency between business and the wider community and of the significant bottom line benefits of corporate social responsibility and indeed going beyond compliance are clearly highlighted through this anecdote. And these trends and expectations are international. Senator Bill Bradley extended and illustrated this thought well.

> What (people) fail to see is that the government and the market are not enough to make a civilization. There must be a healthy robust civic sector, a space in which the bonds of community can flourish. Government and the market are similar to two legs on a three legged stool. Without the third leg of civil society, the stool is not stable and cannot provide support for a vital (society).[6]

A study[7] carried out amongst potential business leaders of tomorrow by AIESEC (the International Association of Students in Economics and Management) and The Prince of Wales Business Leaders Forum provides further evidence of the importance of corporate social responsibility to employee commitment and morale. Highlights from the report indicated that:

- 50 per cent of respondents felt that companies have the greatest responsibility to customers;
- 24 per cent ranked employees as a company's most important stakeholder group;
- 13 per cent ranked shareholders as the most important group.[7]

Business is increasingly recognizing its social responsibilities. George Bull, as Group Chief Executive of Grand Metropolitan prior to its merger with Guinness Worldwide to form DIAGEO, said:

> Increasingly, business people are recognising that their prosperity is directly linked to the prosperity of the whole community. The community is the source of their customers, employees, their suppliers and, with the wider spread of share ownership, their investors.

Governments are in retreat and yet there is little reduction in societies' needs. Business, if it is to continue to be successful in whatever market it is operating, has to invest in the communities in which it operates, from which it draws its resources, be they mineral, vegetable or human, and from the communities in which it hopes to market its products. Quite simply if the business does not have the staff with the requisite skills and resources to produce the goods; if the component parts are not up to standard; if the market to which the business hopes to sell its product is not able to purchase or use that product or service then eventually that business market will disappear as will that business. Chasing new markets around the world, homing in on particular niche markets as existing markets slow down or fold, fails to address the fundamental issues. Ultimately business and the wider community are interlinked. The investment of one in the other and the partnership and investment between the two therefore make sound business sense.

The role, purpose and impacts of business are changing. The argument that business exists solely to produce shareholder value is eroding and developing. As James Collins and Jerry Porras highlight in their book, which studied the common features of visionary companies:

> Contrary to business school doctrine, we did not find 'maximizing shareholder wealth' or 'profit maximization' as the dominant driving force or primary objective through the history of most of the visionary companies.[8]

The conclusion they reached was that 'Profitability is a necessary condition for existence and a means to more important ends, but it is not the end itself for many of the visionary companies. Profit is like oxygen, food, water and blood for the body; they are not the point of life but without them, there is no life.'[8]

The research by Collins and Porras demonstrates that visionary companies that enjoy lasting success have vision which embodies the core ideology of an organization which in turn consists of two distinct aspects: core values and core purposes.

> Paradoxically, the visionary companies make more money than the more purely profit driven comparison companies.[8]

For many of these visionary companies, corporate social responsibility is a core value.

This is further supported by the Tomorrow's Company report which argued that tomorrow's successful companies would be those that concentrated on the intangibles of business rather than those that were purely technically innovative and price competitive.

> If there's one overriding lesson from our experience, I think it's that there are indeed great rewards for organizations that pay as much attention to the engineering going on in the so-called 'soft' side of their business as the 'hard' side.
>
> **Bob Lutz, President, Chrysler Corporation**[9]

Corporate social responsibility is part of that equation. It enables an organization to build loyalty amongst the shareholders and the city; develop strong global partnerships and relationships with government and other institutions and opinion formers; enter new markets more easily; generate positive publicity; act as a market leader whilst at the same time storing up a bank of goodwill which can be drawn upon for the benefit of the doubt in times of need. Indeed, managed well, corporate social responsibility has a positive impact on the full matrix of stakeholders. Conversely an absence of corporate social responsibility will have a significant detrimental impact on an organization's reputation.

> Community contribution, and (crucially) its communication, give companies a competitive edge. Communication should be stressed, because the public generally has little knowledge of what individual companies do – only one in three can think of a single company that makes a community contribution, and no single company is mentioned by more than 12%. When we show people the range of activities companies already undertake they tend to be stunned and impressed.[10]

> **Stewart Lewis, Director, MORI**

Cause Related Marketing is one very high profile and positive way of demonstrating, communicating and leveraging this message.

Enhancing Reputation through Communication – BT case study

BT is a company that is leading by example. Since privatization it has made huge strides in improving operational efficiency, investing heavily in technology and boosting customer service, whilst at the same time investing in the communities in which it's operating through a £15 million a year Community Partnership Programme. Like many large organizations however, BT was reluctant to make much of these initiatives. Following a communications review in March 1996 at a time when pressure to beat off competition, forge alliances, adapt to changing consumer trends and fight for room to manoeuvre within the UK's tight regulatory framework was increasing, things began to change. In such an environment 'reputation' was increasingly seen as key element which would differentiate BT from its competitors. BT found from research that although BT are the largest corporate donor in the UK, few people were aware of it. This raises some interesting questions regarding awareness amongst consumers of other organizations contributions too.

Research showed that while people believe they knew about BT, this knowledge was incomplete or inaccurate. When told the facts, audiences were genuinely surprised. Consumers' change to a positive attitude as a result of being made aware of these facts was very apparent. This led to BT developing a new strategy which 'aimed to demonstrate that BT benefits all kinds of people in all kinds of ways'. This was to be achieved by communicating a broad spectrum of new and unexpected facts about BT, from global success to community investment. The overall aim of the strategy was to contribute to the enhancement and development of BT's reputation amongst key stakeholders.

Balance and tone are critical in this type of communication. There is a fine balance to be found between boasting and apologizing. In developing the final execution of the advertising campaign that resulted from this review, BT found that although the strategy was sound, the balance and tone of the communication were vital. This confirmed the findings of a wealth of research including Business in the Community's own Winning Game and Game Plan research which clearly highlighted the consumer desire, indeed demand, for information.

BT's objective was to position itself as an asset in the eyes of UK consumers; to encourage a positive reappraisal of BT and to position BT as a good corporate citizen. The creative development culminated in December 1996 with the launch of ' Always on my mind', a TV and cinema advertisement featuring Elvis Presley's song, informing the public in an emotional and engaging way of what BT did and why. It was supported by a press campaign which aimed to give customers new reasons to evaluate BT. It includes 'Winston's Wish', a press treatment focusing on helping adults communicate with bereaved children in ways that children understand. Being a communications company, naturally communication had to be at the core of these messages. BT's research had clearly indicated that from the consumer's perspective a real affinity between the cause and the brand was vital. This core thread of communication ran throughout the BT relationships, reinforcing the natural link between BT and their partners which was combined with messages regarding BT's investment in the community. This was made even more effective by providing examples of human stories, bringing real benefit to real people in real communities.

Communicating their corporate social responsibility is benefiting BT whilst at the same time generating further awareness of the causes and issues they invest in. Research has revealed that the campaign has had a significant effect on getting people to reappraise BT.

One in four customers nationally said they were more favourably disposed towards BT as a result of seeing the advertising. High levels of recall were also recorded. The corporate image monitor which historically is relatively static has also shown improvements for BT with key drivers of corporate reputation, such as technological innovation, investing in the community and supporting charities and other causes all improving. BT is clear that continued investment in the communication of their corporate social responsibility is paying dividends.

If communities are to thrive and in turn enable and support the success of businesses, it makes sound business sense for the business to invest in their communities. Communicating this corporate social responsibility and being seen to be actively involved as a responsible corporate citizen also has benefits to reputation which in turn have benefits in terms of stakeholder perceptions of the organization. It is ultimately stakeholder perceptions of an organization which influence their actions and reactions both positively and negatively. Clearly communicating the corporate social responsibility of an organization therefore not only provides business benefits but at the same time, through supporting and enabling communities to thrive, this has benefits for all. Cause Related Marketing is arguably one of the most effective ways of demonstrating corporate social responsibility, by giving life to an organization's values and beliefs and bringing them to the attention of the broadest possible stakeholder groups. As Sir Dominic Cadbury, Chairman of Cadbury Schweppes plc and founder of the Business in the Community Cause Related Marketing Campaign said:

> Cause Related Marketing allows you to contribute to the community while at the same time promoting your own products. I feel that its becoming more and more a normal part of the marketing programme and marketing activity because the company as a totality understands that it's got to be a positive corporate citizen.

Clearly the important point is to ensure stakeholders know about the organization's values and social responsibility. Managed well there is an increasing evidence and support for the notion that being a socially responsible business makes sound commercial sense.

> Corporate responsibility is not a fringe activity. All of us at GrandMet believe business success cannot be defined solely in terms of earnings, growth and the balance sheet. A truly successful company is sensitive to the concerns of all those on whom it depends; investors, employees, customers, trading partners and the countries and communities in which it does business.

> **John B. McGrath, Chief Executive, Grand Metropolitan, now Group Chief Executive, DIAGEO, and George Bull, Chairman, Grand Metropolitan, now Non-Executive Director, DIAGEO**[11]

Notes

1 Mitchell, A. (1999) How brands touch the parts others can't reach, *Marketing Week*, 18 March, p. 22.
2 Logan, D. (1998) 'Corporate Citizenship in a Global Age', lecture at the RSA, 25 March.

3 Handy, C. (1997) Will your company become a democracy? *The World in 1997*

4 Logan, D. (1998) Mapping global corporate citizenship, *Community Affairs Briefing*, Issue 39, April.

5 RSA Inquiry (1995) Tomorrow's Company, The Role of Business in a Changing World.

6 Bradley, B. (1995) New Jersey Senator in a speech to the National Press Club (reported in Shore, B. *Revolution of the Heart*, Riverhead Books, New York, p. 12).

7 Educating tomorrow's global business leaders (1995) report by The Prince of Wales Business Leaders Forum and AIESEC.

8 Collins, J.C. and Porras, J.I. (1977) *Built to Last: Successful Habits of Visionary Companies*, HarperBusiness.

9 Lutz, R. A., President and Chief Operating Officer, Chrysler Corporation, Re-engineering the Corporation for the '90s, The 1994 Christopher Hinton Lecture, Royal Academy of Engineering, p 12. (RSA Inquiry (1995) Tomorrow's Company: The Role of Business in a Changing World, p. 7).

10 Lewis, S. (Director, MORI) (1998) *Does it matter? 1998 Examples of Excellence*, Business in the Community.

11 Grand Metropolitan, Report on Corporate Citizenship 1997.

Chapter 5

Cause Related Marketing in the context of corporate reputation

In the future as increasingly price and technical innovation are eroded and copied at greater speed and therefore no longer endure as the key differentiators, areas such as behaviour, corporate identity, integrity, ethics, and the organization's standing in the community are likely to become central issues for the companies of the future and therefore competitive advantage will be centred on corporate reputation and trust.

The variety of means and speed for transmission of information globally bears no resemblance to the situation 10 years ago.

What can be achieved in the space of a day today[1]

It is estimated that the following are all achieved in the space of one day today:

- a year of US economic output growth achieved in 1830;
- a year of world trade achieved in 1949;
- a year of scientific work undertaken in 1960;
- a year of foreign exchange trading completed in 1979;
- a year's worth of telephone calls in 1983;
- a year's e-mails in 1989.

According to IBM, in 1997 40 million people surfed the Internet. In 1998, 60 million surfed the net. It is anticipated that this will increase 10-fold by the year 2000. The US Department of Commerce in April 1998 reported Internet usage doubling every 100 days. The first report from the DTI Future Unit in the UK shows the time taken to reach 50 million consumers. On the Internet this would take 4 years versus 38 years for radio and 13 years for television.

The information supply doubles every five years[2]:

■ A weekday edition of *The Times* contains more information than the average person was likely to come across in a lifetime during the seventeenth century.
■ A greeting card which plays Happy Christmas, contains more computing power than existed in the entire world before 1950.
■ A Sega Saturn games console has a more powerful processor than the original Cray super computer launched in 1976.

The Information Communications Technology (ICT) revolution means that not only has the speed and access to information increased exponentially but the price of information and good practice can be shared faster and faster, and global benchmarking becomes possible. Businesses will have to manage all parts of their business holistically and ensure that all parts of their organization and indeed their supply chain meet the criteria and values of the parent in all corners of the earth. It also means that businesses will have to differentiate themselves in different ways in the future. This differentiation may be achieved through innovation, and, increasingly, through investment in and communication of reputation through reinforcement and projection of their values and vision, and through building long-term relationships. It is as part of the new business imperative that Cause Related Marketing can make a significant contribution.

In this new reality of fast dramatic change, everyone has to raise their game. Advancing technology means that product development and innovation are more quickly replicated from market to market. As the former Chairman of Ford Motor Company, A. Trotman, explained 'New technologies such as advanced electronics, ultra-light materials, computer-aided design, and a host of others could change cars more radically in the next 10 to 20 years than in the last 100.' If Mercedes Benz developed the technology for in-car air bags, it is interesting to note that virtually all new car models produced today carry air bags as standard. What was value added yesterday is value expected today.

You think you understand the situation, but what you don't understand is that the situation just changed[2].

Corporate reputation is made up of a number of elements including corporate citizenship or corporate social responsibility, and innovation not of itself, but for the sake of the wider community and of investing in the communities in which the organization operates and beyond.

> In a world of proliferating choice where we face a bewildering array of products and services to choose from, stakeholder reputation is becoming an important means of deciding whether to buy those products and services . . . Building a reputation is not about words and fancy value statements communicated via glossy brochures which languish on coffee tables in reception lounges and in the departments of corporate affairs. Reputation with stakeholders is gained by the systematic application of values into normal everyday operations.[3]

As the RSA Inquiry identified very clearly, the world is changing; the dynamics of the marketplace are changing as are the breadth of stakeholders and their needs and expectations.

Good reputation is a vital element in the business success equation. It takes decades to build reputation and only moments to destroy. Price, quality, service and performance are key components that go towards supporting the building of that reputation. Positive interaction with the full range of stakeholders, demonstrating an ethical code of conduct will also positively support that reputation. Failure to appreciate this will hinder the development of that organization.

Internal and external conflicts

In the last few years Shell, like many other multinationals, has faced some very complex dilemmas. We dealt with them to the best of our abilities – we took decisions. In retrospect some of those decisions were mistakes . . .

We were perhaps excessively focused on internal matters and we failed to fully understand the need to provide information to the general public . . .

We were seen as unresponsive and so, to some extent, became targets . . .

We have listened very closely to our customers. We have listened very closely to our government and to our staff. They, after all, were the institutions we had always dealt with.

Of course, we also dealt with environmentalist groups, consumer groups and so-on, but we tended to let the public affairs department deal with them. They were important – but they were not as important as government, industry organizations and so on.

> In essence, we were somewhat slow in understanding that these groups were tending to acquire authority.
>
> We underestimated the extent of these changes – we failed to engage in a serious dialogue with these new groups ...
>
> To-day we have to admit that we have occasionally stumbled – that we have made mistakes, we have not handled some of the new challenges as well as we could have ...
>
> What I am talking about is a series of faulty assessments, of mis-readings of the situation which have led us to take poor management decisions.
>
> Why did they come about?
>
> I think that the fundamental answer lies in our failure to fully recognize the social and technological changes ...
>
> Simply put the institutions of global society are reinvented as technology redefines relationships between individuals and organizations ...
>
> **Cor Herkstroter, Senior Group Director, Shell[4]**

In line with this corporate thinking, in spring 1999, Shell launched a global through the line communications campaign based around the theme of their 1998 report 'Profit and Principles: Is there a Choice?'. The headlines include 'Exploit Or Explore', 'Protect Endangered Species Or Become One' and 'Commodity. Or Community?'.

Brands are a guarantee of a consistent delivery of quality and service. They are not simply product attributes but increasingly a total customer experience. Brands increasingly connect people on a rational and emotional level and in fact some of the world's biggest brands could be defined as experience providers.

> A brand is like any other asset; if it is not well managed it will decrease in value. A well managed brand on the other hand is a great competitive advantage.[5]
>
> **Sally Shire, Head of Brand Management, Barclays Plc**

Nurturing, developing, enhancing and communicating the essence of an organization's corporate reputation is the role of everyone in the organization. Marketing clearly has a lead role to play in the external communication of that reputation and brand and therefore all avenues should be considered, explored and when appropriate employed. These avenues could and should include not only a sound code of corporate social responsibility, clearly and effectively demonstrated, but corporate community investment and Cause Related Marketing strategies should form part of the portfolio.

With the increasing globalization of the economy and the speed of communication, business strategies can have impact and can be seen or heard about literally at the flick of a switch. What one does in the UK will be known about in Australia for instance in a matter of moments. Corporate reputation can be affected both positively and negatively by activities taking place in the furthest corners of the world. The challenge is therefore to ensure a consistency of approach and practice and a clear communications strategy to ensure the benefits and positive impacts of an organization are well understood throughout the markets in which the organization operates or intends to operate.

As Simon Ward, Strategic Affairs Director for Whitbread, said at the Business in the Community Awards for Corporate Community Investment in June in 1998:

> From welcoming new customers to our restaurants to gaining new supply contracts and licensing consents, our reputation as a responsible business has led to measurable benefits for our business.

Consumer expectations of business

One could look for the origin of consumer interest in the ethical behaviour of business by referring to some of the key psychology models. Maslow, through his Hierarchy of Needs, argued that people are not merely controlled by mechanical forces or instinct but that humans strive to reach the highest levels of their capabilities. They seek the frontiers of creativity, and aim to reach the highest levels of consciousness and wisdom. Maslow's Hierarchy of Needs places all the basic needs at the bottom and those needs concerned with man's highest potential at the top. Each level of the pyramid is dependent on the previous level and therefore for instance the person does not feel the second need until the demands of the first have been satisfied.

In applying this model to consumer behaviour one could argue that once the basic needs have been met consumers aspire to the need to belong, brotherhood, self esteem and self actualization. In other words they are looking beyond the functional properties to the emotional values of products and brands.

Alternatively considering Kohlberg's model of levels of moral development Stage 5 (Social Contact) and Stage 6 (Principle Conscience) are the key mindsets driving interest in corporate social responsibility and Cause Related Marketing.

Combine these psychological models with the fact that consumers are increasingly brand literate and socially aware and are focusing less on the tangibles of a product or service, but on the labour to produce it, the renewable resources used to manufacture it, the profit margin and how it is used, and

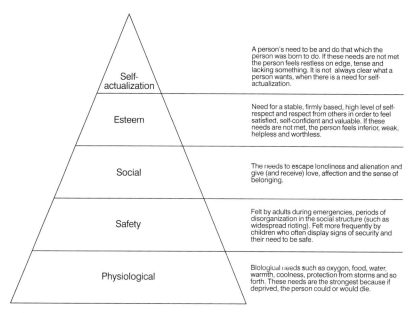

Figure 5.1 Maslow's Hierarchy of Needs. *Source:* Colemand and Hammen, *Contemporary Psychology and Effective Behaviour*

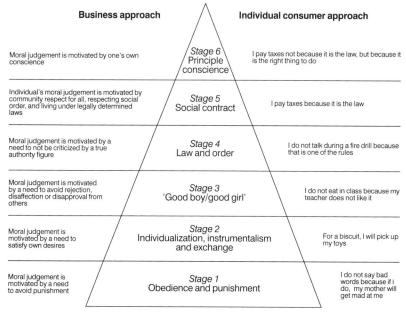

Figure 5.2 Kohlberg's levels of moral development. *Source:* Adapted from a paper by L. Gill and C. Magee, 'Lawrence Kohlberg's Stages of Moral Development', Pepperdine University (taken from the Internet in 1999)

there is a potent and compelling force for business to step up to its responsibilities and affirm its ethical code.

The consumer is concerned about an organization's corporate social responsibility and their perceptions of it or lack of it, that is the corporate reputation, will influence their decisions and actions. MORI research in July/ August 1998 indicated that when forming an opinion about a company 77 per cent of the sample of the adult population said it was very or fairly important for them to understand the activities of corporates in society; 77 per cent of the sample also said the same in terms of making a decision about a product. It is therefore vital for business to make sure that corporate citizenship and corporate social responsibility are well communicated and understood, as they form a critical aspect in the perception and development of a corporate reputation.

Adding value to your values

Cause Related Marketing is about adding value to your values. It is a way of demonstrating the organization's corporate social responsibility and bringing it to the attention of your consumers and other stakeholders.

Organizations spend valuable executive and employee time developing values and mission statements; agonizing over precisely the right words and images that encapsulate and reflect the essence of an organization. They can range from something as elegant as the American Declaration of Independence, to something as simple as Walt Disney's core purpose 'To make people happy'[6].

Whatever the form of the mission statement, it is important to bring the words and vision to life; to demonstrate the values through action, 'to walk the talk' and to ensure that all internal audiences and partners buy into and feel part of that vision, believe it and believe in it. Only then can a business hope to project this externally to all stakeholder groups.

In preparation for a presentation I was to give recently I called a few of the organizations I knew would be present to ask whoever I got through to what their organization's mission statement was. I received some interesting replies; they ranged from 'sorry that is not our department, you need to speak to marketing,' through to a clear explanation that was almost word perfect. The point is that a corporation has to be consistent in the messages both internally and externally with all its stakeholders. An organization has to demonstrate its values by its deeds if it is to be believed by the ever and increasingly scrutinizing and sceptical multitude of stakeholders.

An interesting study conducted by Dragon International in the UK amongst 50 leading brands across drinks, food and household products aimed to test the relationship between the message projected by an organization and the subsequent follow-up. Letters were sent to these various companies asking particular questions. Some were about what the complaints procedure was, some about the ultimate owner of the company, others about pricing policy and advertising whilst other letters asked questions about the environmental policy, community investment and help with a school project. These letters essentially represent the very sort of correspondence any company might receive from its stakeholders during the course of business. Each letter represents an opportunity to reinforce and enhance the consumers' perception of the organization's values and key message. Responses were judged in terms of speed, tone, quality, accuracy and relevance to the question asked or request made and fullness in terms of providing a response beyond what had been expected from the request.

This research essentially provided evidence on whether or not companies were in fact maximizing opportunities to relate positively with stakeholders and enhance their brand reputation. Fifty brands were targeted as part of the exercise and the maximum score any company could receive was 25 points. The results in relation to the community investment requests were as shown in Table 5.1.

Table 5.1 Leveraging reputation building opportunities . . . business response in relation to community investment[7]

Outcome	Number of companies in the category
No replies	21
15 or less points	13
More than 15 points	16

Clearly many opportunities to reinforce the brand message are being missed.

How these values and messages are conveyed and absorbed; how they are demonstrated is important and part of the reinforcement of the corporate brand. As MORI research has shown over time, a key issue for many of those leading organizations with sound corporate social responsibility policies and programmes in place, is to ensure the various stakeholders are aware of these values, policies and programmes and to receive credit for them perhaps in terms of goodwill. MORI research data in September 1998 indicated that despite increasing expectations of companies,

> . . . nearly four in five consumers said knowledge of a company's involvement in this area (corporate social responsibility) is important in their judgement of a company. A third said it is very important. However, two in three of the British public still

believe British industry and commerce are paying insufficient attention to their social responsibilities.[8]

Cause Related Marketing is just one way, and a very public way, of demonstrating those values, and therefore Cause Related Marketing can add value to those values. As John Ballington, Corporate and Consumer Affairs Director, Lever Brothers Ltd, summarized; there is no doubt that Cause Related Marketing can play a major role in building that 'feel good' factor around a brand or a company – it can materially impact on brand value as a result.

Neighbour of choice

Corporate social responsibility, corporate citizenship, values, vision and indeed standing for something are increasingly important differentiators. In an environment where price and quality are increasingly equal and where consumers' demands and expectations of business are ever growing, holistic management of organizations is becoming even more critical.

Overlay this with the appreciation of the shared destiny between business and the wider community and this indicates the potential opportunities and threats in failure to take these factors into account. In the relationship between business and community, business is traditionally perceived as having a greater weight of influence and importance in the equation. With the empowerment of the consumer this can no longer be assumed. Business in the future will be striving to demonstrate its social responsibility in order to develop its 'licence' with consumers and communities. Earning a 'licence to operate' will become increasingly critical in future markets and societies, as it is accepted that the future of successful business depends on a healthy society, peopled with an educated population, skilled labour and with a market with the means to purchase.

A reputation or an association with human, environmental or social abuse, for instance, will count against business in the future; it will no longer be ignored. In today's society if a company is considered antisocial, communities do have the power to block entry and future progress of the company in their markets. Conversely having a positive reputation, as with McDonald's during the Los Angeles' riots in 1992, can lead to community protection of your business; that is the ultimate neighbour of choice.

The need for business therefore to manage all aspects of its activities ensuring at least compliance if not more, is becoming critical. Business will need to strive to be welcomed as a 'neighbour of choice' in the successful thriving communities of the future. This forms the basis of the idea of 'neighbour of choice' – a concept and phrase developed and coined by Ed Burke, former Director at Boston College Centre for Corporate Community Relations.

As much as a business needs to pursue 'Neighbour of Choice Status' so too will communities need to develop strategies of 'Communities of Choice'. They will want to ensure that they are identified as thriving communities with the assets required for the successful development of future businesses. Whilst it is therefore in the business interest to demonstrate their corporate social responsibility and indeed invest in communities in which they operate or wish to operate, it is similarly in the interest of communities to tackle local economic and social issues not just for the sake of the stability of that society but also for the future economics of that community.

Businesses will be striving to demonstrate their corporate social responsibility not only because of the obvious business benefits already discussed but also because they will want to be the first choice business for the most successful communities. In other words businesses want to be welcomed with open arms, receive planning permission speedily and have the pick of the most successful communities in which to establish themselves.

> In the global marketplace, it is societies not economies which compete. You have to consider economic, social, technological and environmental indices in order to understand a community's competitiveness . . .[9]

Good practice: turning community hostility into support

We believe that building relationships with our surrounding communities through sponsorship and participation in community activities is essential to our business. However, establishing long-term relationships and an open dialogue is even more important in times when relationships can be strained. An example of this comes from a recent planning application in which Unipart sought permission to develop a factory on the edge of its headquarters site at Cowley, after the opposition of another community had forced the abandonment of the original site.

Initially, local residents were apprehensive about the plans. Unipart developed an open dialogue with the community to discuss concerns. Literature about the development plans was circulated to the homes of all local residents. A reply card asked for residents' views, and each card was answered with a personal letter. The team also established a set of working meetings with representatives from the Parish Council and other interested groups. Four meetings were held during which aspects of the plan were amended to meet residents' needs. As a result, the planning approval for the new factory was applauded by local residents as well as the business community.

The leader in the local newspaper, *The Oxford Mail*, summarised the experience: 'Unipart and Horspath Parish Council have proved that civilised discussion can make everyone a winner. The village gets its protection, Unipart its factory and the area 200 new jobs. Not bad, eh?'[9]

Notes

1 Unchartered Waters – Chatham House Forum (from Nelson, J. (1998) *Building Competitiveness and Communities*, published in the UK by the Prince of Wales Business Leaders Forum, p. 10).

2 Pritchett, P. (1996) *New Working Habits for a Radically Changing World*, London, Pritchett and Associates Inc.

3 Glen Peters, Head of Future Strategy at PricewaterhouseCoopers.

4 Cor Herkstroter, then Senior Group Director of Royal Dutch/Shell Group of Companies: 'Dealing with contradictory expectations – the dilemmas facing multinationals', Amsterdam, 11 October 1996.

5 Sally Shire, Head of Brand Management, Barclays, in a speech at the Business in the Community Cause Related Marketing Conference, November 1998.

6 Collins, J.C. and Porras, J.I. (1996) Building your Company's Vision, *Harvard Business Review*, September–October, pp. 65–77.

7 Dragon International presentation at Business in the Community Cause Related Marketing seminar 1996.

8 MORI Corporate Social Responsibility study, conducted among 2000 British adults, September 1998.

9 Grayson, D. (1998) Communities and Partnerships, A Business in the Community paper prepared for Committee of Inquiry: Into a New Vision for Business and *The Oxford Mail*.

Chapter 6

Cause Related Marketing in the context of corporate community investment

Your involvement in the communities in which you do business is more than an act of charity. Involvement in the community is about giving better definition to the purposes and practices of business in the modern world.

The Rt Hon. Tony Blair MP, Prime Minister

Corporate community investment is a strategy of sustained corporate investment focusing on an alignment of the business objectives with the social, environmental and economic needs of the community in which it operates with the objectives of promoting its long term corporate interests and to enhance its reputation.

There are many ways in which a business can invest in the communities in which it operates and these have been summarised by Business in the Community as the 7Ps. These 7Ps are illustrated in Table 6.1.

In an effort to bring some rigour into the management and reporting of community investment, Business in the Community developed its Principles of Corporate Community Investment. These represent a framework upon which an organization's Corporate Community Investment programme can be managed and improved. Aligned to the European Foundation for Quality Management Model for Business Excellence, there are nine principles.

Table 6.1 The 7Ps for business involvement in the community

7Ps for leveraging resources	How it works	Example
Power	Power of a business and/ or brand's reputation and networks to encourage others to support and participate	Every charity knows the benefits of the power and influence the name and image of a FTSE 100 company can have. In addition to this, on a consumer level, the power of brands as a 'call to support' can not be underestimated, i.e. Cadbury Strollerthon (see Chapter 16, Case Study 11)
People	Using the potential army of employee volunteers as well as expertise	NatWest UK employee volunteers help in schools – as school governors, as headteacher mentors, and especially through the bank's interactive programme to tackle financial illiteracy
Promotions	Marketing promotions and strategies to leverage corporate support, raise funds and resources and engaging the commitment of others	TESCO Computers for Schools has contributed the equivalent of one computer for every school in England, Scotland and Wales (see Chapter 16, Case Study 1)
Purchasing	Using the purchasing and supply chain	Sainsbury, as the retailer for Comic Relief in 1999, used their purchasing and supply chain to enlist the support of manufacturers in using Cause Related Marketing to support Comic Relief in their stores
Profits	Cash	BT contributed more than £15 million
Product	Gifts in kind	Whitbread have equipped 200 bedrooms in 15 foyers (accommodation/employment projects for young people)
Premises	Donating facilities and premises	BP's former D'Arcy Refinery has been converted into a business incubator

Table 6.2 The Business in the Community Principles of Corporate Community Investment

Principle	Explanation
Leadership	How leaders inspire, develop and facilitate achievement in community investment and create a culture where community investment is an integral part of the organization.
Policy and strategy	How the organization implements its community investment mission and vision through a clear stakeholder focused strategy, supported by relevant policies, plans, objectives, targets and processes.
People	How the organization uses community investment as a tool to manage, develop and release the knowledge and full potential of its people at an individual, team-based and organization-wide level.
Partnerships and resources	How the organization plans and manages its community investment partnerships and internal resources effectively and efficiently.
Processes	How the organization designs, manages and improves its community investment processes in order to satisfy and create value for its stakeholders.
Community partner results	What the organization is achieving in relation to its community partners.
People results	What the organization is achieving in relation to its people.
Society results	What the organization is achieving in relation to the communities in which it operates.
Key performance results	What the organization is achieving in relation to its planned community investment objectives.

Introducing the Business in the Community Principles of Corporate Community Investment, Sir Peter Davis, Group Chief Executive of Prudential Corporation and Chairman of Business in the Community, said: 'The investment of companies in the community in which they operate is vital to the health of society and the competitiveness of the business.'

Corporate community investment is effectively one aspect of corporate social responsibility. In order to be socially responsible a company must invest in the communities in which it operates and that responsibility clearly ranges across all aspects of the business conduct from environmental to employee codes of conduct and products.

There are clearly altruistic and business motives for investing in the communities in which a company operates, and a key question might be which should be the key motivation for a company. In my view and in the view of others, it should be both; it makes sound business sense and provides clear demonstrable benefits to the community.

Hostile take-over bid between two companies

One of the first examples 'caught' by MORI was in 1991, when a battle developed between two major companies. Our survey among MPs at the time showed Company A with an outstanding reputation for social responsibility and Company B with a bad one. Although not the only factor, those reputations were significant in forcing Company B (Hanson) to drop its take-over bid for Company A (ICI).[1]

Stewart Lewis, Director, MORI

As David Logan of Corporate Citizenship International argues, 'Community involvement is a "natural" activity for companies, because companies are incorporated citizens who, like other citizens, have social responsibilities, defined partly by law and partly by custom.'[2]

Caring capitalism, as it has been termed by some, has long been promoted by companies like Ben and Jerry's and The Body Shop and it is increasingly becoming a mainstream business strategy which provides business benefits for all. Cause Related Marketing is a clearly commercial activity providing double benefit, that is benefit to businesses and the wider community. The London Benchmarking Group, a collection of 18 leading companies whose mission is to better define the measure of efficiency and effectiveness of all types of community involvement activity by using benchmark techniques, have developed templates for measuring corporate community investment. Cause Related Marketing is placed within the commercial segment suggesting the relationship between the commercial discipline of Cause Related Marketing and the positive impact it can have on the wider community (see Figure 6.1).

It would seem that to date, in the UK at least, few organizations have achieved effective communications of their corporate social responsibility and corporate community investment with stakeholders. MORI research[3] has found that despite increasing expectations of companies by consumers and opinion leaders, awareness of specific company involvement has not changed over the last four years, with only a third of the public aware of any specific initiative or programme.

As Rosabeth Moss Kanter writes in her book *World Class, Thriving in the Global Economy*:

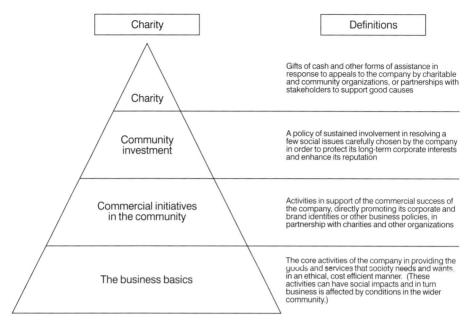

Figure 6.1 A characterization of the company in society. *Source:* The London Benchmarking Group

> The global economy compels a broader conception of community and business leadership in it – greater local engagement whilst recognizing the need of cosmopolitan companies – equated not simply with money, but with involvement activities that contribute to quality of life.

She goes on to note that 'In the global economy, community service has become another set of weapons in the strategic arsenal, more intimately connected with the business mission, more highly integrated with a variety of business functions and sometimes not even local in scope.'[4]

Integration and communication: therein lies a key opportunity. To integrate the social responsibility and community investment strategy across the organization providing benefits to all parts of the business as well as the wider community. It is important to create awareness and understanding internally of the current policies, strategies and attitudes and to define the integrated strategy going forward. That is, it is vital to communicate. These policies and activities must be effectively marketed and communicated both internally and then externally in order to enhance the organization's reputation; demonstrate its values; build positive perceptions, loyalty and relationships amongst stakeholder groups and indeed potentially increase customer traffic and sales. In other words marketing and communication must be used to promote these corporate social responsibility and corporate community investment messages; that is leverage these strategies through Cause Related Marketing. To fail to do so is to miss an opportunity to leverage the return on investment.

The reasons for and the way in which business invests in the wider community clearly fall under the organization's approach to corporate citizenship and corporate social responsibility. It is from this foundation that all the strategy for investment in the community should emanate and it is also these principles on which the marketing strategy and other strategies of the business should be based. The strength of Cause Related Marketing over perhaps corporate community involvement and investment is that it is very clearly visible and therefore can support these programmes and indeed leverage them through the engagement of additional resources and additional skill sets.

As Geoffrey Bush, Group Community Relations Director, DIAGEO commented:

> Cause Related Marketing is usually led by the marketing department with clear commercial objectives but has community value too. Providing the company is open and clear in its motives from the outset, and that the community partner has an equal footing in the partnership, this commercially led approach is not inconsistent with good corporate citizenship. A well planned Cause Related Marketing programme such as the Tanqueray American Aids Rides can attract a new type of customer who is well informed, thoughtful and active and who sees a greater interdependence between business and society.

Over time however, a number of complimentary approaches have developed. Strategic philanthropy, corporate community investment and indeed Cause Related Marketing are at best approaches which are or should be founded on a deep sense of corporate self; on a profound understanding of corporate and/ or brand values.

Notes

1 Stewart Lewis, Director of MORI.
2 David Logan, Corporate Citizenship International, London Benchmarking Group.
3 MORI corporate social responsibility study conducted among 2000 British adults, September 1998.
4 Moss Kanter, R. (1995) *World Class, Thriving in the Global Economy,* Simon & Schuster, New York, p. 191.

Chapter 7

Cause Related Marketing in the context of marketing

Cause Related Marketing can be a highly potent tool for achieving the marketing objectives of a business. It is important therefore that marketers understand as much about Cause Related Marketing and apply as much discipline to it as is used in relation to sponsorship, advertising, sales promotion, public relations and the many other aspects of the marketing mix. As consumers become increasingly demanding of business, as there is greater parity on price and quality, as marketing noise increases and the competition for share of consumers' attention reaches new levels and as the thrust of marketing tends towards loyalty, it will be increasingly important to develop new levels of relationships with stakeholders. Cause Related Marketing provides that opportunity for the emotional as well as rational engagement of stakeholder groups and as such therefore Cause Related Marketing will be key to future marketing strategies.

> Cause Related Marketing will continue to grow in importance as a marketing tool because it embraces consumer trust, providing the opportunity to enrich the lives of many in the community, as well as adding value to the task of sustaining brands.
>
> **Mark Smith, Marketing Director, Cadbury Ltd**

Traditionally it has been argued that providing a product or service which consistently does what it says it should do on the packaging, will increase consumers' trust and the brand will prosper. Consumers, it is argued, will only become disenchanted should the product or service fail to deliver its promise.

This may have been the case in the past, but in today's world where price and quality are increasingly equal and value for money is taken as a pre-requisite, consumers are increasingly looking at the brand behind the product or service and the business behind the brand.

As Alan Mitchell argues[1] 'New emerging models of branding, however, wittingly or unwittingly reach into parts of consumers' lives which traditional brands just don't reach, asking for a much bigger share of life in a variety of ways.'

Clearly there are a huge number of factors which influence the customers' perceptions and desires. The weighting of these factors may differ according to sector or category, but one vital factor that is common across all sectors and products is the level, importance and type of trust. Recent research in the USA[2] found that two-thirds of Americans report having greater trust in those companies aligned with a social issue.

Trust is intrinsically linked to compliance, moral and legal, that is playing by the rules. It is also fundamentally based on ethics, integrity, transparency, sincerity, mutual respect, partnership and mutual benefit. There is a direct relationship between the increasing expectations of honesty and the ethical behaviour of a business.

> In a world of limitless choice, the value of a brand that consumers trust is inestimable, but that trust must be continually earned.

Michael Eisner, The Disney Company

Consumer trust and confidence in companies is being called into question. According to MORI research conducted amongst a sample of the British adult

Table 7.1 Responses to the question, Do you agree that the profits of large British companies help make things better for everyone who buys their goods and services?

Year	Response	Percentage
1970	Yes	53
	No	25
	Undecided	22
1999	Yes	25
	No	52
	Undecided	23

Source: MORI research amongst adult population 1999

Q: 'Industry and commerce do not pay enough attention to their social responsibilities.'

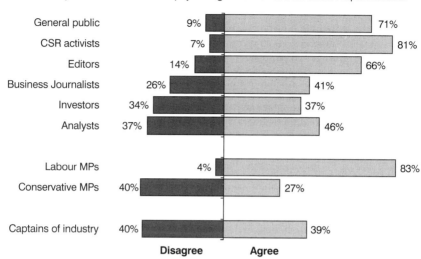

Figure 7.1 Importance of social responsibility. *Source:* MORI, 1998

population in 1999, it is clear that consumers are no longer confident, or trust the assertion that what is good for business brings a benefit to the consumer (see Table 7.1).

MPs are similarly sceptical (see Figure 7.1). Business therefore needs to firstly communicate what it is doing and to do more. Cause Related Marketing, as has been suggested, is an extremely effective way of promoting, profiling and leveraging an organization's corporate social responsibility.

Against this background where price and quality are equal and value for money and compliance are taken as prerequisites, I would like to suggest a hypothesis which describes the relationship which I believe is now emerging in relation to consumers (stakeholders) and business (brand, products, services). The hypothesis is quite simply this:

> The greater the influence a business (brand, product or service) has on our lives, the more consumers (stakeholders) expect an honest and ethical approach, delivering compliance plus, and the greater the consumer scrutiny to ensure it exists and is being delivered. The greater the influence, the greater the expectation and the greater the scrutiny.

Having explored Cause Related Marketing in the context of corporate social responsibility and corporate community investment, the question is how and where does Cause Related Marketing fit into marketing?

Marketing is defined by Kotler[3] as 'a social and managerial process by which individuals and groups obtain what they need and want through creating and exchanging products and value with others.' In today's environment, marketing encompasses anything from sales promotion, direct marketing, sponsorship and PR, and can involve tools such as advertising, be it satellite, TV, press, radio and other communications vehicles including the Internet, intranets, internal newsletters, etc. According to Webster, marketing has three roles: to assess market attractiveness; promote customer orientation and develop the firm's overall value proposition[4].

In the last decade the scope and thrust of marketing and what constitutes marketing has developed. Marketing is increasingly based on relationships and repeat purchase and has therefore moved beyond the focus on a single transaction to developing sustainable relationships. As Webster (1992)[5] argued although most transactions occur in 'the context of ongoing relationships between marketers and customers, there has been a long standing tendency for marketing practice and theory to focus on the sale, the single event of a transaction . . . the pure transaction'. By taking such an approach there is no need to consider a relationship. Things have changed however and relationship marketing is now seen as the key. If a business is to ensure repeated transactions, a relationship needs to be created and a clear differentiation and value proposition need to be developed. Naturally building a relationship takes time and is based on a clear understanding of the intrinsic values of the brand and it is here in building and communicating the overall value proposition that Cause Related Marketing has a key role to play.

There are a whole series of relationships, both internal and external, that organizations may be involved in. To illustrate this Morgan and Hunt[6] developed a model showing the relational exchanges in relationship marketing. To develop its relationship, an organization needs to consider and nurture each of these relevant relationships.

Relational exchanges in relationship marketing[6]

1. The relationship between manufacturers and their suppliers, in relation to 'just in time' procurement and 'total quality management' for example.
2. The relationship between service providers, for instance advertising or market research agencies and their respective clients.
3. Strategic alliances between companies and their competitors, as in technology alliances, co-marketing alliances and global strategic alliances.
4. Alliances between a company and non-profit organizations, as manifested through public purpose partnerships or indeed Cause Related Marketing.
5. Partnerships for joint research and development, as between companies and local, state or national governments.
6. Long-term exchanges between companies and ultimate customers, particularly apparent in the services marketing area.
7. Relational exchanges of working partnerships, as in channels of distribution.

8. Exchanges involving functional departments.
9. Exchanges between a company and its employees, as in internal marketing.
10. Within-company relational exchanges involving such business units as subsidiaries, divisions, or strategic business units.

Successful relationship marketing requires a relationship based on commitment and trust. Strategic Cause Related Marketing can play a key role in developing the value proposition, in building and maintaining many of these relationships, both internally and externally and whether business to business, consumer or other.

Strategic alliances, that is strategies based on the concept of the sum of the parts being greater than the whole, is one that is growing in importance as business develops into the next millennium. Strategic alliances, both internal between departments and external with suppliers and partners, can deliver greater benefits. Extend this concept to marketing and indeed to Cause Related Marketing relationships and the positive impact is magnified.

Strategic alliances between non-competing companies are increasingly prevalent, and the advantage of such relationships are being recognized. Cross-promotions, data-sharing, sampling and TV advertising are just some of the benefits. As brand demarcation lines that traditionally existed are eroding, these forms of relationship are becoming more important. As the 'Leader' in *Marketing*[7] pointed out

> Your customer may bank with a supermarket, take out a pension with a football club and go on holiday with a car company ... If you know where your customer lives, their name and how much they earn this is useful. But if, through a deal with a non-competing company you discover they have three kids, drive a Peugeot and read *The Daily Telegraph*, that could move your marketing to a different level.

These strategic alliances are not just externally focused either through the supply and distribution network or between non-competing companies. Strategic alliances are also highly relevant internally.

Stakeholder relationships with and perceptions of organizations can be formed as a result of a whole variety of interactions and interfaces with the business. These can range from advertising and in-store or on-pack promotional messages, to direct mail and customer care. It is the role of marketing to manage these interfaces to ensure a consistent delivery and reception of message amongst all groups over time and to capitalize and leverage all these opportunities.

There is no question that an organization's philanthropy, corporate social responsibility and community investment not only provide opportunities to connect with stakeholder groups but they fundamentally support the enhancement and development of the corporate reputation, brand and message. They each add value to and potentially impinge on the holistic marketing message. Marketing should therefore have a clear and important role to play in developing these strategies, messages and activities. Where these activities primarily impact on the corporate or brand image, values, reputation, loyalty and relationships with stakeholders, marketing should take the lead. This is, after all, all about managing corporate reputation and brand equity. In this context, as Cause Related Marketing has the potential to have a direct impact on corporate reputation, it is clearly essential to ensure that such opportunities are explored and that such issues are managed by appropriate individuals within the organization. With the ability to enhance corporate and brand reputation, demonstrate values, build loyalty and relationships, generate trial, awareness, PR, provide product differentiation and sales, Cause Related Marketing clearly falls with the remit of marketing, but should not be developed in isolation of other departments.

Combining these strategies and objectives with a charity cause or issue is where you have Cause Related Marketing. Some would argue, as Bartels did in 1968, that 'it is marketing processes which promote an effective and efficient resolution of society's needs'. Today I would suggest it is a combination of those responsible for marketing, and corporate affairs and/or community investment which is likely to achieve the best resolution.

Consistency of message and values needs to be managed. It impacts on reputation and is the responsibility of marketing, corporate and community affairs and chief executives. It needs to be understood in the context of customer or stakeholder needs. Whilst obviously firmly within the scope of marketing, the value of community affairs and community investment colleagues must not be underestimated. To fail to fully appreciate and utilize this expertise and skill is to fail to fully leverage the opportunity. Being responsible for understanding the trends and needs of the community, combining this knowledge and understanding with the skills that exist within the marketing department, provides the ideal basis for the creation of effective Cause Related Marketing.

Cause Related Marketing is intrinsically linked to corporate social responsibility, corporate affairs, community investment and marketing. It can be represented as shown in Figure 7.2.

Cause Related Marketing intersects with marketing, philanthropy, corporate affairs, and corporate community investment. Together they all form part of the overall matrix which makes up corporate social responsibility which in turn forms part of the overall business strategy.

The intersection of all spheres is the ultimate point providing maximum return on investment and opportunity for all concerned. Awareness, support and provision of resources can all be enhanced if departments work in concert with each other. The benefits to each department, the charity or cause partners and therefore to the wider community can all be enhanced through

Figure 7.2 The fit between Cause Related Marketing, marketing, corporate community investment, philanthropy and corporate social responsibility

communication, co-ordination, co-operation and by taking a holistic view of the business. Cause Related Marketing therefore represents a challenge to business as it straddles organizational, functional and decision-making boundaries.

Within the marketing context of the business, Cause Related Marketing can clearly add value and have relevance to any of the disciplines within marketing, depending on the nature of the particular objective of the programme. The question about whether, for instance, an activity is sponsorship or Cause Related Marketing I would suggest has missed the point. One may choose to use sponsorship as the vehicle or one of the vehicles to activate, facilitate, communicate or demonstrate the Cause Related Marketing programme along with perhaps advertising, direct mail and PR. Indeed Cause Related Marketing may be used to activate, facilitate, communicate or demonstrate a sponsorship or other marketing or corporate affairs activity. Sponsorship, like sales promotion, PR or direct marketing or any other marketing activity, is part of the marketing mix, and is just one of the many ways in which a Cause Related Marketing programme may be manifested. Assuming the reason for the Cause Related Marketing activity is to market the product, image or service to a specific audience, where the particular marketing tool interacts with the cause or charity, there you have Cause Related Marketing. Where business and the cause come together for mutual benefit, this is Cause Related Marketing. In relation to the marketing mix therefore I would suggest Cause Related Marketing fits, as shown in Figure 7.3, with as many new aspects of marketing as are created, fitting equally well within the framework.

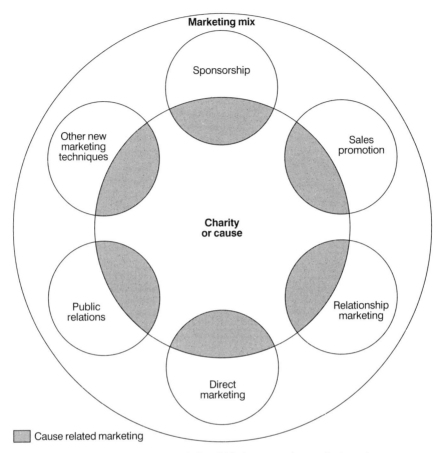

Figure 7.3 The relationship of Cause Related Marketing in the marketing mix

Marketing, like community investment and corporate social responsibility, is not defined by the department from which strategies and programmes originate but are rather defined by its objective, activity and outcome. This is also the case for Cause Related Marketing.

The bottom line is when there is a relationship between a business and charity or cause which is driven by a marketing imperative and is based on partnership and mutual benefit; the result is Cause Related Marketing regardless of the particular marketing tool or combination of tools used.

Cause Related Marketing is simply a strategy that provides additional marketing opportunities for businesses and an additional fundraising tool for charities or causes. It can achieve the individual partner's goals whilst at the same time making a significant positive impact on our wider community. That is why Cause Related Marketing is described as 'a commercial activity by which businesses and charities or causes form partnerships with each other to market an image product or service for mutual benefit'.

Notes

1 Mitchell, A. (1999) *Marketing Week,* How brands touch the parts others can't reach, 18 March, p. 22.
2 Cone/Roper (1999) Cause Related Trends Report: The Evaluation of Cause Branding^{SM}.
3 Kotler, P., Armstrong, G., Saunders, J., and Wong, V. (1996) *The Principles of Marketing,* The European Edition, Prentice Hall.
4 Webster, F.E. (1992) The Changing Role of Marketing in the Corporation, *Journal of Marketing,* **56**, October. Quoted in Collins, M. (1994) Global Corporate Philanthropy and Relationship Marketing, *European Management Journal,* **12**, No. 2, June.
5 Webster, F.E. (1992) The Changing Role of Marketing in the Corporation, *Journal of Marketing,* **56**, October.
6 Morgan, R.M. and Hunt, S.D. (1994) The Commitment-Trust Theory of Relationship Marketing, *Journal of Marketing,* **58** (July), pp. 20–38.
7 Leader, *Marketing,* 4 February 1999.

Chapter 8

Impact on society

To misquote John Donne, 'No business is an island, entire of itself; every business is a piece of the continent a part of the main.'

> BT's continued success depends on the skills and resources of our people, the loyalty of our customers and the health and prosperity of the communities of which we are part. Successful companies need successful communities.
>
> So BT is committed to being a good corporate citizen. We try to be as business-like in managing our community relations and impact on society as in all our commercial activities; the communities of which we are part deserve nothing less.
>
> Sir Iain Vallance, Chairman, and Sir Peter Bonfield, Chief Executive, BT[1]

As has already been argued, business does not operate in a vacuum. It has a significant impact on society and this impact needs to be understood, quantified and managed. Business and the wider community are interdependent. Without a healthy community providing the employees with the skills that a business requires, or the consumers that they desire with the necessary purchasing power, the business will ultimately fail. Of course in the short term other markets in other corners of the world can be sought but ultimately the communities in which the business trades and operates have to be thriving. This concept is becoming firmly embedded in leading organizations around the world. To take the UK as an example, Business in the Community[2] is an organization whose very foundations are based on these principles. Its mission is to 'inspire businesses to increase the quality and extent of their contribution to social and economic regeneration by making corporate social responsibility an essential part of business excellence.'

Clive Morton, Anglian Water's Director of Learning, said recently at a Tomorrow's Company event: 'It used to be thought that the greatest potential for improving productivity lay within the company. That is no longer the case. The really under-utilized resource now lies in the space between the company and other organizations.'

A prominent banker is quoted in Rosabeth Moss Kanter's book *World Class, Thriving in the Global Economy*[3] as saying 'We have no customers unless the community is vital'. In the same book, Alvah Chapman Jr, former CEO of Knight-Rider in Miami, also made the link between community investment business and a thriving economy, and was reported as saying, 'You can't publish a successful newspaper in a community that's dying on the vine. If you want a successful company that's involved in the community, and a newspaper certainly is, then you have to contribute to that community's success, too.'[4]

The concept of every business for itself is certainly erroneous in today's environment. However competitive an industry sector may be, it has a foundation of common mutual interests and codes of conduct. Competition therefore occurs in the context of these 'rules'. Competition is not about guerrilla warfare, in fact business life is fundamentally co-operative and this drive for co-operation is increasingly important. Collaboration passes beyond the boundaries of business, supplier and distributor to involve and depend on other stakeholders including consumers, employees and communities. All need to thrive in order for one to thrive.

Business and the wider community have a symbiotic interdependency. The business, shareholders, stakeholders and the community are intertwined. Companies can have both a positive and negative effect on society, they can therefore add or subtract from societal value. The goal is therefore to create a virtuous circle to encourage a holistic approach to the management of companies in order to maximize both shareholder value added and societal value added.

The ways in which a company impacts on society include financial, natural, human, social and political aspects. There are a range of different stakeholders on whom these impacts are made ranging from customers, employees, communities, shareholders and government. Equally society can have many impacts on a business. This interdependency and flow of the various relationships is elegantly illustrated through Jane Nelson's diagram (Figure 8.1)[5].

Increasing understanding and acknowledgement of symbiotic relationships is another reason for the development in corporate social responsibility, corporate community investment and Cause Related Marketing. A business needs to understand what impact it is having on society and why, where and how in terms of which aspects of the business are causing the impact. It also needs to understand who these impacts are on, that is which stakeholders. Clearly apart from economic, these impacts are environmental and social. Critically, companies also need to understand the relationship their impacts on society have with their long-term business performance.

Figure 8.1 Virtuous cycles of shareholder and societal value creation.[5] *Source:* Nelson J. *Building Competitiveness and Communities* (1998)

As John Ballington, Corporate and Consumer Affairs Director, Lever Brothers Ltd, argued at a Business in the Community Cause Related Marketing conference in November 1998:

> In this so called 'stakeholder society', companies are scrutinised not only for the quality of their products, but also for the rigour of their financial, social, ethical and environmental practices. If any of these practices are found wanting, there can be serious consequences for the company's reputation and it's brands.

Understanding the nature, size and location of these impacts enables a business to manage and improve its record, incorporate this understanding into its strategic decision making and thereby help to grow, develop and/or sustain a thriving environment and community which in turn enables and supports a thriving business. Understanding better the environment in which the business operates and responding to the changes in that operating environment enables the business to be more effective.

According to a PIRC survey[6] of FTSE 350 in the UK, 93 companies report on community issues in their report and accounts, 32 companies in the sample provided copies of separate reports relating to social or community affairs and 79 companies produced a separate policy or report on environmental issues; 31 companies in the sample provided copies of statements on ethical policy or codes of conduct – over half of these were FTSE 100 companies.

Those organizations which have reported include companies like BT, Co-operative Bank, DIAGEO, The Body Shop, BP, Shell and RTZ who are beginning to embrace this approach and have carried out and published both environmental and social audits, and indications are that this is set to become a trend for business. Consumers have much greater expectations of business than they did 20 years ago. Gone are the days when it was only niche values-based organizations like The Body Shop and Ben and Jerry's that were concerned about these aspects of their business. Social and environmental audits are now mainstream; incidents and issues around the world add further fuel to this trend.

Twenty years ago, large companies were granted trust. There was respect for the idea of ownership, and as long as they stayed within the law, businesses had freedom to do what they wanted. People who asked questions were seen as interfering busybodies who lacked legitimacy.[7]

Demonstrating an appreciation of an organization's impact on society and by taking an inclusive approach to the society in which it operates, investing in that society through community investment and Cause Related Marketing programmes in turn generates goodwill amongst that community and therefore reinforces and builds corporate reputation.

McDonald's situation during the course of the 1992 Los Angeles' riots is an excellent case in point. During the course of the riots entire blocks of businesses were burned down and looted, but neighbourhood residents protected McDonald's stores because of their franchisees' reputation for community service projects.

And it is not just large companies that can benefit and employ such strategies. In Rosabeth Moss Kanter's book *World Class, Thriving in the Global Economy*[8] she quotes the CEO of Lau Technologies in regard to the benefits to smaller companies from local community investment. 'Neighbours come to understand the business; if you need something, it's not the first time they've seen you.'

One can imagine a similar comment being relevant to an organization that is perhaps seeking new planning permissions. If they are an organization that is considered to be a good neighbour or 'neighbour of choice' and responsible, this can only count in their favour.

Bill Cockburn, Group Managing Director of BT at the launch of the Business in the Community Impact on Society Task Force which he chairs, compared the precariousness of corporate reputation and the importance of understanding and measuring an organization's impact on society, to a game of snakes and ladders.

> I suppose it's like a game of snakes and ladders; you know how it is, you work your way up the board to the top and lo and behold you can trip over something, and that great big snake on square 99 takes you right back down to 2 again. And you've got the long laborious journey up. And I think that's exactly what can happen to any company. Just watch out; some event could cause your reputation to take a real plummet.[9]

The challenge is to make sure that the social responsibility demonstrated and the community investment made by a company is understood and that people are aware of it. Cause Related Marketing is one way of bringing these messages to the attention of the various publics or stakeholders. Cause Related Marketing provides the means to leverage and communicate some of these programmes by bringing them to the public eye. This may be through a variety of marketing tools including PR, sponsorship of linked activities, or a transaction based activity which serves to add to the funds for a particular community investment programme or initiative.

Notes

1 BT Cares, Community Partnership Programme Report 1997.
2 Business in the Community is a charity established in 1982, which aims to inspire businesses to increase the quality and extent of their contribution to social and economic regeneration by making corporate social responsibility an essential part of business excellence. It is a membership organization with over 600 members including more than 75 of the FTSE 100. HRH the Prince of Wales is the patron.
3 Moss Kanter, R. (1995) *World Class, Thriving in the Global Economy*, Simon & Schuster, New York.
4 Whited, C. (1984) Alvah Chapman, Business and Community Leader, *Miami Herald*, 29 September, p. I.C.

5 This argument is further developed through Nelson, J. (1998) Building competitiveness and communities – How world class companies are creating shareholder value and societal value, The Prince of Wales Business Leaders Forum.

6 Pensions Investment Research Consultants Ltd (1998) Environmental Social Reporting: a survey of current practice at FTSE 350 companies.

7 Peter Hunt, Shell UK.

8 Moss Kanter, R. (1995) *World Class, Thriving in the Global Economy*, Simon & Schuster, New York.

9 Business in the Community (October 1998) Impact on Society Task Force, speech made at the launch breakfast.

Part Two

Who Cares, Why Care?

Chapter 9

Introduction

Communities care, charities and causes care, consumers care, the media care, the city cares and businesses care. They care or should care because Cause Related Marketing has the potential to make a positive difference to all of them.

In 1998, 75 per cent of community affairs directors, 72 per cent of marketing directors and 67 per cent of chief executives predicted that Cause Related Marketing will grow in importance to achieving objectives over the next 2–3 years[1].

In the USA[2], 90 per cent of executives surveyed said their companies' commitment to Cause Related Marketing will continue, with over half (57 per cent) saying Cause Related Marketing will stay the same in the future.

It is estimated by IEG that in North America, Cause Related Marketing is projected to be worth 8 per cent of sponsorship spending which is expected to be $7.6 billion[3]. Similar figures are not yet available in the UK, but this estimate from the USA gives an indication of the potential for Cause Related Marketing to make a real positive difference both to business and the wider community in the UK. The challenge is to ensure that this potential is released.

The reasons that an organization gets involved in Cause Related Marketing are many and varied. There are a range of business imperatives and a range of stakeholders to consider. Whilst the particular drivers, stakeholder focus, attitudes and perceptions, will differ according to the organization and its sector there are many core themes. These core themes may include some of the following.

General business drivers:

- Build or demonstrate corporate social responsibility and corporate citizenship
- Build or reinforce reputation or image
- Demonstrate organizational values

Marketing and fundraising drivers:

- Building and/or reinforcing the brand, its value and its personality
- Build awareness

- Generate trial
- Increase traffic
- Add value
- Build relationships
- Develop loyalty
- Product/service differentiation
- Product/service promotion
- Deflect negative publicity
- Build business relationships
- Emotional engagement of the customer
- Increase sales, income, volume
- Increase profile
- Develop understanding
- Provide finance
- Provide other resources
- Increase membership

Community affairs drivers:

- Build licence to operate
- Leverage corporate community investment programmes and strategies
- Build local community relationship
- Build government and opinion former relationships

Human resources drivers:

- Build team work
- Build staff motivation and morale
- Attract the best potential employees
- Use opportunity for skills development
- Use opportunity for transition

Whether a business, a charity or cause, the organization needs to take into account a whole variety of stakeholders in order not only to market its goods and services but also to ensure goodwill and licence to operate. As has been suggested stakeholders include not just shareholders but everyone who is 'affected by corporate policies and practices and who sees themselves as having a stake in the business'[4]. Clearly this idea was developed from a business perspective but replace the word business with organization thereby including charities and causes, and the concept of stakeholder still holds. Stakeholders can therefore include shareholders, the community in which the organization operates, the wider community, opinion formers and pressure groups, government and other political bodies, trade associations, suppliers and distributors as well as the employees and consumers. In addition in the case of charities and causes, stakeholders can include volunteers, beneficiaries and support groups, carers and the family of the beneficiary (see Figure 9.1). As argued in The Two Way Street:

> The concept of stakeholding provides a way of seeing how business and voluntary organizations relate and how they can benefit from good working partnerships. Fundamental is the appreciation that no organization operates in isolation. Each organization or institution is dependent for its health and prosperity on many inputs. Many interest groups have a 'stake' in an organization's activities, not necessarily because of financial interest. These various stakes, which may sometimes conflict with each other, need to be recognized by all involved.[5]

Clearly there are many issues that influence these various groups and their attitudes towards and relationships with an organization. The motivation therefore for considering Cause Related Marketing as a strategic part of the organization's approach and development will vary accordingly.

In order to develop the business case for Cause Related Marketing and to understand the attitudes of some of these stakeholder groups, Business in the Community, with the *pro bono* support of Research International (UK) Ltd, conducted and published as series of substantial reports on Cause Related

Figure 9.1 An organization and its stakeholders

Marketing, focusing on two of the stakeholder groups: the corporates and the consumers. This series of reports include:

- The Corporate Survey (1996) and The Corporate Survey II (1998), a quantitative survey into corporate attitudes towards and involvement in Cause Related Marketing, which gauged business awareness, understanding and involvement in Cause Related Marketing providing comparative data.
- The Game Plan (1997), an in-depth qualitative research study which involved focus groups, in-store interviewing and observation of supermarket shoppers in the UK, to provide a detailed understanding of consumer attitudes and responses towards Cause Related Marketing.
- The Winning Game (1996), quantitative research on Cause Related Marketing, which investigated consumer attitudes towards Cause Related Marketing, probing whether it is appropriate, what types of causes are most important to consumers and how Cause Related Marketing can affect buying habits and perceptions.

The evidence uncovered through these studies and others provides a vital insight into the motivations, issues, concerns and opportunities that Cause Related Marketing provides to businesses, charities, causes and the consumer.

The business case for Cause Related Marketing in relation to the different departments of a business are entirely intertwined, but in an attempt to draw on some of the key motivating arguments for each group, I have positioned the evidence under the headings of the chief executive, the marketing function, the corporate and community affairs function and the human resources function. Clearly however all evidence is relevant to all groups depending on their objective, remit and motivation.

Notes

1 The Corporate Survey II (1998), Business in the Community quantitative Cause Related Marketing research conducted by Research International (UK) Ltd.
2 Cone/Roper II Study (1996) Executive Attitudes Toward Cause-Related Marketing.
3 IEG Sponsorship Report, 21 December 1998, Volume 17, Number 24.
4 Sturdivant, F.D. (1981) *Business and Society: A Managerial Approach*, Irwin, USA. Quoted in Collins, M. (1994) Global Corporate Philanthropy and Relationship Marketing, *European Management Journal*, **12**, No. 2, June.
5 The Two Way Street (1998) Report by Taskforce 2002, Business in the Community and NCVO.

Chapter 10

Why the chief executive should care

As the chief executive of Levi Strauss said, 'Companies of the future must have soul'.

As the person responsible for the overall direction of the business, arguments based on value creation in terms of shareholder value added, societal value added (referred to as SVA[2])[1] and the importance of corporate social responsibility, corporate citizenship, building corporate and brand equity and protecting and enhancing corporate reputation will perhaps have greatest resonance.

It is the holistic management and appreciation of all stakeholder relationships that will support the development of the successful company of the future. In the words of Tomorrow's Company:

> As the world business climate changes, so the rules of the competitiveness race are being rewritten ... only through deepened relationships with – and between – employees, customers, suppliers, investors and the community will companies anticipate, innovate and adapt fast enough, while maintaining public confidence.[2]

The Body Shop's environmental management report (1991) summarized this, stating that 'The Body Shop believes that any enterprise, profitable or not, has an obligation to ... offer something of tangible benefit to the community.' Anita Roddick in her autobiography, *Body and Soul*, argued that 'Business should do more than just make money and create jobs and sell good products; it should help to solve major social problems ...We have a long way to go in Britain before business in general accepts that success and social responsibility are not incompatible.'

Since then many more blue chip organizations appreciate the validity of this argument. In 1997, the former Chairman (George Bull) and Chief Executive (John B. McGrath) of Grand Metropolitan through the Grand Metropolitan Report on Corporate Citizenship stated:

> Corporate responsibility is not a fringe activity. All of us at GrandMet believe business success cannot be defined solely in terms of earnings, growth and the balance sheet. A truly successful company is sensitive to the concerns of all those on whom it depends; investors, employers, customers, trading partners and the countries and communities in which it does business.[3]

In 1998 Bob Ayling, Chief Executive of British Airways (BA), wrote in the introduction to BA's Changing for Good – World Community Relations, 'British Airways is committed to serving consumers around the world. Of our corporate values, two in particular, summarize our community aims – to be a good neighbour, and to be global and caring.'

The argument for corporate social responsibility is clearly being understood by business. The next stage of the process is ensuring that this responsibility is understood by and communicated to stakeholders. This is where Cause Related Marketing comes into play. What motivates different stakeholder groups in terms of change in perception and action will vary. These influences could range from actual or predicted financial performance on the Stock Exchange, the level of dividend paid out, the corporate reputation, whether the organization makes a positive contribution to the local community in which it operates, the treatment of its suppliers, distributors and other parties and whether performance, price and quality of a particular product or service is appropriate.

From the point of view of the chief executive, research indicates that corporate social responsibility can indeed influence this group of stakeholders' perceptions of an organization, including city analysts, and Cause Related Marketing can be one of the ways in which it is communicated.

MORI research conducted amongst analysts and the city, presented at the Business in the Community Annual General Meeting 1998, showed that when asked to what extent does knowing about a company's contribution to society affect opinion of it, analysts and investors responded as shown in Figure 10.1.

The MORI research went on to explore the extent to which analysts and investors felt a company's contribution to society and the community impact on its financial performance. Well, over a quarter of each group responded that they felt that the impact was either to a great or certain extent (Figure 10.2).

If city analysts are influenced as they clearly are by awareness of corporate social responsibility, and Cause Related Marketing is a key way of projecting and communicating corporate social responsibility, then, Cause Related Marketing is an important strategy for the business to consider.

Q: 'To what extent does knowing about a company's contribution to society
and the community effect your opinion of it?'

Figure 10.1 Effect on opinion – the city. *Base:* 129 analysts, 98 investors (Summer 1998); 27 business press (Winter 1997). *Source:* MORI

Q: 'And to what extent do you feel a company's contribution to society
and the community impacts on its financial performance?'

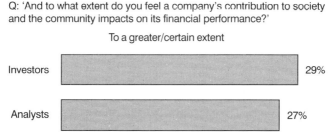

Figure 10.2 Impact of financial performance – the city. *Base:* 129 analysts, 98 investors (Summer 1998). *Source:* MORI

In terms of other key opinion formers and influencers, MORI questioned 100 MPs in 1997 to understand what the drivers for favourability were for this group. Social and environmental responsibility were shown without doubt to be the key drivers (see Figure 10.3).

MORI, who have been conducting research amongst a variety of other stakeholder groups, have reported developments in the trend for greater expectations and demand for business to behave in a socially responsible way, and that by so doing it can have a positive effect on the constituent groups.

From an opinion former's point of view, MORI, through regular research on corporate social responsibility found that in 1998 over 70 per cent of the general public, two-thirds of editors and over 80 per cent of Labour MPs amongst others felt that businesses were not paying enough attention to their social responsibilities (see Figure 7.2).

Support for corporate social responsibility is not just demonstrated amongst the city analysts, politicians and journalists. Leaders of business themselves are

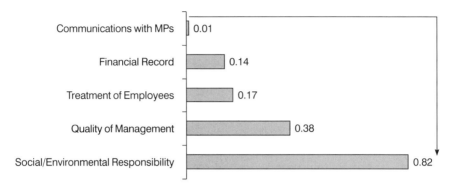

Figure 10.3 Drivers of favourability – MPs: correlation between specific attributes and overall favourability (1.0 = perfect correlation). *Base:* 100 MPs, November 1997. *Source:* MORI

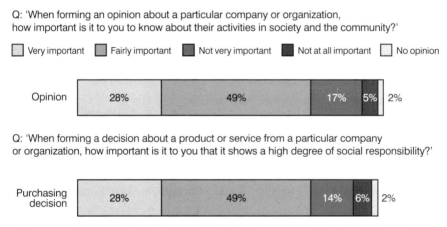

Figure 10.4 Importance of social responsibility. *Base:* 996/939 British adults aged 15+. July–August 1998. *Source:* MORI

showing greater interest and appreciation of its benefits. From both the corporate research surveys conducted by Business in the Community/Research International (UK) Ltd it is clear that chief executives see Cause Related Marketing as an area of growth over the next two to three years[4]. Clearly, however, as a relatively new discipline there may be sharp learning curves for some chief executives, boards and businesses to really test and appreciate the approach both for themselves and the community.

The number of chief executives who thought that Cause Related Marketing would grow in importance in achieving business objectives is increasing, from 60 per cent in 1996 to 75 per cent in 1998, when looking at comparative samples. Over 50 per cent of chief executives, in both 1998 and 1996, when using comparative samples, regarded Cause Related Marketing as very or fairly important to the company's objectives; 51 percent of chief executives in 1998 felt that Cause Related Marketing was important to the marketing objectives of a company, being best able to achieve the objectives outlined in Figure 10.5.

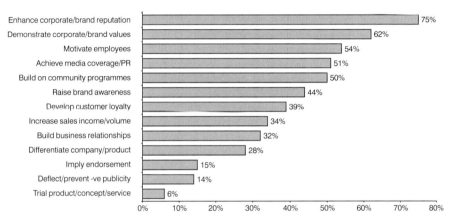

Figure 10.5 Business objectives Cause Related Marketing can achieve. *Base:* 437 chief executives, marketing and community affairs directors. *Source:* The Corporate Survey III, Business in the Community/Research International (UK) Ltd

The fact that 67 per cent of chief executives feel that Cause Related Marketing will grow within their company over the next two to three years and combined with the potential impact corporate social responsibility can have on city analyst perceptions of an organization, these are very clear indications that the chief executive cares. It is in the interest of the rest of the organization to investigate the potential, and as is seen by further research, the aspects of the business are alert to the opportunity.

Clearly it is not only shareholders and city analysts that drive the chief executive's interest; the wider community and all its stakeholders are also vital constraints in the equation. As has been argued at length, consumers expect businesses to shape up to their social responsibilities. If businesses do, research indicates that this can have a very positive effect on perception, attitudes and ultimately on their behaviour and buying habits. Indeed business responsibility for addressing the social issues of the day rated higher in importance than charities and religious institutions[5].

Notes

1 Nelson, J. (1998) Building competitiveness and communities – How world class companies are creating shareholder value and societal value, The Prince of Wales Business Leaders Forum, p. 7. See also pp. 53–54 of this book.

2 RSA Inquiry (1995) Tomorrow's Company, The Role of Business in a Changing World.

3 John B. McGrath, Chief Executive Grand Metropolitan, now Group Chief Executive, DIAGEO, and George Bull Chairman, Grand Metropolitan, now Non-Executive Director DIAGEO, Grand Metropolitan Report on Corporate Citizenship (1997).

4 The Corporate Survey (1996) and The Corporate Survey II (1998) Business in the Community quantitative Cause Related Marketing research conducted by Research International (UK) Ltd.

5 The Winning Game (1996) Business in the Community quantitative Cause Related Marketing research conducted by Research International (UK) Ltd.

Chapter 11

Why marketing should care

In today's environment, marketing is focused on lasting relationships between the 'customer' and the corporation, where 'customer' is synonymous with the concept of stakeholder (see Figure 9.1). Loyalty is the key objective as the recognition of the cost of attracting new customers versus retaining and developing existing ones is appreciated. Lifetime relationships, where the value of that relationship is calculated not just in terms of repeat purchase and cross-selling but also in terms of customer satisfaction which in turn leads them to act as ambassadors for the company. The marketing function is focused therefore not simply in identifying, anticipating and satisfying customer requirements profitably, but on identifying those customers most valuable to the organization over the long term and understanding how best to ensure their satisfaction, retention and development. Conversely therefore marketing is also about understanding the motivations behind corporate or brand defection and addressing them.

In this context therefore, where we know clearly from various research reports that stakeholders' perceptions and ultimately buying habits can be affected by business attitudes and actions in regard to social responsibility, it is essential that marketing consider how to develop and maximize these potential benefits in the pursuit of long-term stakeholder relationships.

Irrespective therefore of whether the marketing function leads in the development of an organization's corporate social responsibility, clearly the potential impact it has on stakeholders' perceptions and ultimate value and performance of the business, the challenge is for marketing to understand how it impacts on each stakeholder group and maximize the strategy. Cause Related Marketing, which is often the visible manifestation of corporate social responsibility, is therefore a key strategy.

The research conducted by Research International (UK) Ltd for Business in the Community provides clear evidence on the marketing perspective of Cause Related Marketing. Consumers are increasingly sophisticated, cynical and demanding of everything they come into contact with including businesses.

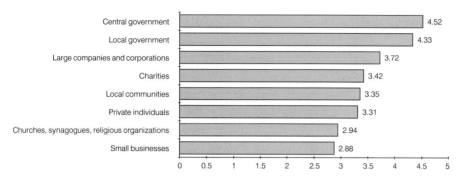

Figure 11.1 Level of responsibility for helping to solve society's problems (mean score, 5-point scale). *Base:* 1053 consumers. *Source:* The Winning Game, Business in the Community/Research International (UK) Ltd

When asked through The Winning Game research about the responsibility for addressing the social issues of the day, consumers had no doubt that businesses had a significant role to play.

From the marketing point of view, 81 per cent of marketing directors in the UK feel companies should address the social issues of the day; 58 per cent agree that a Cause Related Marketing strategy enables companies to address business issues at the same time addressing social issues; 39 per cent believe that Cause Related Marketing is important to achieving their overall marketing objectives, and over 70 per cent are devoting part of their marketing budgets to Cause Related Marketing (see Figure 11.2).

Clearly, significant groups of marketing professionals are beginning to appreciate the benefits and the opportunity. Comparative data is available from the USA, which indicates that there is a similar level of support and interest amongst US executives.

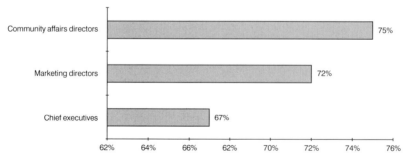

Figure 11.2 Extent to which the importance of Cause Related Marketing to achieving objectives will increase over the next 2–3 years. *Base:* 447 UK chief executives, marketing and community affairs directors. *Source:* The Corporate Survey II, Business in the Community/Research International (UK) Ltd

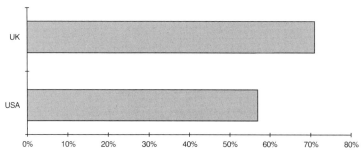

Figure 11.3 Respondents predicting that their company's commitment to Cause Related Marketing will increase. *Base:* 447 UK chief executives, marketing and community affairs directors and 70 US executives involved in Cause Related Marketing. *Source:* UK, The Corporate Survey II, Business in the Community/Research International (UK) Ltd; USA, Cone/Roper

Building strong brands is a core responsibility for the marketing team. Finding new and sustainable ways to enhance and build the brand, to imbue it with meaning and reinforce its personality, to emotionally engage the consumer and to build their trust is key. The building and maintenance of trust is a key marketing imperative in today's environment. Maslow developed a theory about the hierarchy of needs which are: physiological, safety and security, affiliation or acceptance, esteem and self-actualization (see Figure 5.1). He argues humans are driven by unsatisfied needs, so when lower needs are satisfied, higher needs become more important. Applying this theory to brand management and Cause Related Marketing, if the functional issues are satisfied, that is the physiological, safety and security issues are covered, then the importance of affiliation, esteem and self-actualization come to the fore. Cause Related Marketing is about engaging individuals on these higher levels; it is about affinity and reinforcing consumers' identity and beliefs. Trust is a vital element of the marketing and reputation mix and can not be taken for granted (see Figures 11.4 and 11.5).

As has already been mentioned, there is, I believe, a direct correlation between the level of trust and honesty a consumer (stakeholder) expects from a business depending on its size and share of purse. In other words as businesses bid for greater share of the individual consumer's spending, the more important the trust element and the higher the expectation from the consumer for levels of honesty, integrity and trust. There is of course a fundamental level of expectation which is of compliance and basic ethical behaviour. Beyond that, however, the more powerful or extensive the relations between the business and the consumer, the greater the consumer expectation in terms of ethics and levels of trust. Clearly there are risks and rewards in this strategy.

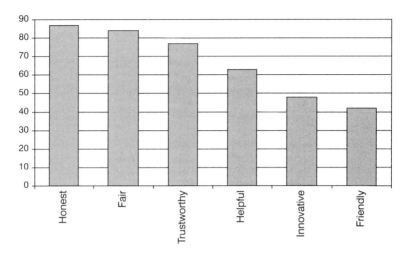

Figure 11.4 What people want from their ideal company. *Source:* New Britain, New Millennium, New Consumers ... New Marketing? (1998) The Future Foundation/Consumers' Association

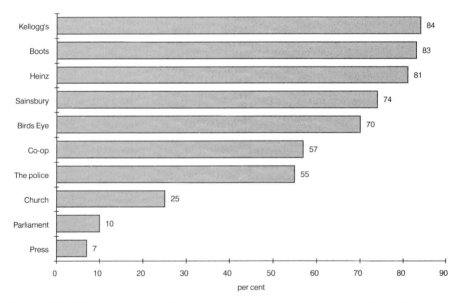

Figure 11.5 Who do you trust? Percentage who have a 'great deal' of confidence in... *Source:* The Henley Centre, Planning for Social Change (1997/98)

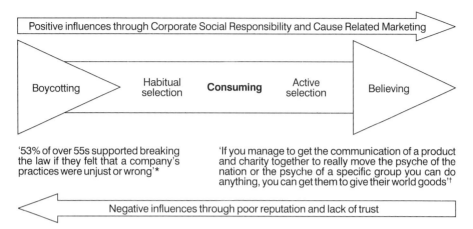

Figure 11.6 The positive effects of corporate social responsibility and Cause Related Marketing strategies. *The Vigilante Consumer and The New Honesty (1996) research by GGT; †The Game Plan (1997) Business in the Community qualitative research into Cause Related Marketing conducted by Research International (UK) Ltd

Depending on the market more and more, brand management is less about product attributes and more about emotional engagement of the consumer. Brand management is increasingly about connectivity: connecting with consumers (stakeholders) on many different levels; from the functional to the emotional; from consuming to believing. It's about engaging the consumers' emotions, their passions and their trust. This is when Cause Related Marketing has a strategic role to play (see Figure 11.6).

The debate continues over what constitutes and influences brand value and the balance between performance and functional benefit vis a vis affinity. A global study[1] conducted by Research International (UK) Ltd in the credit card market revealed that affinity constituted 52 per cent of the brand equity with the functional benefits accounting for just 48 per cent (see Figure 11.8).

Whilst this is based on research in the credit card market, a market which has generated more than £40 million for various organizations in the UK[2], it is an interesting indication of the trend that seems to be developing in which consumers are looking for affinity as well as, or more so, than the purely functional aspects of a product. The trends indicate the importance of affinity in the building of the brand and its relationships with stakeholders[3]. It also therefore heightens the importance of strategies like corporate social responsibility and Cause Related Marketing.

The marketing benefits of Cause Related Marketing are significant. They can range from enhancing reputation, image and demonstrating core values, to making corporate social responsibility and corporate community investment visible. It can also increase loyalty, build relationships with stakeholders,

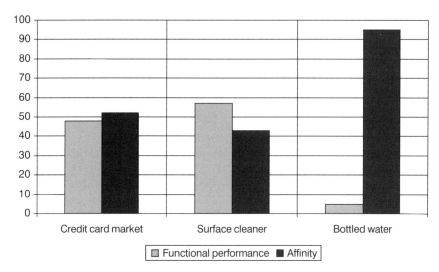

Figure 11.7 Building strong brands and Cause Related Marketing – the importance of brand equity. *Source:* Research International (UK) Ltd

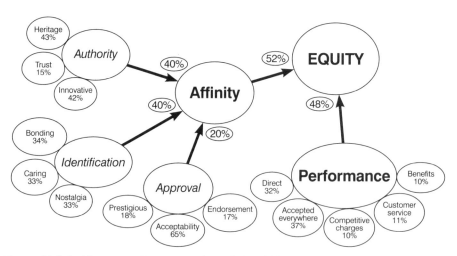

Figure 11.8 Building strong brands and Cause Related Marketing – credit card model. *Source:* Research International (UK) Ltd

provide differentiation and indeed increase sales. Case study evidence clearly illustrates this, as do the results of the research[4]. Since the original Business in the Community/Research International (UK) Ltd 1996 corporate research, Cause Related Marketing seems to have become a much more focused business activity. The survey went to chairmen, chief executives, marketing and

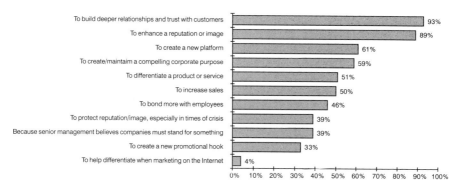

Figure 11.9 Reasons companies in the USA engage in Cause Related Marketing. *Base:* 70 executives involved in Cause Related Marketing in the USA. *Source:* Cone/Roper Executive Attitudes Toward Cause Related Marketing

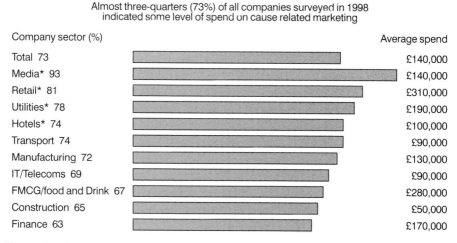

Almost three-quarters (73%) of all companies surveyed in 1998 indicated some level of spend on cause related marketing

Company sector (%)		Average spend
Total 73		£140,000
Media* 93		£140,000
Retail* 81		£310,000
Utilities* 78		£190,000
Hotels* 74		£100,000
Transport 74		£90,000
Manufacturing 72		£130,000
IT/Telecoms 69		£90,000
FMCG/food and Drink 67		£280,000
Construction 65		£50,000
Finance 63		£170,000

Figure 11.10 Cause Related Marketing – who is doing it? Levels of investment (by sector). *Base:* all answering (412 chief executives, marketing and community affairs directors); * = small bases. *Source:* The Corporate Survey II, Business in the Community/Research International (UK) Ltd

community affairs directors and across all groups respondents indicated a number of the benefits of Cause Related Marketing (see Figure 10.5).

The similarities with the US market are fascinating. There is therefore a growing recognition in both the UK and USA that Cause Related Marketing can deliver against clear corporate objectives both externally and internally, for marketing, communications, community affairs and human resources (see Figure 11.9).

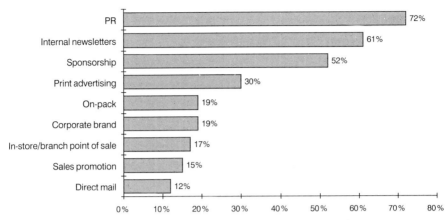

Figure 11.11 Marketing methods used to maximize Cause Related Marketing programmes. *Base:* 118 marketing directors, 71 community affairs directors. *Source:* The Corporate Survey II, Business in the Community/Research International (UK) Ltd

Investment in Cause Related Marketing in the UK would seem to be widespread and growing with 73 per cent of respondents in the UK indicating some level of investment. The level of investment however is relatively low, with the average being £180,000.

Taking comparative samples from the original Business in the Community Corporate Survey and Corporate Survey II on average marketing budgets have grown from £24.57m in 1996 to £28.34m in 1998 and community affairs budgets have grown from £1.64m in 1996 to £2.17m in 1998. Marketing budgets are

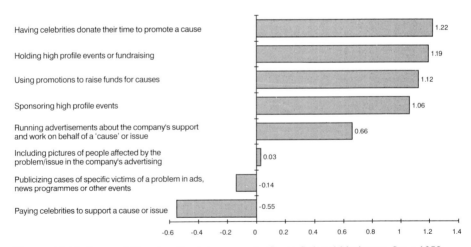

Figure 11.12 Acceptability of methods to promote Cause Related Marketing. *Base:* 1053 consumers. *Source:* The Winning Game, Business in the Community/Research International (UK) Ltd

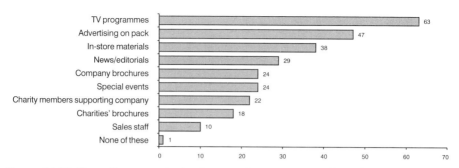

Figure 11.13 Most effective methods of communicating a company's involvement with a cause. *Base:* 1053 consumers. *Source:* The Winning Game, Business in the Community/ Research International (UK) Ltd

therefore almost 8 times the size of community affairs budgets and therefore represent a rich source of opportunity. Considering the tools available for the marketing of the business, the breadth and depth of potential communication is also significant[5].

According to the corporate research conducted in the UK, the key methods for maximizing a Cause Related Marketing programme are as detailed in Figure 11.11.

From the consumers' point of view, the most acceptable methods for communicating these types of relationships are through, television, or print advertising and point-of-sale material.

The most effective means are presented in Figure 11.13. The balance of communication, between the business and the cause, the tone of the message, the weight of the communication package *vis à vis* the benefit to the cause are all vital elements to get right for effective Cause Related Marketing. This is covered in detail in the communication section (see Figure 11.13).

The consumer cares

The consumer demand and expectation for corporates to be socially responsible can not be underestimated. When the public were asked how appropriate it was for companies to address the social issues of the day, the consumer response was overwhelming. Businesses' role and responsibility for the addressing the social issues of the day is second only to that of central and local government and above that of charities, or religious institutions for instance (see Figure 11.1).

Consumers were also quick to point out that for companies which did try to do something 'to make the world a better place', 86 per cent of consumers claimed that they would have a much more positive image of that company, regardless of specific 'cause' or issue being addressed. Almost nine out of ten

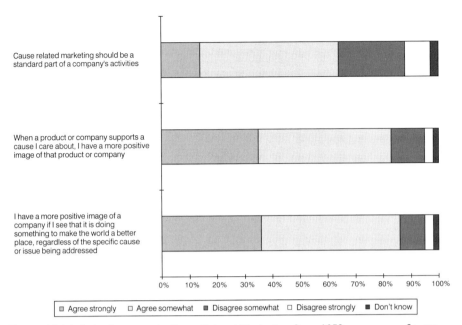

Figure 11.14 Attitudes towards Cause Related Marketing. *Base:* 1053 consumers. *Source:* The Winning Game, Business in the Community/Research International (UK) Ltd

consumers therefore indicated that Cause Related Marketing and corporate social responsibility had a highly positive impact on their perceptions of a company.

MORI research conducted in August 1998 further corroborated the importance of business involvement in the wider community. When asked about the influence this type of activity had on forming an opinion about a particular company or organization, 77 per cent of consumers felt that knowing about a company's activities in society and the community was either very or fairly important and three in ten of the British public chose or boycotted a product or company for ethical reasons in 1998. That equates to 12 million consumers. In addition to this over a third of the public believe it is extremely or very important for companies to make donations to charities linked to sales of a product (i.e. Cause Related Marketing).[6]

The idea of communicating an organizations' investment in the community is one which does not sit well with some companies; it appears to contradict a sense of philanthropy. This is an interesting dilemma. If the programme or activity is meant as a philanthropic contribution, clearly no return on that donation is expected. If however, the organization is investing in the programme and/or community, and expects this to benefit its reputation locally or nationally for instance, or if continued investment is dependent on image enhancing objectives, then the programme clearly needs to be communicated. The issue is therefore to be clear why the programme is being supported from the outset, and then to develop the communication appropriately, taking care to get the balance, tone and content just right. MORI research also indicated that 77 per cent of British adults felt it was very or fairly important for a company to show a high degree of social responsibility when making a decision about a product of service.

There is no question from various research studies that consumers find it acceptable, indeed appropriate for business to derive some benefits through their relationship with a charity or cause and the wider community. Business in the Community research indicated that 63 per cent of consumers felt Cause Related Marketing was an acceptable way of a company doing business and MORI research[6] indicated that 61 per cent of adults felt that it is acceptable for companies to derive some benefit. Business should be in no doubt therefore of the consumers' support for such strategies and for them to be communicated. Suspicions can be aroused in fact if such programmes are not communicated.

Corporate social responsibility therefore certainly seems to be striking an important chord amongst consumers, and, managed and communicated appropriately, has the potential to influence their perceptions and actions positively.

The vigilante consumer

The consequences of failing to behave in what is deemed a 'socially responsible' way can be serious. Research undertaken in 1996 by advertising agency GGT[7], and questions asked through MORI research clearly indicate that the consumer can and will act if they regard a company as doing something inappropriate (see Figure 11.15).

The research confirms the ability and potential strength of consumer power and empowerment. Over 70 per cent of consumers indicated they were prepared to complain by telephone or letter. Indeed almost two-thirds of respondents claimed that they were more likely to take action against a company which behaved badly than they were five years ago. Over half the respondents claimed that as a protest they would stop doing business with a company; this rose to almost two-thirds of the 45–54 age group who tend on average to have greater spending power.

The GGT research indicated that 59 per cent of respondents agreed that there are times when people may be justified in breaking the law as a form of protest against practices which they find unjust or wrong. This was not something that only the 18–35 age group considered appropriate but was supported by people of all ages, including the traditionally conservative group of over 55s, of whom 53 per cent were in agreement.

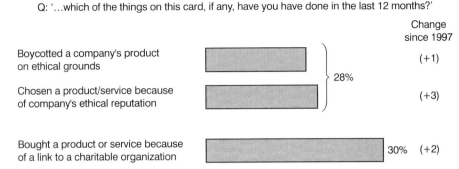

Figure 11.15 Corporate social responsibility and purchasing behaviour. *Base:* 1935 British adults aged 15+, July–August 1998. *Source:* MORI

Clearly when combined with the arguments about the number of people a consumer tells of a bad experience, the potential impact could be significant. It also represents a significant shift in consumer behaviour and willingness to take action which if not considered and handled with care could have significant repercussions for business. With the speed and availability of technology and the Internet, these repercussions could be stronger, faster and more damaging. As GGT concluded at the time, 'consumers of all ages are becoming more vociferous and active in protesting against corporations and institutions. They are more willing than ever to back up an ethical judgement or a sense of injustice with action rather than simply turning the other cheek.'

From the marketing perspective this represents a significant watershed in consumer behaviour and a response needs to be carefully considered. The vigilante consumer is born out of a marketing-literate society who understand their own powers of persuasion. From the marketing perspective, this requires a 'new honesty' which recognizes the consumer's interest in making moral and ethical judgements and their willingness to back these up when necessary with positive action. Business behaviour, indeed business ethics, are under the spotlight like never before. The notion of consumer empowerment and the stakeholder society are becoming more firmly established. Customers have recognized their power and are exercising their rights to challenge how companies behave. The information, communication and technology revolution simply makes it faster, easier and even more effective.

The attitudes and perceptions of the consumer are vital and there is no question that they can be strongly influenced by Cause Related Marketing and corporate social responsibility.

Effects of Cause Related Marketing on consumers in the UK

- 86 per cent of consumers indicated that when price and quality were equal, linking with a cause would make the difference.
- 86 per cent had a much better perception of a company trying to do something to make the world a better place.
- 73 per cent would switch from one brand to another and 61 per cent would change retail outlets.
- 63 per cent felt that such strategies were appropriate means of business addressing society's causes and issues.

Source: The Winning Game (1996), Business in the Community quantitative Cause Related Marketing research conducted by Research International (UK) Ltd

These findings are reinforced by research carried out amongst potential business leaders by The Prince of Wales Business Leaders Forum and AIESEC[8] which found that:

- 57 per cent of respondents had made buying decisions based on environmental or social influences.
- 46 per cent had not bought products because they were not environmentally or socially responsible.

Research conducted in the USA in 1998, by Cone Communications[9]/Roper Starch Worldwide, found that as in 1993, nearly two-thirds of Americans, approximately 130 million consumers, reported they would be likely to switch brands or retailers to one associated with a good cause, when price and quality are equal compared to 73 per cent of the UK population.

Similar research has also been conducted by a consortium[10] of organizations in Australia, by The Explorer Group in Italy and by Bates-Roulata in Belgium. The evidence is consistent and overwhelming. As a core stakeholder group from the marketing function point of view, if Cause Related Marketing can influence consumer perceptions and buying habits then clearly it is a vital strategy in the marketing mix. If it can enhance corporate reputation, brand equity, increase loyalty, build sales and benefit the community at the same time it becomes an intrinsic part of the marketing and indeed corporate social responsibility strategy.

Clearly there is some interesting debate about whether and when price and quality are equal. One just needs to look at the price part of a luxury car

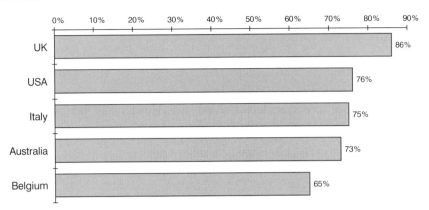

Figure 11.16 International consumer propensity for brand switching based on Cause Related Marketing. *Base:* 1053 British consumers, 2000 American consumers, 1000 Australian consumers, 1000 Italian consumers and Belgian consumers. *Source:* The Winning Game, Business in the Community/Research International (UK) Ltd

through to a washing powder to illustrate how similar price and quality and innovation are. Whilst a product may hold a price of quality differential for a week, a month indeed a year, the rate and speed at which these periods of differentiation can be eroded is accelerating.

Taking comparative data across the UK, USA, Australia and Europe, it is clear that acting in a socially responsible way can have significant effects on the consumer. This is a worldwide trend (see Figure 11.15).

These numbers and messages coming back from consumers are similar around the world; more than eight out of ten consumers are clear that linking with a cause makes a difference. Were that number to be quartered, that still indicates that more than one in five members of the adult population aged 15+ internationally say that price and quality being equal, and increasingly they are, linking with a cause would make a difference to their buying habits. Can one afford to ignore such a potentially significant finding? One need only consider what share of that market needs to be attracted in order to affect market share.

The most recent Cause Related Marketing research carried out in the USA by Cone/Roper[11] confirms the popularity of Cause Related Marketing amongst consumers over time.

- Eight out of ten Americans have a more positive image of companies who support a cause they care about, and this figure has been consistent from 1993 to 1998; compared to 86 per cent of consumers in the UK.
- 94 per cent of Influential Americans™ have a more favourable image of companies who are committed to a cause, up 6 per cent from 1993.

- Overall acceptability of Cause Related Marketing programmes as a business practice has increased 5 per cent since 1993, growing from 66 per cent to 74 per cent.
- Nearly two-thirds of Americans agree that Cause Related Marketing should be a standard business practice, and this figure has been solidly consistent since 1993, compared to 64 per cent of consumers in the UK.
- Two-thirds of Americans report having greater trust in those companies aligned with a social issue.

Source: The Winning Game (1996), Business in the Community quantitative Cause Related Marketing research conducted by Research International (UK) Ltd and 1999 Cone/Roper Cause Related Trends Report, The Evolution of Cause Branding[SM]

Who cares about what?

Clearly understanding which particular issues are of concern to the consumer can influence the route that a Cause Related Marketing programme may take. On the one hand, an organization may decide to champion one of the top three

Consumer ranking (%)		Corporate ranking 1998	Change since 1996
1. Medical/health		2	↑
2. Schools/education		1	=
3. Environmental		4	=
4. People with disabilities		6	
5. Children's disabilities			
6. Poverty and social in the UK			
7. Housing/homelessness		10	↓
8. Animal rights and protection		10	↓
9. Alcohol and drug abuse			
10. Community issues			
11. Third world causes			
12. Youth development			
13. Urban regeneration		9	↓
14. The arts		5	↓

Figure 11.17 Most important causes and issues to consumers. *Base:* 1053 consumers, 57 marketing directors and 80 community affairs directors. *Source:* The Corporate Survey II, Business in the Community/Research International (UK) Ltd

	Energy/water supply	Manufacturing /vehicle	#Construction	Hotels, catering, leisure	Distribution, transport	#IT/telecoms	Banking, finance, insurance	Retail	#FMCG, food and drink	#Media, communications, publishing
Medical/health	◉	◉◀	◉	◉	◉◀	◉	◉◀	◉◀		◉
Environmental	◉◀	◉◀	◉	◉◀	◉◀	◉	◉◀	◉◀	◉	◉
#Crime prevention	◉	◉	◉	◉	◉		◉	◉	◉	◉
Third world	◉◀	◉	◉		◉◀		◀	◉	◉	◉
Animal rights/protection		◉	◉	◉	◉◀		◀	◉◀		◉
School education	◉◀	◉◀	◉	◉◀	◉◀	◉	◉◀	◉◀	◉	◉
Children	◉◀	◉◀	◉	◉◀	◉◀	◉	◉◀	◉◀	◉	◉
#People with disabilities	◉	◉	◉	◉	◉	◉	◉	◉	◉	◉
#Older people	◉	◉	◉	◉	◉	◉	◉	◉	◉	◉
Urban regeneration	◉◀	◉	◉	◉◀	◉◀	◉	◉◀	◀	◉	◉
The arts	◉◀	◉◀	◉	◉◀	◉◀	◉	◉◀	◉◀	◉	◉
Homelessness/poverty	◉◀	◉◀	◉	◉◀	◉◀	◉	◉◀	◉◀	◉	◉
#Alcohol/drug abuse	◉	◉	◉				◉	◉	◉	◉
Other	◉	◉	◉		◉	◉			◉	◉

Key: ◉ supported in 1996; ◀ supported in 1998; # indicates that the cause or industry information was not reported in 1996.

Figure 11.18 Cause supported by industry sector. *Base*: 1998, 209 marketing and community affairs directors, and, in 1996, 250 chief executives, marketing and community affairs directors. NB: small bases in some sectors. *Source*: The Corporate Survey and The Corporate Survey II, Business in the Community/Research International (UK) Ltd

areas because so many consumers seem to identify with them. On the other hand the market saturation, the opportunities for share of voice, the ability to make a unique, significant impact and the opportunity to be synonymous with or own a particular cause or issue may lead to an organization selecting a different cause.

Business in the Community/Research International (UK) Ltd research in the UK asked both consumers and corporates to rank the area of greatest concern to them and the issues they support. Comparative data between the first and second corporate report and the consumer report showed fascinating discrepancies between the causes businesses supported and those that the consumer identified. Since the 1998 Corporate Survey, the picture looks very different (see Figures 11.17 and 11.18).

It is fascinating to see that the causes that feature at the top of issues consumers care about around the world show very little difference (Table 11.1).

This expectation and demand by consumers is therefore not a factor that is peculiar to the UK, but indeed a global trend. With the speed of communication, and effectively the 24 hour day, businesses increasingly have to monitor their policies and activities in all markets on which they have an impact or influence. Mistakes or contradictions in attitudes in one country or on one continent can within a moment be common knowledge around the world amongst consumers, opinion formers, advocacy groups and governments to name but a few. Appreciating that consumers are consistent in their expectations and demand for responsibility around the world has increasingly encouraged companies to appreciate, understand and audit their activities and impact in the markets in which they operate. It is interesting to note that increasingly companies are looking at social audits as a way of tracking and measuring their performance in this regard.

Table 11.1 International comparison of causes of most concern to consumers

UK	USA	Australia	Italy
1. Medical/health	1. Crime	1. Medical research	1. Youth training
2. Schools/education	2. Environment	2. Homelessness,	2. Medical research
3. Environment	3. Education	poverty & hunger	3. Social exclusion
4. Disabled people	4. Poverty	3. Care for elderly	4. Care for elderly
		people	people
		4. Child protection	

Source and base: 1053 British consumers in The Winning Game, Business in the Community/Research International (UK) Ltd; 2000 American consumers in the Cone/Roper Cause Related Marketing Trends Report, 1000 Italian consumers in the Explorer research and 1000 Australian consumers in *The New Bottom Line*, Cavill & Co./Worthington Di Marzio

- A weekday edition of *The Times* contains more information than the average person was likely to come across in a lifetime during seventeenth-century England.
- A greeting card that plays 'Happy Birthday' contains more computer power than existed in the entire world before 1950.
- Today's average consumers wear more computing power on their wrists than existed in the entire world before 1961.
- Computer power is now 8,000 times less expensive than it was 30 years ago. . .if we had similar progress in automotive technology, today you could buy a Lexus for about $2. It would travel at the speed of sound, and go about 600 miles on a thimble of gas.

    Source: Pritchett, P "The Employee Handbook of New Work Habits for a Radically Changing World, 13 Ground Rules for Job Success In the Information Age", Pritchett & Associates Inc.

Consumers not only increasingly expect business to assume its responsibility in addressing the social issues of the day but as part of the research, 86 per cent of consumers stated that they had a much better perception of a company that was doing something to make the world a better place.

The process for identifying and selecting a cause has many elements which are described in more detail in Part Four of this book. As part of this, it is vital to be clear about the business objective; to have a sound understanding of the areas of interest for particular target audiences and to understand which stakeholders the business is trying to influence and why, and thereby build the strategy accordingly.

Notes

1 Research conducted by Research International in Australia and New Zealand.
2 *Marketing Week* (18 March 1999) p. 43.
3 *Marketing Week* (14 August 1997) p. 28.
4 The Corporate Survey II (1998) Business in the Community quantitative Cause Related Marketing research conducted by Research International (UK) Ltd.
5 Please note that these budgets relate to those usually larger companies surveyed.
6 Conducted in July–August 1998, MORI.
7 The Vigilante Consumer and The New Honesty (1996) GGT consumer research.
8 Educating tomorrow's global business leaders (1995) report by The Prince of Wales Business Leaders Forum and AIESEC.

9 Cone/Roper (1999) Cause Related Marketing Trends Report: The Evolution of Cause Branding[SM].

10 Cavill & Co, Worthington Di Marzio, Sydney City Mission, Mutual Community, World Vision Australia, ICI Australia, Spastic Society of Victoria.

11 Cone/Roper (1999) Cause Related Marketing Trends Report: The Evaluation of Cause Branding[SM].

Chapter 12

Why community affairs should care

Much of what has been said regarding the case for the chief executive and marketing director has equal resonance with the community affairs director. Building corporate reputation, enhancing image, finding new ways to connect with stakeholders are vital issues to the community affairs function, therefore Cause Related Marketing can add value to the community affairs director's role strategy. To say that everyone's attitude towards Cause Related Marketing is positive would be an exaggeration. There are those who are uncomfortable with the concept of marketing and communicating an organization's contribution, investment and support of a cause, charity or community. This may be because the activity is entirely altruistic and philanthropic. It is therefore absolutely appropriate that this is not marketed. If however the programme is about delivering against clear marketing objectives by partnering with a cause, that is, Cause Related Marketing, then clearly the benefits to the business will only accrue if stakeholders know about it and therefore it needs to be marketed and communicated.

The community affairs director's role can cover a whole multitude of activities, ranging from liaison with government departments to managing relationships with local communities in which the organization operates, and strategies are developed accordingly. With the spectrum of activity that falls to the corporate affairs department, the business case will vary. I would suggest the key role for Cause Related Marketing in terms of the community affairs function, is to leverage further existing community affairs strategies. Taking the example of TESCO Computers for Schools, this programme generated well over 250 Computers for Schools Presentations involving local MPs, thus providing a major boon to the community affairs strategy.

Considering these areas that community affairs directors tend to be involved in, the opportunity to leverage their impact and effectiveness through Cause Related Marketing is an interesting and a yet generally untapped strategy. To take a different perspective, using employee involvement, fundraising and

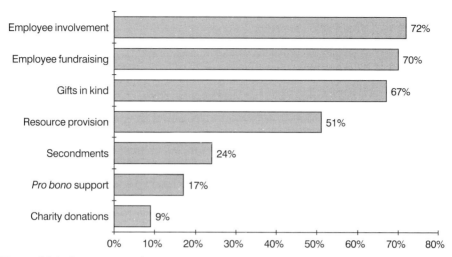

Figure 12.1 Corporate involvement in community investment. *Base:* 103 community affairs directors. *Source:* The Corporate Survey II, Business in the Community/Research International (UK) Ltd

secondments, etc., to further leverage a Cause Related Marketing partnership also provides scope for opportunity and again this is generally untapped.

Adams Childrenswear use staff fundraising and employee involvement to enhance their core Cause Related Marketing strategy which is intrinsic to the brand proposition; TESCO PLC have used Cause Related Marketing to support their charity of the year relationships. These companies that employ the full mix of community investment and marketing in support of their business objectives and of a particular cause or issue are few and far between. This is a major opportunity that should be further developed.

ASDA and Breast Cancer Awareness Month

ASDA have supported Breast Cancer Care (BCC) throughout Breast Cancer Awareness Month in October since 1997. This has involved a full mix of marketing, corporate affairs and employee fundraising including: Cause Related Marketing promotions, sale of charity pin badges, staff fundraising and other support.

To date this has raised over £730,000 for BCC and the aim is to take the total over £1 million in 1999. In 1998 alone:

■ ASDA raised a total of £281,783 for BCC during October.
■ George at ASDA donated 50 pence from all sales of its womens' wear to BCC for one week in October.
■ Staff engaged in fundraising activities.

- Pink ribbon pin badges, attached to a card with the BCC helpline number on were distributed for a £1 donation in all stores.
- BCC and the partnership were featured on an ASDA in-house video.
- Archie Norman issued a 'Chairman's Challenge' to encourage colleagues to fundraise.
- ASDA hosted a party for BCC at the Labour Party Conference.

As has been seen from previous evidence, whilst community affairs investment strategies are extremely high profile in those communities in which their benefit is being received, often the public at large are not aware of the particular programme. Cause Related Marketing could be extremely effective in leveraging these programmes, bringing the consumers' attention to the contribution that particular organizations are making, and this I believe is a key strength and opportunity for Cause Related Marketing and the community affairs function.

Clearly, moving from a low to a high profile strategy requires serious consideration, and may not be appropriate in all cases, but I would suggest there are many cases in which it is appropriate and therefore Cause Related Marketing should be considered.

From research recently carried out by Business in the Community/Research International (UK) Ltd[1], evidence suggests that almost three-quarters of all

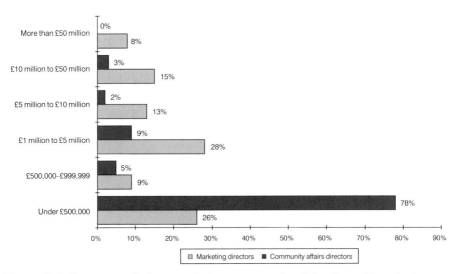

Figure 12.2 Comparative budgets: marketing to community affairs. *Base:* 191 marketing directors and 105 community affairs directors. *Source:* The Corporate Survey II, Business in the Community/Research International (UK) Ltd

marketing directors and community affairs directors devote some part of their budget to Cause Related Marketing, with community affairs directors spending something in the region of 3 per cent (see Figure 12.2).

Evidence also suggests that in a highly competitive market place from the point of view of charities, Cause Related Marketing proposals need to be well targeted. As 79 per cent of community affairs directors and marketing directors receive at least one proposal a month, and of those who do receive proposals on average seven are actually being received. It is therefore vital that community affairs has a clear policy for dealing with such approaches. Again, from the research conducted by Business in the Community/Research International (UK) Ltd it was clear that there are a number of methods being used (Figure 12.3).

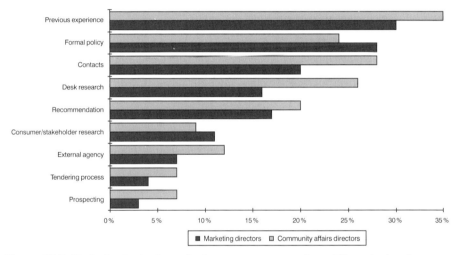

Figure 12.3 Methods of selecting a charity or cause partner. *Base:* 192 marketing directors and 103 community affairs directors. *Source:* The Corporate Survey II, Business in the Community/Research International (UK) Ltd

Two-thirds of community affairs directors and over a half of marketing directors approve of Cause Related Marketing and believe it has obvious benefits for both the wider community. Indeed 57 per cent of community affairs professionals felt that Cause Related Marketing was important to achieving their community affairs objectives and 75 per cent said it would grow[1].

Community affairs budgets in the UK are much smaller than marketing budgets. This means that from the charity or cause point of view the financial ceiling for the potential activity is lower but this of course doesn't impede the opportunity to secure alternative sources of support from within the business.

The research in fact tends to suggest that there is a greater incidence of community affairs teams looking across departments to find additional sources of funds to support initiatives. Thirty-nine per cent of community affairs directors indicated that they sought budget support from other areas with 27 per cent looking towards marketing.

The overlap between general business, marketing and community affairs objectives is incredibly wide, and therefore the benefits of Cause Related Marketing are potentially highly applicable. In terms of the specific objectives that community affairs teams felt that Cause Related Marketing addressed[1], these were very much in line with those of the marketing directors in terms of enhancing corporate reputation and demonstrating brand values. The tension between the departments as to who has responsibility for the corporate reputation and values should, in the best case scenario, lead to a high degree of management. The worst case scenario could be management of corporate reputation falling out of any department's or individual's portfolio of responsibility and resting with junior management. Corporate reputation and value is a key concern of the chief executive, the marketing and the corporate and community affairs departments. The challenge is to ensure it is managed and at the appropriate level which reflects its importance and impact on the business.

It is also clear from the research, that the shift of Cause Related Marketing has moved in the last two years from community affairs towards marketing. On the one hand this is very encouraging from the charities and cause point of view, as marketing budgets are somewhere in the region of eight times larger than community affairs budgets, but clearly community affairs have a vital role to play in the development of effective Cause Related Marketing programmes. It is after all, their role to understand the many stakeholders in communities in which the organization operates or hopes to operate, and this is exactly where community affairs can add value to the marketing team, as Cause Related Marketing programmes are developed.

Whilst this is positive when looking at the size of budgets available and the skills, strategies and techniques being applied to Cause Related Marketing partnerships, there is a danger however that the pendulum moves too far towards marketing and the value of the community affairs team is eroded. Community affairs teams have enormous value and experience to add in the planning, preparation, development, implementation and leverage of these programmes. They are also guardians of the corporate brand and reputation and indeed in many cases can act as the counter-balance to the tactical 'sales promotion' of some marketers.

During the course of my work, I have picked up some sense of reservation from some community affairs teams where there is a concern that Cause Related Marketing has a rather more overt approach than traditional community investment programmes. This may very well be the case in some instances, and in some instances may be very appropriate, if the purpose of the community affairs function is to build relationships between the business and the communities in which they operate, and to build and develop relationships between stakeholders and the organization, and clearly if Cause Related Marketing should be regarded as an opportunity to help leverage some of the existing programme, and to provide more funds, support and resources to existing programmes.

Note

1 The Corporate Survey II (1998) Business in the Community quantitative Cause Related Marketing research conducted by Research International (UK) Ltd.

Chapter 13

Why human resources should care

The benefits and impacts of corporate social responsibility, corporate and brand reputation cannot be separated from the impact they have on the human resources of an organization. Similarly the marketing and community investment strategies have a similar influence on, for instance, the ability to recruit the best employees from graduates through to senior managers and on the ability to positively or negatively affect the attitudes of existing employees towards the business. The ability therefore of Cause Related Marketing to have a positive impact on human resources, and help human resources achieve its objectives, should not be overlooked. It represents a significant opportunity.

Research undertaken by MORI in 1997 amongst 882 British adults, illustrated in Figure 13.1, clearly shows the importance of a company's support of the community in terms of employee relations.

The Prince of Wales Business Leaders Forum survey of business studies graduates (Table 13.1) further reinforced the message coming from the potential business leaders of tomorrow.

Evidence of a company's Cause Related Marketing, like evidence of a company's corporate social responsibility and corporate community investment motivates employees, builds morale and generates pride, all of which have an impact on loyalty and retention – key issues for human resources. Cause Related Marketing, being more overt, more public and generally more vigorously communicated, has demonstrated itself as being an effective way of demonstrating a company's corporate social responsibility and corporate community investment. As such therefore Cause Related Marketing adds value to the strategies of the human resources function. Often however, the potential is not recognized and remains untapped.

Q: 'A company that supports society and community is probably a good company to work for.'

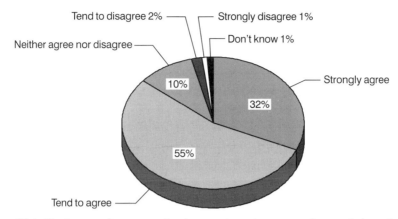

Figure 13.1 The impact of corporate involvement in society on employee relations. *Base:* 882 British adults, August 1997. *Source:* MORI

As a key measurement, the Business in the Community/Research International (UK) Ltd research[1] indicates that employee satisfaction is something that community affairs and marketing directors consider important in the evaluation of Cause Related Marketing programmes and I am sure this will grow. Often as part of the process of identifying the cause, employees' views are surveyed, building ownership therefore of the outcome by involving, engaging and motivating staff right from the start.

The most up to date research that explores the connection between Cause Related Marketing and human resources is the Cone/Roper 1999 study[2].

Table 13.1 What are the most important factors in considering a future employer?

Factor	Ranking
Career growth potential	1
Good corporate reputation	2
Starting salary	3
Fringe benefits	4
Record of high yield for shareholders	5
Good sports and social facilities	6

Source: Cone/Roper (1999)[2]

Effect of Cause Related Marketing on employees

- Nine in ten workers whose companies have a cause programme feel proud of their company's values versus 56 per cent of those whose employers are not committed to a cause.
- 87 per cent of employees whose companies have a cause programme feel a strong sense of loyalty to their companies versus 67 per cent of those employed in companies without a cause association.
- More than half of all workers (56 per cent) wish their employers would do more to support a social cause.
- Nearly half of all large corporations currently have programmes associated with a social issue, as reported by their employees.

Source: Cone/Roper (1999) Cause Related Marketing Trend Report, The Evolution of Cause Branding[SM]

Cause Related Marketing can generate a sense of pride, which, as the research shows, is directly correlated to employee loyalty and therefore retention. Cause Related Marketing has therefore fantastic potential to deliver against key human resources objectives, and, as has been covered in numerous studies, the key to future competitiveness will be in the ability to attract and retain quality employees. It is therefore in the interest of human resources professionals to support, encourage, collaborate and possibly even initiate such programmes as they clearly make sound departmental sense.

Looking at the evidence from both the UK and abroad, Cause Related Marketing makes sound business sense. With the increasing sophistication and perhaps cynicism of consumers, individuals feel and are empowered to act. With the speed of global communication, news travels fast and therefore stakeholders are able to act and react much more quickly.

In the drive to enhance corporate reputation and build licence to operate and to develop customer loyalty, long-term stakeholder relationships, create product differentiation, develop promotions, awareness, PR, provide added value, increase sales, volume build customer traffic and attract the best employees, organizations should use the full range of marketing advertising, community affairs and human resources strategies. The research evidence is clear. Cause Related Marketing programmes have demonstrated success against each of these imperatives and many more and should therefore be part of the armoury.

There seem to be global pressures from the consumer for business to take up its responsibilities and executives everywhere are appreciating that this trend will develop rather than abate.

From the UK point of view, there is no doubt that chief executives, marketing directors and community affairs directors think that Cause Related Marketing will grow in importance in the next two to three years and this has also been reflected internationally.

There is clearly a business rationale for acting in a socially responsible way and for utilizing Cause Related Marketing strategies. Increasingly more and more businesses, and departments within businesses, are understanding this and developing strategies and approaches accordingly.

Notes

1 The Corporate Survey II (1998), Business in the Community quantitative Cause Related Marketing research conducted by Research International (UK) Ltd.
2 Cone/Roper (1999) Cause Related Marketing Trend Report, The Evolution of Cause Branding[SM].

Chapter 14

Partners not patrons: why charities and causes should care

Charities and causes are working with the same demands as business, it's simply that the market sector, and products are different. Corporate fundraising teams are therefore working with the same type of objectives as their marketing colleagues. The same objectives are driving both the fundraising and the marketing strategies. Image enhancement, awareness, relationship building and loyalty are key to all, as are sales and income. The strategies and mechanics for both fundraisers and marketing colleagues alike are drawn from the same tool kit with the addition perhaps for fundraisers of being able to draw on the addition of legacies, covenants and donations. Cause Related Marketing is therefore one of the strategies that is available to fundraisers. Like marketing however it is not the only solution and should be used appropriately and in concert with other aspects of the fundraising mix.

The terms may be different, the means are often similar and the ends are ultimately the same: for the product, service or image to be enhanced; to have a greater share of the market, to deliver the most effective solution and to increase sales and income.

Concern has been voiced amongst some sectors of the charity world that Cause Related Marketing is taking resources away from the foundations, philanthropic funds and donations that individuals and corporates have made in the past. It is felt by others that it has the potential to erode traditional philanthropy, that Cause Related Marketing encourages a charity to sell its soul and that smaller less 'fashionable' charities will suffer.

Evidence suggests both in the UK and elsewhere that donations to charities and causes are under significant pressure and indeed in some cases they are falling. There is also clear evidence that conditions upon which philanthropic monies are being donated and community investment monies being invested are becoming far more focused and stringent. The traditional source of funds is therefore by no means secure and with a growing number of charities chasing fewer funds, the need to be well targeted, focused and creative becomes even more important.

A reduction in the source of funds when the needs are growing is a major concern for all charities and causes regardless of size. Cause Related Marketing however is and should be providing additional funds which are drawn from entirely new budget sources – that is, marketing budgets which are based on different sets of objectives. As has been mentioned earlier, the marketing budgets are in the region of eight times the size of community affairs budgets and therefore if charities and causes are able to attract a percentage of these larger budgets the potential for increased funds and support is enhanced. If the charity or cause whilst at the same time as attracting the new funds from marketing, is able to present and argue the case that both the marketing and the community affairs objectives can be achieved through the same partnership, the size of the potential funds and resources is further enhanced. Building on this, it may also be possible to attract the support from human resources and other parts of the business thereby encouraging collaboration across the different parts of the business to achieve their objectives. Such a vision and strategy provides the potential to leverage the opportunity, thereby increasing the size of the overall funds and support package. This concept of leverage is key.

The National Council for Voluntary Organizations (NCVO) in the UK, who track trends in charitable giving, report that since the National Lottery started, individual donations to charity have fallen by 20 per cent. The NCVO figures in 1997 indicated that whilst large charities were growing at around 7 per cent in real terms, since 1994, medium sized charities have suffered a drop in income of approximately 3.4 per cent between 1994 and 1997, whilst small charities have only just managed to keep pace with inflation. The NCVO report that charitable income from business is still very small, representing only 4 per cent of voluntary sector income.

According to the Corporate Citizen/Directory of Social Change report for 1997[1], of the top 50 corporate fundarising charities, the amount of money raised from companies was estimated as £91 million, an 8 per cent increase on 1996/7. According to this study, donations account for the majority of this corporate income, and of the charities who responded, they reported that Cause Related Marketing was a growing area. For instance in 1997/8, over 90 per cent of UNICEF's income, £2,100,000, was linked to Cause Related Marketing.

Early indications from the analysis of the figures from the Corporate Citizen/Directory of Social Change 1998 annual survey show that Cause Related Marketing has more than doubled from £5.49 million to £14.5 million, although £5.6 million is attributable to Comic Relief 1999. Taking this out of the equation, charity income from Cause Related Marketing has increased by 63 per cent.

The environment in which charities are competing for funds is increasingly competitive and therefore it is important to consider all appropriate sources of support and revenue from individuals, corporates, foundations or elsewhere. Looking to business as an area of potential, if a percentage of these larger marketing budgets can be diverted towards addressing the social issues of the day, the size of the overall budget for impact on the wider community could grow exponentially.

> Backing social causes, . . . moves corporations onto a moral plain. You may not like profit-minded chief executives deciding which charities get all the loot. But in an era of shrinking government responsibility for the welfare of its citizens, somebody has to pick up the tab.[2]

The opportunity that Cause Related Marketing potentially provides the charity sector is fantastic, but it must be considered thoroughly. The risks are as significant as the potential rewards. The strategy therefore must be clearly considered and assuming it is approved, it is essential that proposals are relevant, well thought through and clearly targeted. This need is reinforced by the findings of The Corporate Survey II[3]. This study revealed the high levels of Cause Related Marketing proposals that companies are receiving, with each business receiving on average seven proposals a month. This average camouflages the fact that many of the blue chip organizations receive hundreds a month.

Volume of Cause Related Marketing proposals received by businesses

- 79 per cent of business respondents receive at least one Cause Related Marketing proposal each month.
- 61 per cent of respondents receive between 1 and 10 proposals every month.
- 6 per cent of respondents receive over 20 Cause Related Marketing proposals a month.

Source: The Corporate Survey II (1998), Business in the Community quantitative Cause Related Marketing research conducted by Research International (UK) Ltd

---

To attract marketing budgets there needs to be a sound business argument that meets the objectives of the business, whilst at the same time meeting those of the charity or cause. The proposals need to outline the specific reasons for a partnership with the particular charity or cause versus the other 200,000 voluntary organizations in the UK, not to mention competing with more traditional marketing strategies. At the most basic levels, marketing teams can for instance be considering the Cause Related Marketing strategy or tactical opportunity against the tried and tested 'Buy one, get one free' or 'X% extra free' sales promotion mechanic. It is a competitive market. Cause Related Marketing can of course deliver so much more than short-term sales – indeed the purely tactical use of Cause Related Marketing undersells the opportunity completely.

If the case can be made, and the mutual objectives achieved through a partnership based on sound ethical principles, then a Cause Related Marketing solution could lead to new and additional funds, marketing funds. Indeed the challenge is to get both the business and the charity or cause to independently take a holistic approach to their business and then together look at how to leverage their Cause Related Marketing strategies. Encouraging collaboration across all of the different divisions of the organization to channel their efforts, energies, budgets and resources to support particular strategies will of course provide greater resource to support such strategies. The integrated strength of marketing, community affairs, human resources, chairman budgets and others with the combined focus of corporate fundraising, donor relations, legacies and covenants all working together to address a specific challenge or issue, has the potential to make a fantastic positive impact both for the cause or issue and the business, providing a greater return on the investment of all involved.

The question has been raised as to whether Cause Related Marketing is only relevant or available to larger more fashionable charities and causes. I do not believe this to be the case. There are many examples where local corner shops, pubs, restaurants and even estate agents have got behind a particular local hospital or school to raise funds by giving a portion of their sales or through a percentage donation from a particular product or service. This has been proven to be extremely effective for all involved. I believe the issue is about synergy and affinity; creativity and passion; energy and commitment.

As for the more fashionable charities, defining what is fashionable for one group versus another is interesting. Recently at a conference, a breast cancer charity asked how it could attract Cause Related Marketing funding when it was clearly a less fashionable cause. I cited Avon Crusade Against Breast Cancer as a demonstration of first what sort of commitment could be attracted for the apparently 'unfashionable' cause. I also drew attention to the superb example of the thirty-five staff at Nambarrie Tea Company Ltd in Northern Ireland who through their total partnership with Action Cancer, a breast cancer charity, doubled their funding. Through the course of their partnership they also closed the factory for the day to help make the collection boxes and pink ribbons and also funded an advertising commercial. Vision, synergy, imagination, creativity, passion, energy and commitment is what it takes.

There is further evidence from organizations like Tusk who negotiated and benefited from successful programmes in the UK with the *Young Telegraph* and Debenhams, or with Crisis who have developed and achieved important objectives through Cause Related Marketing partnerships with New Covent Garden Soup Company; Whizz-Kidz with BT; The Medical Foundation for the Victims of Torture with Waterstone's; and The Terrence Higgins Trust with Selfridges.

I am also aware of a large multinational which when researching what cause or issue to support provided research groups with a range of options with a particular emphasis on what some describe as the less obviously 'attractive' charities, causes or issues. The question was asked whether associating key consumer brands with these issues would have a negative affect on the brand or on consumer perceptions of the company. Consumers gave overwhelming approval of the idea of supporting this particular group of charities. The multinational is currently considering the next steps in developing their Cause Related Marketing strategy.

The message to those causes and issues that feel that corporates would not want to align their marketing to them is, think through the likely objectives that the prospective business might be trying to meet and how you can support these. Consider what benefits you can provide; collaborate with each other and do some consumer research, indeed collaborate with each other and offer yourselves as a package or one unit. This provides a greater entity which has the potential for greater spread and impact and can in some cases provide a more attractive proposition to the corporate.

The Children's Miracle Network in the USA and Canada is a great example of how, rather than operating as individual hospitals focusing on a small local market which is likely only to be able to attract small and local businesses, by the 170 hospitals (which treated over 14 million kids in the USA in 1998) coming together as one, The Children's Miracle Network are able to offer a nationwide reach for a prospective partner and therefore in some cases represents a much more attractive opportunity. In 1998 the Children's Miracle Network retail programme has now developed to work with over 100 grocery, drug and mass retail chains along with five major packaged goods sponsors and in 1998 this retail campaign generated over $50 million. In addition to these 100+ retail champions the Children's Miracle Network have agreements with over 70 corporate sponsors.

Another example of collaboration would be the Jeans for Genes alliance in the UK which currently uses a 'dress down' fundraising technique as well as Cause Related Marketing to raise funds for relatively unknown organizations. The organizations involved in the Jean for Genes Campaign, which is a registered charity, include Great Ormond Street Hospital Children's Charity, The Chronic Granulomatous Disorder Research Trust, The Primary Immuno-deficiency Association and The Society for Mucopolysaccharide Diseases. All of these charities, apart from Great Ormond Street Hospital Children's Charity, are small in themselves, but together provide a larger opportunity. In 1998 alone, this partnership, with the support of Levi, Lee, Pepe Jeans, Falmer Original Jeanswear, Burton Menswear, Dorothy Perkins, Evans, Hawkshead, Principles, Racing Green, Top Shop/Top Man, Boots, New Look and TESCO PLC, raised over £2.3 million with Top Shop, Burton, Principles and Dorothy Perkins all donating £1 for every pair of jeans sold during Jeans for Genes week. This partnership illustrates how small charities can raise their profile and their donation earnings opportunities through collaborating with each other within the umbrella of another well known charity brand.

This said, from a business point of view naturally these collaborative Cause Related Marketing opportunities have to be turnkey. Helping a group of organizations organize and run themselves is a very different proposition for a potential business partner from presenting them with the opportunity at one stroke to be able to benefit sick children throughout the country whilst at the same time enhancing the corporate, brand or product reputation and increasing loyalty and sales. It is essential therefore to be clear what is being offered, what is being asked for and what the mutual benefits might be *vis à vis* the various organizations' objectives. I repeat, vision, synergy, imagination, creativity, passion, energy and commitment reap results.

Whether or not Cause Related Marketing will work for a particular charity or cause will for instance be based on creativity, imagination and thinking through the objectives and how to communicate to the various stakeholders. From a communications point of view one needs to consider the merits of communicating what the overall objective of the cause or charity is, rather than, for instance, focusing on how the charity or cause achieves this. This does not mean sell your soul, this means consider how best to communicate with whatever potential partner or stakeholder group you wish to attract or call to action. Consider for instance the difference between asking for help in raising funds for audio tapes for the blind and dyslexic versus talking about workforce readiness. The fact is the tapes are the means to achieving the vital ends of enabling people to take a full and active part in all aspects of life and with access to audio tapes of books, articles, etc., that the sighted are able to read, this group of society are kept equally informed and up to date, and are thereby able to take an even fuller more active role in the workplace. To lead on the message which focuses on the ends not the means is for some stakeholders including potential corporate partners an attractive proposition. In fact a charity in the USA working in this area by turning round the way it was communicating its message was able to see direct benefits in terms of corporate support.

The point is therefore, understand the target market, the potential business partner, what motivates them and their target markets and adapt the balance of your message accordingly. By so doing this may increase the success rate in attracting corporate partners for all charities and causes including the less 'fashionable' or smaller organizations.

Those that argue that 'the growth of joint-marketing ventures involving business and charities is a sign of real weakness in the fundraising profession'[4] are, I believe, misguided. On the contrary, those fundraisers that see and develop the potential of Cause Related Marketing are adapting to the new social and economic environment. Such partnerships are and will continue to be a key constituent in the fundraising strategies of the future.

Times change, markets change, the environment changes and it is vital for all to understand these movements and the implications thereof. As mentioned earlier the trends in corporate philanthropy and individual donations are not encouraging. In the UK the profile of philanthropic giving has shown a marked decline over the last few years (Figure 14.1).

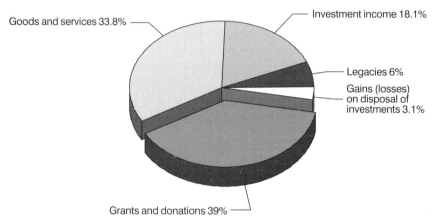

Figure 14.1 Income streams for general UK charities as a percentage of total income for 1997 (total income £13,074.8 million). *Source: NCVO Almanac 1998*

Taking the overall picture of UK charities' income streams, the category 'grants and donations' represents the largest share, worth £5095 million of the total £13,075 million.

The 0.1 per cent growth in grants and donations income hides the fact that the traditional forms of charitable income from individuals is shrinking, indeed the profile for this key source of income has been shrinking significantly over the last decade. According to NCVO figures, the percentage of UK population donating to charity has fallen from 81 per cent in 1994 to 65 per cent in 1997.

The income generated from this key, traditional source has also declined dramatically since 1993, according to the NCVO research, representing a 31 per cent fall in real terms (see Figure 14.3).

The same 0.1 per cent growth in grants and donations disguises the significant 27.9 per cent growth in income from trading subsidiaries. Trading

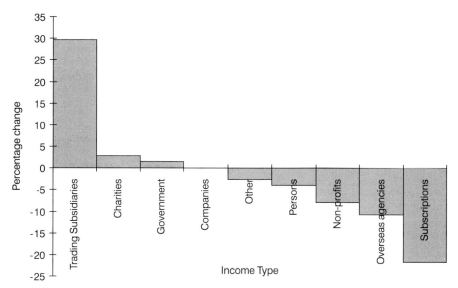

Figure 14.2 Percentage change in grants and donations income 1994–97. *Source: NCVO Almanac 1998,* p. 77

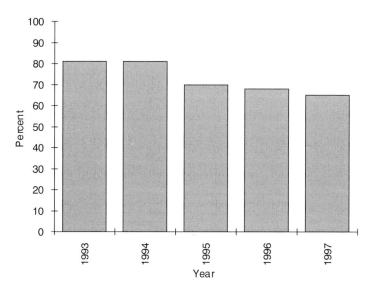

Figure 14.3 Profile of percentage change in number of individual donors 1993–97 as a percentage of UK population. *Source: NVCO Research Quarterly,* Issue 3, September, 1998

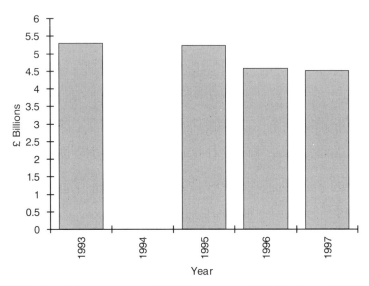

Figure 14.4 Profile of change in total charitable donations 1993–97. *Source: NVCO Research Quarterly,* Issue 3, September, 1998

subsidiaries often receive the funds generated by Cause Related Marketing initiatives, to be covenanted to the parent charity. It is interesting therefore to speculate just how much of the growth is attributed to the increase in Cause Related Marketing and other such commercial activities which are providing new sources of income (see Figures 14.2 and 14.4).

It would seem from the *NCVO 1998 Almanac* figures that it is the larger charities that are seeing particularly strong growth from their trading subsidiaries. Perhaps as with the blue chip businesses of the FTSE 100, these larger charities and the fundraising methods they use to generate income, will have a domino effect on smaller charities over time. This may be through setting up trading subsidiaries, trading activities and using Cause Related Marketing and other dynamic strategies, tools and techniques.

The 0.1 per cent growth in income from grants and donations also includes a 0.1 per cent growth in income from companies. Combined with the growth in income from trading subsidiaries which, as described earlier, often receives the income from Cause Related Marketing programmes, this growth, although marginal, would seem to confirm the fact that Cause Related Marketing is not eroding corporate donations to charity and does in fact provide an additional source of income.

From the point of view of charitable funding with its trend of decline in key and traditional sources of funding, it is vital that appropriate alternative income sources are sought and explored. There would seem to be clear indication that Cause Related Marketing presents an interesting and potentially valuable option to work in concert with the other income strategies.

> Cause Related Marketing is not yet fully utilized in the United Kingdom. The vast potential it has to offer is unique and it will probably be the biggest growth area for charities in their efforts to increase revenue and profile in the years to come.

> **Assaf Admoni, Marketing Director, The National Autistic Society**

In the USA the trends are similar. Corporate donations to non-profits are rising in terms of value although there is some concern that this increase does not reflect the corporates' increases in profits. The American Association of Fund-Raising Counsel's[5] estimate of 1997 corporate giving of $8.20 billion, represents a 7.5 per cent increase over 1996. However, $8.20 billion only represents 1.1 per cent of pretax income, which is a low percentage when placed in historical context. The increase in mergers and acquisitions has been blamed[6] for some of the decline in terms of the percentage of pre-tax profits being donated as companies are reluctant to make financial commitments during these lengthy processes. These figures however do not include funding non-profits received from businesses through marketing, community relations and advertising budgets which is regarded as a business expense, not a tax-deductible charitable contribution. Charities and fundraisers particularly – ignore these trends at your peril.

Cause Related Marketing is just one of the fund raising tools available to the corporate fund raiser and should be used as appropriate. As Ellen West of the Charities Aid Foundation in the UK said in July 1998 when talking about the newly launched Business in the Community Cause Related Marketing Guidelines:

> Cause Related Marketing is an exciting concept that has great potential to generate additional resources for funding the voluntary sector. It should complement traditional corporate philanthropy and help companies meet their business objectives more fully.

Further, Stuart Etherington, Chief Executive of the National Council for Voluntary Organizations, said:

> Although charities are becoming more and more business aware, partnerships with business are still an unexplored, sensitive territory for many . . . Public confidence in charities depends on the maintenance of the sector's good name; it only takes one unsuccessful partnership to tarnish this good name and dent the public's trust in charities as a whole. However much charities are attracted to business partnerships to increase income, especially in the present challenging economic climate, we would urge any organization contemplating such a venture to be clear and realistic

about the outcomes, to take every step to ensure that the organization is fully aware of what the joint endeavour entails, to get the backing of their members, and, most importantly, to be clear that the partnership does not run counter to what the charity was set up to achieve. That way they are sure to get the most out of their partnership.

Stuart Etherington, Chief Executive, NCVO, on the launch of the Business in the Community Cause Related Marketing Guidelines

Clearly Cause Related Marketing is not appropriate for all circumstances but obviously it is for some. The case studies mentioned in this book attest to that and the results speak for themselves. Cause Related Marketing is not without risk however, and these risks should be clearly understood before embarking along the Cause Related Marketing road[7]. If the risks are understood; if the relationship is based on the key principles of integrity, transparency, sincerity, mutual respect, partnership, and mutual benefit; providing the planning and preparation are sound; the implementation, management and communication are thoroughly managed then there is every chance that an excellent mutually beneficial Cause Related Marketing partnership and programme will result.

Clearly there are some fairly significant ifs, but as you will see in the course of this book, many have achieved very successful programmes. Successful Cause Related Marketing partnerships depend on both partners understanding their own mission, vision and objectives and understanding what unique features advantages and benefits they can bring. It is essential to build the case as to why organization (a) is the most appropriate to form an alliance with rather than organization (b). Clearly a lot of homework and desk research needs to be done in order to build the case and understand the strategies, needs and likely objectives of a prospective partner, but it is possible. It is also important to consider collaboration.

Size and manpower are not the crucial factors to success as some would argue; rather its a foundation based on the key principles[8], a sound strategy with a clear synergy and raison d'être that provides benefits and meets the needs of all parties. Imagination and creativity, planning, preparation, passion, energy and commitment, professionalism and attention to detail – none of which have anything to do with size or manpower – are then the keys to success.

As has been suggested, there is concern that if Cause Related Marketing succeeds at the expense of other forms of corporate fundraising this will have a significant and detrimental affect on the less fashionable causes, which, it is argued, will fail to reap the benefits. This argument seems to be based on either/or premises which I believe to be unfounded. It is not necessarily a question of corporate donations reducing as a result of increased Cause Related Marketing, but rather a new opportunity has come into the mix which targets new budgets and is based on partnership not patronage.

Concerns have been raised concerning whether Cause Related Marketing forces a charity or case to sell their soul. In this concern there appears to be an implication perhaps that business has the upper hand in this relationship, but as Ken Madine, Head of Corporate Partnerships at Age Concern, reported in an article in *Corporate Citizen*[9]: 'Don't be surprised if charities occasionally say no to a relationship ... some charities receive several approaches each week.' Clearly no one is forced into anything within a Cause Related Marketing partnership. The partners involved should be professional, competent individuals who understand the vision, mission, values and objectives of their organization. Provided the key principles and elements of the process are attended to in the development of the relationship, there is every likelihood that a successful Cause Related Marketing programme will result that provides benefits for all[10]. It is clearly up to the charity or cause concerned to be clear about what its values are, what it is and is not prepared to do; what is and is not negotiable. Clearly whoever is negotiating the relationship needs to have the authority to do so and the support of the organization, be they a business, charity or cause. If the resulting agreement leaves either side feeling aggrieved or abused, the reason will lie in failing to base the relationship on the key principles and the failure to follow a sound and thorough process, but at no point is anyone forced to do something they are unhappy about.

I would suggest that Cause Related Marketing does not encourage organizations to sell their souls. With sound research, planning, preparation and a clear understanding of one's own organization's vision and values combined with a thorough understanding of those of the potential partners; with a clear, open, honest and transparent discussion and appreciation of the mutual objectives to be achieved enshrined in a clear and formal agreement; with a creative, targeted, well balanced programme that is based on partnership and mutual respect there is every chance that success will result and that souls remain well intact. If a charity sells its soul that is not, I would argue, the fault of Cause Related Marketing, but rather of the understanding, ability, competence, integrity and ethics of those involved in planning, negotiating, implementing and communicating the programme.

A corporate fundraiser who sees the opportunities that Cause Related Marketing presents, is a corporate fundraiser who understands the market realities. Apart from the key principles, caution, appropriateness, balance, being true to core values and planning and preparation will be central to this future. There is no question that the future of corporate fundraising will sees a significant shift from patrons to partners.

Notes

1 Corporate Citizen/Directory of Social Change report of the top 50 corporate fundraising charities, Spring/Summer issue 1998.

2 van Voorst, B. (1997) The New World of Giving, Time, May 5.
3 The Corporate Survey II (1998) Business in the Community quantitative Cause Related Marketing research conducted by Research International (UK) Ltd.
4 Warner, I. *Art of Fund Raising* (from van Voorst, B. (1997) The New World of Giving, Time, May 5).
5 *Giving USA 1998*, produced by the American Association of Fund-Raising Counsel.
6 Reported in *Philanthropy Journal Alert*, Vol. 3, No. 62, April 14 1999, from the Chicago Sun-Times.
7 See Part Four of this book.
8 The Cause Related Marketing Guidelines – Towards Excellence (1998) Business in the Community.
9 *Corporate Citizen*, Issue 25, Winter 1999.
10 The Cause Related Marketing Guidelines – Towards Excellence (1998) Business in the Community.

Part Three

Application of Cause Related Marketing

Chapter 15

Cause Related Marketing models

Cause Related Marketing can appear in many different guises and from different parts of an organization, as has been mentioned before. It is important to be clear about the objectives for a particular partnership or programme and use the most appropriate mechanic for the circumstances. As has been argued earlier, the most effective Cause Related Marketing is when it is developed as part of a long-term strategy, thereby providing a maximum return on the investment of time, effort and money put in by all parties concerned. Tactical use of Cause Related Marketing does have its place. It can for instance satisfy the short-term need of either party or indeed serve as a pilot for a longer term scheme. Cause Related Marketing should always be considered within the context of the strategic implications of the link. Those involved should be clear of potential stakeholder reaction. Clear, open, honest and balanced communication is key, whether a programme be tactical or strategic.

In the following paragraphs I have attempted to outline some of the most frequently used mechanics as well as some of the more innovative.

Some writers on the subject of Cause Related Marketing have suggested that there are three or four types of Cause Related Marketing. Professor Alan Andreasen suggests in an article written for the *Harvard Review* in November–December 1996 that there are three key forms of alliance: transaction based promotions, joint issue promotions and licensing[1]. This covers part but not all of the spectrum of Cause Related Marketing. There are a number of other forms of Cause Related Marketing including the advertising, PR or sponsorship led programmes. It is possible to perhaps try and summarize where Cause Related Marketing is at any given point in time but the rate at which developments are taking place in marketing mean that such a statement will shortly be out of date. Marketing is developing at a rate and therefore with that so are the potential forms of Cause Related Marketing. Cause Related Marketing is precisely that. It is entirely about marketing related to a cause and within that, the limits of Cause Related Marketing are created or are defined only by the limitations of one's imagination. If one accepts that the marketing mix consists of the 4Ps of product, price, place (distribution) and promotion or promotional mix, Cause Related Marketing falls within this promotional mix. The promotional mix is ever growing and therefore so is the scope of Cause Related Marketing. The promotional mix includes advertising, sales promotion, public relations or publicity, sponsorship, licensing and direct marketing, which includes loyalty and relationship marketing etc.

I would suggest that Cause Related Marketing can be demonstrated under these six broad headings as a minimum.

Advertising

Advertising clearly includes a variety of media; anything from TV and satellite or Internet advertising to print and press campaigns. Cause Related Marketing advertising therefore can include any or all of these media. From a content point of view, Cause Related Marketing/advertising may focus on communicating a particular sales promotion, as in the TESCO Computers for Schools programme. Alternatively Cause Related Marketing/advertising can also refer to the advertising of a particular cause or issue where the business aligns itself with a particular good cause and uses its advertising to communicate the cause message. Apart from raising awareness of the particular cause or issue, the objectives from the organization's point of view can range from anything from building, reinforcing or demonstrating corporate or brand reputation to providing differentiation and encouraging relationships and loyalty between the product, service or charity, cause or corporate.

From a TV commercial point of view, a particular favourite example of mine of this form of Cause Related Marketing was created by Members Only, an American clothes manufacturer of men's outerwear.

Members Only

For several years all of Members Only marketing funds, including the advertising budgets, were pooled together to create powerful TV advertisements encouraging people to vote. Hitler, Nuremberg rally and Mussolini footage were used to create incredibly powerful images with an end line that said: '200 years ago the constitution of the United States suggested a very simple way to keep idiots like these out of our government. There is no excuse not to vote.'

Members Only clearly differentiated and distinguished itself in a crowded market place, evidenced through prime time TV coverage. Fox News of Los Angeles began a news item at the time with:

'Getting a little tired of all those negative campaign ads on the TV these days, Yes? Well, Eric Burns says he's found one, mind you only one, that is actually positive. And as you might imagine it comes from no-one's campaign.'

A variety of ways have been tried over the years to persuade people to vote. In nineteenth-century America men were sometimes 'couped'; the word refers to drugging and sometimes intoxicating men and dragging them to the polls. In twentieth century Australia, non voters are fined unless they have a good excuse for not voting. Back in America, late in the twentieth century all we do is beg people to vote, plea with them in phrases that sound like small town 4th July speeches. Well, Members Only, a clothing company of all things has decided to do something different. Watch … (shows video) … That is the best 30 second television inducement to vote I have ever seen. Well, congratulations to Members Only for not mincing their words, for having an impact on the screen which one can only hope will have an impact at the polls.

In the years when there was no election, Members Only ran a campaign entitled 'Say No to Drugs' featuring well known celebrities.

Avon in the USA has taken the concept of using television and satellite channels in promoting a cause message even further by funding documentaries on breast cancer as part of the Avon Crusade Against Breast Cancer[2].

In the UK we have not yet seen such powerful applications. Norwich Union[2] however led their Cause Related Marketing partnership with St John Ambulance with a wonderful TV commercial. The commercial aimed to create differentiation in the market place, reinforce their positioning that 'No one cares for you more' and so develop associations and relationships with their market. At the same time by promoting the Norwich Union link with St. John Ambulance and the free first aid courses that were part of the programme available to the 25,000 members of the public who responded to the advertisement in each market it was shown, Norwich Union were responsible for getting St. John Ambulance on TV for the first time in their history. This was therefore a fantastic opportunity to generate awareness of their name and mission to a broad section of the public.

In each case referred to, use of the TV commercials has added enormous value, not only to the business but also to the cause.

From a press advertising point of view, many Cause Related Marketing partnerships use this medium which clearly serves to bring the message to a wide audience and therefore increase the impact of the message.

Public relations

Public relations is often cited as a key benefit and indeed a key objective of Cause Related Marketing and in some cases represents the leading discipline in defining, creating and implementing a Cause Related Marketing programme. Cadbury Ltd's strategic partnership with Save the Children[2] demonstrated through the Cadbury Strollerthon and pantomime season, the Tanqueray Aids Rides[2], the London Electricity Winter Warmer Campaign with Age Concern, Persil and their Go Red for Comic Relief programme[2], Adam's Childrenswear and Save the Children[2], Avon and Fashion Targets Breast Cancer[2] and New Covent Garden Soup Company Cause Related Marketing relationships with Crisis and the National Trust[2], are all prime examples.

The key to getting the PR coverage for Cause Related Marketing is the same as for any other PR activity. Newsworthiness, innovation and excitement are all crucial but there is a significant difference for Cause Related Marketing, and that is that the balance in the communication must be absolutely appropriate. This is dealt with in more detail in Chapter 25 on communications, but suffice to say that both the media and the public have to be clear that any Cause Related Marketing partnership is sincere, open, transparent and honest; that the relationship is based upon a partnership of mutual respect and that there is balanced benefit to be accrued by both sides. It is not appropriate for the corporate organization to spend more time and effort publicizing their involvement in the activity than it is investing in. As has been argued in Chapter 11, the army of vigilante consumers is thriving and growing; consumers are more cynical and sophisticated and therefore messages have to be communicated openly and honestly if the public and the media are going to support the partnerships and for the maximum benefit to be achieved.

Sponsorship

A key way of realizing a Cause Related Marketing partnership is often through sponsoring a particular event or activity. What makes it Cause Related Marketing as opposed to standard sponsorship is the fact that, first, what is being sponsored is a good cause or charity. Second, that the organizations are actively marketing this relationship to meet their own objectives and those of their partner. Objectives, as have been highlighted earlier, can range from awareness, PR, demonstrations of corporate and brand values, consumer engagement, generating trial, providing a differential etc. In some cases the sponsorship might be straight commercial relationship with cause links interwoven within it.

Coca-Cola's 'Community Heroes'

Coca-Cola's sponsorship of the Atlanta Olympics in 1996 is an example of this. Through the extension of this sponsorship, Coca-Cola sponsored the Olympic Torch Relay. This included the 'Community Heroes' whereby in association with the Atlanta Committee for the Olympic Games, Coca-Cola through this sponsorship, funded the search for thousands of local community heroes to be Olympic torchbearers, honouring their work as volunteers and their achievements. This programme was supplemented by Coca-Cola's own 'Share the Spirit' programme.

The 'Community Heroes' concept, managed by United Way, aimed to identify 'local heroes who everyday, in every action, bring to life the meaning of the Olympic Spirit'. All Community Heroes possessed one or more of the core values and ideals and were people who: perform outstanding volunteer work; serve as a community leader, role model or mentor; perform acts of generosity or kindness; perform extraordinary feats or accomplishments, locally or nationally.

In extending the concept Coca-Cola developed 'Share the Spirit' through which a further 2500 people were identified by individuals nominating someone who was special in their lives. Coca-Cola put the marketing and PR investment behind this to promote the concept and opportunity for local heroes. Entry was driven through Coca-Cola branded entry forms available in retail stores, inviting the public to make their nominations. PR, awareness, store traffic and indeed sales all benefited for both Coca-Cola and their partners whilst at the same time involving key target audiences in the brand and the concept, celebrating community heroes.

The Torch Relay travelled more than 15,000 miles over 84 days, through 42 states and the District of Columbia, via 29 state capitals and came within a 2 hour drive of 90 per cent of the United States population.

Coca-Cola naturally benefited from the halo effect generated by such a community spirited activity, and from the reinforcement of their core values whilst at the same time building sales. This relationship therefore incorporated both the commercial sponsorship as well as the community celebration and benefit, thus demonstrating the application of Cause Related Marketing within a much wider commercial sponsorship.

BT Swimathon

BT Swimathon is the largest fundraising swim marathon in Europe, raising over £12 million; 27 national charities have benefited and over 300,000 people have taken part at an average of 500 pools, leisure centres or health clubs across the UK. The neatness of the idea behind BT Swimathon makes it a true community event where everyone wins.

A charity is chosen each year which will be the main beneficiary, receiving 70 per cent of the funds raised. The remaining funds raised are shared each year between

Disability Sports England (DSE), the British Paralympic Association (BPA), the UK Sports Association (UKSA) and the Amateur Swimming Association (ASA).

A strong partnership has developed during the nine-year relationship between BT and LEA Events, who own and operate the event. In 1998, BT invested £500,000 in the programme, the return on this investment was almost £2 million in terms of the sponsorship money generated and hundreds of thousands of pounds worth of positive publicity for BT. Eighteen per cent of the general public questioned have heard of BT Swimathon in the last year, second only to Comic Relief, a TV led campaign. The BT Swimathon is now the leading BT sponsored activity in terms of media coverage for community projects and as a result of this sponsorship the public's perception that BT takes its responsibilities to society and the community seriously has moved from 42 per cent in 1991 to 59 per cent in 1997.

Licensing

In a licensing relationship, the corporate pays for the licence to use the charity logo or identity on its product or service. The corporate generally wants to use the charity logo to sell more product or services; to benefit from the implied endorsement and halo effect of the charity or cause and the positive values that it projects. This is very much a commercial relationship. The charity or cause can decide whether or not to sign up to the deal and as part of that process put a price on the opportunity and consider the effects on their own brand and reputation.

Licensing can sometimes form part of a much broader strategy or programme where the purchase of the rights to use a charity's logo is just part of an overall package of activities that together represent the Cause Related Marketing partnership. It is important to understand that there are tax and VAT rules that impact on this; it can be that certain aspects of a Cause Related Marketing relationship fall under different tax rules. Individuals concerned in negotiating such arrangements should ensure that they are clear about these implications[3].

Examples of the use of licensing as part of an overall Cause Related Marketing relationship would include many of those examples already referred to throughout this text where the charity's logo is included on the packaging and communication. First Direct's Anorak Amnesty is an example where the company paid a licensing fee to use Shelter's logo as part of the partnership and then made further donations. There are numerous other examples including for instance New Covent Garden Soup Company's relationship with the National Trust[2] and Crown Wallcoverings and WWF. Crown have developed the 'Go Wild!' range of wallcoverings which feature wildlife designs through a licensing arrangement with WWF. Crown make a donation to the WWF for every 'Go Wild!' roll sold up to an annual total of £25,000.

Direct marketing

Direct marketing is clearly one of the methods that could be employed to communicate Cause Related Marketing messages. Many charities are experts in the field, managing databases with millions of records. Often access to the charity's database is considered the big prize for the corporate in a Cause Related Marketing relationship. Clearly it is very much up to the charity or cause whether or not it makes this database available and if so under what circumstances.

Those who have concerns about Cause Related Marketing as a way of forcing charities or causes to sell their souls often refer to the abuse of charities' databases as a key concern. Relationships with one's customers or supporters whether one is a charity or cause are crucial and should be guarded with enormous care.

Affinity credit cards probably represent the largest group in this aspect of Cause Related Marketing. To date more than 1000 organizations have launched affinity or co-branded credit cards in a bid to raise funds, extend their brand awareness and give something back to their supporters, members or fans. Starting in the UK in 1987 when Bank of Scotland Direct launched the NSPCC card, nearly 20 per cent of all UK credit cards are now affinity cards and since 1987 more than £40 million has been generated for various organizations. It is said that there are over 350 charity affinity cards in the UK market with charities currently accounting for more than 50 per cent of affinity cards in circulation[4]. Jonathan Moakes of Affinity Solutions cautions: 'Don't rush into it – you could end up wearing a plastic albatross around your neck.'

This is a significant market opportunity; the Bank of Scotland recent affinity cards have apparently raised more than £12 million for good causes. It is of course not without risk. David Williams-Jones of Trans National suggests that such a relationship is akin to a marriage:

> When searching for an affinity partner, supplier or marketer, organizations need to be sure that their programme will be handled professionally. After all you are handing over your brand, logo and reputation to another company.[5]

For every financial organization arranging these affinity card deals, access to the charity or cause database is a pre-requisite. Clearly the charity or cause must decide whether or not the terms of the deal suggested are advantageous or not.

Basic affinity card mechanic

The basic mechanic for an affinity card is that in signing up for the particular card a donation is made to the charity or cause, and in using the cards further donations are made for every £100 or so spent. The charity therefore earns an income dependent on the applications and usage of the card. The credit card company gains access to a new universe of potential users and makes its money in the usual way, donating a percentage of this to the charity or cause.

Cause Related Marketing affinity credit cards generally take one of three forms. Either they represent a purely monogamous relationship where a uniquely branded card is designed and produced for a particular charity. It is then targeted at that charity's database of members and supporters, as in the case of the Royal National Institute for the Blind (RNIB) and the Bank of Scotland affinity card.

From a marketing point of view I think this is one of the more interesting cards of its type as it actually demonstrates a real appreciation of the loyalty dimension these cards can have. Rather than just the one-off sign-up and usage payments to the charity and perhaps an annual further donation, the RNIB card continues to reward the charity and incentivizes the card holder to continue their ownership and use of the card through its first year and beyond. Donations to the charity are triggered provided the card holder continues to hold the card at three, six and nine month intervals as well as at the end of the first year. From the credit card organization's point of view this clearly keeps the momentum of usage going and helps to develop a habit from the holder's point of view. The holder continues to feel like a hero because through their holding and using the card, they cause donations to continue to be made to the charity. The charity also receives larger donations and has a very clear incentive to encourage members to use the card.

A second form of Cause Related Marketing affinity card is one that provides the consumer with a set group of charities that they can choose to benefit. In the case of The Halifax Visa Charity Card, customers are given a choice of any one of three charities to whom funds will be donated. These are currently The British Heart Foundation, Imperial Cancer Research and Mencap. Customers choose which charity they wish to benefit and then the process is fairly standard. A sign-up donation is made at the beginning of the year and donations are triggered for every £100 spent. In fact to celebrate having raised over £10 million for the three charities it supports over the last 10 years, The Halifax has committed to double their donation from 25p to 50p for every £100 spent until they have donated a total extra £1 million.

A third approach is that used by The Co-operative Bank. Through the 'Customers Who Care' programme the bank donates 0.25 per cent of any transaction from a current or savings account to charities. Customers are invited to nominate charities to benefit, both at national and local levels, and money raised through the same mechanic is donated to the charities in relation to the votes received. The list changes every quarter.

Other examples of where direct marketing has been used as a vehicle for Cause Related Marketing include using the latter as an incentive for market research questionnaires, and where, as with London Electricity, the bill is used as the communication vehicle and the return of the masthead or coupon triggers a donation to Age Concern.

London Electricity and Age Concern

To ensure optimum customer involvement and awareness, a tear-off coupon was included on London Electricity's 1.7 million customer bills over a three month period. For every coupon received London Electricity, guaranteed to donate £1 towards the Age Concern Winter Warmer campaign up to the agreed ceiling level. Customers were also able to make their own donations to a specifically set-up Midland Bank fund or directly to Age Concern.

Foxes Biscuits 'Don't be a Stranger'

The Don't be a Stranger campaign was developed to show how biscuits can be used to cheer and encourage sharing in the local community. To date the campaign has consisted of three elements:

1 A series of television advertisements were developed to convey the 'Don't be a Stranger' message and the link with Foxes Biscuits.

2 This was followed up with an integrated below the line direct mail campaign which used money-off coupons and a prize draw to encourage consumer participation. The direct mail campaign was a door drop to 500,000 households which included a money-off coupon that could be redeemed either on its own or was worth a free pack of Foxes biscuits when redeemed with a neighbours' coupon. Winners of the four prize draws entitled customers to a year's supply of Foxes Biscuits for themselves and a charity of their choice.

3 Following the direct mail campaign, Foxes leveraged the campaign further by joining forces with TESCO PLC to raise money for Help the Aged's Brighter Futures Appeal. Help the Aged was the TESCO PLC charity of the year at the time, and the two companies pledged to donate 2p to the appeal for every pack of Foxes Biscuits sold in a TESCO PLC store.

Sales promotion

Sales promotion is such a broad category that it is almost impossible to cover every possible option, but in the next paragraphs I will aim to illustrate some of the most frequently used mechanics and some of the more innovative.

Purchase triggered donations

Cause Related Marketing is probably most often demonstrated within this broad category. Donations to causes are triggered by purchase, as is the case in the New Covent Garden Soup Company and Crisis[2]; Persil and Comic Relief[2]; Daddies Tomato Ketchup and NSPCC which, over two and a half years, raised £250,000 by donating 1p from every purchase of their tomato sauce, and Cormar Carpets who make a donation to Care for the Wild from the purchase of every roll of 'Solemate' recycled underlay.

The range of examples using this type of mechanics is endless and includes companies, charities and causes of all sizes. Examples range from biscuits, books, bank accounts and bath oils to sauce, soup and soap powder, and everything in between. They range from a local pizza restaurant in Barnes wanting to encourage sales by promising to donate a percentage from the sale of wine to the local school, to the tens of thousands raised for Comic Relief through the sale of Persil.

Barnum's Animal Crackers and The World Wildlife Fund USA

This 93 year old brand was aiming to revitalize itself and create excitement, thereby stimulating sales. From April 1995 the packaging changed from the traditional red and yellow to green and introduced 16 new animal crackers. The new packs invited consumers to 'Help save endangered animals around the world every time you buy this product. Nabisco will donate 5 cents from the sale price of this package up to $100,000 to World Wildlife Fund to help protect endangered animals and their habitats.' The programme was so successful they ran out of product in the first 6 weeks and exceeded their targets. The programme was extended to the new line of 'Jelly Jars' (jam) using the same mechanic. Clearly the speed at which these products moved off the shelf demonstrated a clear sales benefit.

James White Apple Juices and the National Trust

James White Apple Juices, a company employing just 11 people, make donations to the National Trust from the sales of bramley apple and elderflower, apple and blackberry and apple and cinnamon fruit juices. The money raised, at least £40,000 over three years, is funding the restoration of a National Trust walled garden local to the company.

Examples don't just include consumer products but also relate to the business to business market too.

BT and Whizz-Kidz and The World Wildlife Fund[2]

BT Mobile's link with the disability charity Whizz-Kidz generated £50,000 through a three month promotion offering £4 to Whizz-Kidz for every new connection made. BT also used Cause Related Marketing to increase sales of its call diversion product to *BT***Business***connections* customers offering £1 donation to WWF for each sign up. Taking these two examples, BT engaged its sales staff, increased its connection, enhanced its profile and raised significant funds for both causes.

Waterstone's and The Medical Foundation for the Victims of Torture

Waterstone's, building on the success of their charity of the year and Cause Related Marketing partnership with Crisis in 1997/8, linked with The Medical Foundation for the Victims of Torture in 1998/9. Cause Related Marketing was used to leverage this partnership and two books were created, a celebration of the 50th anniversary of the Universal Declaration of Human Rights and The Book of Light, a collection of short stories for Christmas. All profits from the sale of these books were donated to the charity. This message is clearly communicated on the cover of the book:

£1.60 of the £1.99 price will be donated to The Medical Foundation for every copy sold of The Book of Light. This represents the entire profit after production and distribution costs.

Thorntons and The Children's Society

Thorntons, the chocolate company, as part of their charity of the year relationship with The Children's Society, produced an advent calendar and an Easter egg with a donation from each product sold to the charity. The product differentiation was such that the advent calendars sold-out completely when showcased at the International Festival of Chocolate.

Trial triggered donations

Cause Related Marketing can also be used to trigger donations through trial, application or signing up to a product or services and through usage. The American Express Restoration of the Statue of Liberty programme and the Charge against Hunger programme (see Chapter 3) that followed demonstrate this model in action, as do The Visa Read Me a Story programme in the USA[2] and SurfAid, the partnership between the Internet service provider Global Internet and Christian Aid whereby £1 of customer's £7.50 monthly subscription fees is donated to Christian Aid.

Voucher collection schemes

Voucher collection schemes are also frequent mechanics for Cause Related Marketing, with the TESCO Computers for Schools programme[2] being an exemplary demonstration but many others have used similar mechanics including a number of other retailers in the UK and abroad.

Using the voucher in another way, London Electricity have raised funds to support the teaching of maths and have also raised funds for Age Concern. Consumers were simply invited to send in a coupon from their bill and this automatically triggered a donation to the particular cause. In the case of London Electricity, apart from easily reaching the fund raising target of £30,000 for Age Concern, the key objective of active customer participation and significant PR for London Electricity were also achieved.

Walkers Crisps and News International's Free Books for Schools

To support the Government's National Year of Reading, Walkers Crisps and News International's Free Books for Schools promotion ran in the first quarter of 1999. This gave customers the opportunity to collect tokens from crisp packets, *The Times, The Sun, The Sunday Times* and *The News of the World*, redeemable by schools for free books. The promotion created a collecting frenzy across the UK with 99 per cent of schools in the UK registered for the scheme and with stories of token collection being published in the newspapers.

Cause Related Marketing as an incentive to action

Cause Related Marketing has been effectively used as an incentive to promote interest dialogue and sales from markets as diverse as banking, with for example Barclays Plc's 'Savings to Make You Smile'[2], and insurance to telecommunications. Examples range from organizations wanting to increase the response rate to research surveys, where a donation was promised to charity in return for the survey's completion, to Cause Related Marketing as an incentive on a mortgage product. Another example of Cause Related Marketing as an incentive is the way in which Selfridges, a large department store in the UK, has used it when running a series of shopping evenings over the last two years. On some evenings the incentive to attend is focused around a make up offer or is run in conjunction with a women's magazine. In other cases the promise of 10 per cent of all proceeds going to The Terrence Higgins Trust has been used. It was said in 1997 when this was first done, that attendance and sales on the evening when donations were being made to The Terrence Higgins Trust far outstripped those of other evenings.

The Leeds Building Society and NCH Action for Children

In 1994 the NCH Action for Children in partnership with a mortgage provider (The Leeds) tested the effects of offering a cash incentive to the consumer versus a donation to charity. The two options were test marketed at the same time in similar markets. The performance of the mortgage providing a donation to the charity was reported as being significantly better than the direct cash incentive.

Toyota and the Muscular Dystrophy Group

When sending market research surveys to lapsed customers, the car manufacturer Toyota offered a donation to the Muscular Dystrophy Group for every completed survey returned. This acted as an incentive for consumers to participate and return the forms. This was highly successful, significantly increasing the usual response rate to their surveys. The returned survey provided Toyota with detailed customer information which could be used to target lapsed customers and to improve customer satisfaction in the future. It also had the added benefit of the 'feel good factor' felt by customers returning the survey. This was also a success for the cause through raised awareness and understanding of the charity amongst a specific target group and also through the financial donation of £10,000 they received from Toyota.

Cable & Wireless Communications and Barnardo's

Cable and Wireless Communications donated 50p to Barnardo's for every completed telecommunications survey they received as part of their launch campaign in the UK in 1997. As well as the information provided by the market research, and raising £150,000 for Barnardo's, this served to build a positive corporate image amongst external publics in the UK.

Cause Related Marketing as an incentive to action has been used by a range of organizations across the full industry and sector splits to great effect. The opportunity to evaluate the effectiveness of a widget incentive versus the use of a charitable link as an incentive for responses, has been tested in the past by, for instance, Macmillan Cancer Relief where a retail voucher, a pen and a charitable donation were tested against each other with the charitable donation proving very successful. The benefits to the business are not only increasing the number of returns and the gathering of useful information, and the potential start of a dialogue with customers or potential customers but also reinforces the organizations' values and commitment to the wider community, by making a real contribution.

Competitions, games and draws

Charitable donations have also been included in competitions, games and draws when for instance a prize is won by the individual and a donation is made by the business to charity, which enables both the winner and the competition organizer to be seen as heroes. The Sunlight example given in Chapter 2 illustrates such an approach as does one aspect of the Barclays Plc 'Savings to make you Smile'. Additional examples range from toilet tissue manufacturers to Christmas trees. For example Andrex, a toilet tissue manufacturer, ran a Cause Related Marketing promotion linking with Barnardos, a children's charity, and Nouvelle, a manufacturer of recycled kitchen and toilet tissue, combined the competition mechanic with a self-liquidating promotion run with Care for the Wild. In another example over Christmas 1998, The British Christmas Tree Growers Association ran a competition and a promotion with The Variety Club children's charity to increase sales of British Christmas trees. The charity received 25p from the sale of every British Christmas tree and on each there was the chance to win a 'kids go free' offer at family attractions around the UK.

Barclays Plc 'Savings to Make You Smile'

Barclays Bank in the UK have used this type of mechanic in a number of ways including running a programme in partnership with Save the Children to encourage the public to review their savings arrangements during November 1998. Simply by arranging to see a Barclays Plc personal banker to discuss savings, customers received a free set of Christmas cards supporting Save the Children. Inside each of the cards could be a financial prize, for each prize claimed Barclays Plc made a matched donation to Save the Children. The results exceeded expectations:

- over 150 per cent of the sales forecast achieved;
- almost double new business was recorded compared to 1997;
- over £175,000 raised for Save the Children;
- the promotion generated £49,000 worth of PR with an impact on 6.7 million consumers.

Persil Funfit

To leverage the Persil Funfit programme, run by the detergent brand, Lever Brothers Ltd formed a partnership with the Early Learning Centre. This involved an advertorial in parenting media on Persil Funfit and targeted mailing to schools and playgroups within the Early Learning Centre catchment area. This mailing included a competition with a prize of £5000 worth of Early Learning Centre activity items for schools and playgroups registered with the Persil Funfit scheme.

Birds Eye Wall's Smile & Win

Over the 1998/9 winter, Birds Eye Wall's customers were encouraged to return their ice cream wrappers. Wall's donated 5p to Great Ormond Street Hospital Children's Charity for every ice cream wrapper returned to them. In addition to this every wrapper returned represented an entry for the customer into four prize draws for a holiday of a lifetime.

Self-liquidating Cause Related Marketing promotions

Another means of integrating Cause Related Marketing into the marketing mix
is through the use of self-liquidating promotions, whereby companies provide
consumers with a special offer which is available at a small cost. The small
price the consumer pays, finances the offer. Examples of this type of
application include the savoury snack Hula Hoops, in support of Comic Relief
1999, running a promotion on crisp packets offering consumers the chance to
purchase a Comic Relief video. For every video bought, Hula Hoops donated
£1 to the charity.

Similarly the detergents manufacturer Ecover formed a Cause Related
Marketing partnership with The Meadowland Trust. This promotion encouraged consumers to preserve British meadowlands by planting seeds in their
own gardens. With two proofs of purchase from Ecover products, and a small
payment, customers could purchase a pack of Meadowlands seeds, with The
Meadowlands Trust receiving the proceeds from the sale of the seeds.

Nouvelle and Great Ormond Street Children's Hospital

Nouvelle, manufacturers of recycled kitchen and toilet tissue, developed a self-
liquidating Cause Related Marketing promotion in conjunction with Great
Ormond Street Hospital Children's Charity. An on-pack offer encouraged
customers to buy Peter Pan room decorations and raise money for the charity. To
send off for the decorations customers needed to collect tokens from
promotional packs and send them with payment to Nouvelle, each token
representing a donation to the charity, and Nouvelle doubled the value of these
tokens for each completed order. Customers who did not wish to purchase the
decorations but wanted to make the donation to charity could send in their
tokens and Nouvelle would make the donation.

'New for old'

Another mechanic often used under the sales promotion umbrella is what I
have termed 'new for old' where, with the objective of encouraging perhaps
footfall, trial, awareness, differentiation or reinforcement of the brand values,
etc., consumers are encouraged to trade in their old products for a new one.
Examples would include the Cause Related Marketing partnership between
Austin Reed and Shelter which was built around a suit exchange. Also,
Gestetner, the office supply company, have run two schemes to provide schools
with much needed printers and fax machines. Essentially businesses were
encouraged to donate their old equipment, and Gestetner collected, serviced

and cleaned it before installing it in schools, free of charge. Laserlife, a company which sells original and recycled printer cartridges, uses a similar mechanic, collecting used cartridges from businesses. For each one collected they donated £2 to Great Ormond Street Hospital Children's Charity.

Hanna Andersson – 'Hannadowns'

The American children's clothing mail order company Hanna Andersson developed 'Hannadowns', a Cause Related Marketing programme. This programme encourages the return of outgrown clothes so that they can be passed on to children in need through more than 250 organizations, ranging from local shelters to national and international charities.

The 'Hannadowns' concept reinforced the core product values of Hanna Andersson clothing – that it was of such a robust quality that it would last for more than one childhood. Apart from feeling good by contributing old clothes to a worthy cause, originally the programme offered customers a 20 per cent credit note too.

This programme is a core part of the way Hanna Andersson do business and is now run continually. Customers are therefore now encouraged to donate their old 'Hannas' directly to local charities or alternatively to one of two organizations that they recommend to customers who do not have a preferred local charity. Since the programme began, Hanna Andersson have distributed close to one million pieces of clothing to charitable organizations.

Austin Reed Suit Exchange with Shelter

The Suit Exchange was developed to provide a complete win:win:win:win. For a two week period consumers are offered £30 off any new suit in Austin Reed stores up to £300, and £50 off any suit over £300 when trading in an old suit. The old suits are then dry cleaned and donated to Shelter, a charity addressing homeless issues. For every suit donated Austin Reed make a £5 contribution to Shelter. The old suits are then resold in Shelter shops.

The suit exchange benefits Austin Reed through driving in-store traffic, prompting more sales of an infrequent purchase and enhancing their corporate profile through the association. At the same time there is a donation to Shelter and old suits are put back into circulation for the benefit of Shelter's shops and their customers.

The Castrol 'Spaza' Shops

The Castrol 'Spaza' Shops operate in South Africa; the word is in fact based on township slang meaning semi, imitation or an informal business. Spaza Shops are business outlets operated from an owner's house, a garage, backroom or even a shack in the predominantly black populated areas by disadvantaged people who use them to earn a living and support their families. In this case the Castrol Spaza Shop is a second hand marine container converted to the operator's specification to meet his business requirements. The Castrol Spaza Shops are situated in the townships, are open late at night and aim to service the taxi market. They are managed by local people and stocked with Castrol lubricants and other allied products, e.g. spark plugs, oil fibres. Generally the formal business outlets are far away from the townships and therefore not only are Castrol providing opportunity for individuals through these shops, but they are also meeting a market need.

The Castrol Spaza Shops contribute to the spirit of the Reconstruction and Development programme in South Africa by empowering emerging business people with skills and opportunity to generate income in order to support their families and grow their communities. Castrol also meets its business objectives, which, although subordinate to the community objectives, increase brand awareness and provide new distribution channels for Castrol products.

Depending on the area, the Spaza Shops have met with varying degrees of success; however with the exception of one unit, all operators' businesses are self-sustaining and are able to provide for the operator's family as well as increase capacity. As Stanley Zulu, the driving force behind the concept stated:

Our quest is to improve the living conditions of the communities in which we operate. Through our Spaza Shops we encourage economic self reliance and independence, by empowering previously disadvantaged people with skills and opportunities with the objective that over time they also will become players in the business mainstream of our country.

Stanley Zulu, Consumer Brand Manager, Castrol South Africa.

Facilitated giving

Cause Related Marketing can also take the form of 'facilitated giving' whereby the business partner provides a vehicle to facilitate customer donations to the charity.

BA Change for Good is a classic example. At its simplest, it consists of in-flight appeals by video, envelopes and on-board announcements for customers to donate their unwanted foreign currency. This currency is then donated to

UNICEF and to date this programme has raised over £7 million for needy children around the world by exposing over 40 million passengers a year to the partnership. Other examples include utilities, restaurants and hotels to name but a few. UK water companies are partnering with Wateraid and then inviting customers to make donations to Wateraid through a standard form sent out by all water companies in the UK, with customer bills. StreetSmart, a concept developed by Forward Publishing and the Groucho Club, raises funds for projects for the homeless by working in conjunction with restaurants around the UK. In the run-up to Christmas, participating restaurants added an optional £1 to customer bills which was donated to the charity. StreetSmart have just announced that in 1998 they raised over £50,000, with the Oxo Tower in London raising over £11,000. On the other hand Amari Hotels, the chain of luxury hotels and resorts in Thailand, provide a collection envelope in hotel rooms encouraging guests to leave unwanted Thai currency in the envelopes as they check out. All proceeds are donated to the Duang Pratheep Foundation which is a charity helping needy children in Thailand. The mechanics are straightforward, the potential funds raised significant and the benefit to the brand manifold.

Sheraton Hotels Check Out for Children

Guests at Sheraton hotels are invited to add $1(or local currency equivalent) to their bill as a donation to UNICEF in 154 Sheraton hotels in 123 cities in 48 countries. Guests are of course free to choose to increase, decrease or opt out of the donation. This mechanic has raised over US $3 million to date. Following the take-over of Sheraton by Starwood Hotels & Resorts Worldwide this programme has been extended to Westin Hotels, adding a further 113 hotels and taking Check Out for Children to the USA for the first time.

Clearly in an age where information held on consumers' interests and habits is growing at an incredible rate, the opportunity to understand what motivates an individual from a charity or cause point of view and to communicate with them accordingly is there. We know from research[6] that 86 per cent of consumers have said that price and quality being equal, linking with a cause would make the difference; they would change brands, switch retail outlets and have a much better perception of a company trying to do something to make the world a better place. The opportunities to build the business whilst making a real positive difference to the wider community are therefore significant.

Notes

1 Andreasen, A.R. (1996) Profits for Nonprofits: Find a Corporate Partner, *Harvard Business Review*, November–December, pp. 47–59.
2 Detailed in the case study section.
3 See Part Four of this book (especially Chapter 23 'The Formal Agreement'), or The Cause Related Marketing Guidelines – Towards Excellence (1998), Business in the Community.
4 Datamonitor, from article in *Marketing Week* by Steve Hemsley, 18 March 1999.
5 *Promotions News*, March 1999.
6 The Winning Game (1996), Business in the Community quantitative consumer research on Cause Related Marketing.

Chapter 16

Case studies

There is no better way to demonstrate the effectiveness of Cause Related Marketing and highlight the issues than by looking at case studies for the evidence of what has actually happened in Cause Related Marketing partnerships.

Cause Related Marketing partnerships can be effective whether linking large businesses to small charities; small businesses with large charities or any combination in between. The ultimate Cause Related Marketing partnership is clear about the objectives, is conceived on the grounds of The Key Principles, is developed on the basis of a long-term commitment and a thorough process is followed. Based on this solid foundation, the team involved in creating and implementing the partnership should then use their imaginations, consider all aspects of the marketing mix and all the stakeholders involved and use them to the full to ensure maximum impact and return on investment.

In the following sections case studies are provided from a variety of sectors and causes, highlighting the range of objectives and mechanics. Apart from raising funds, awareness and helping to spread the message of the cause etc., the business objectives were as follows:

Case study summary

Case studies (UK)	Business objectives
TESCO Computers for Schools	■ Reinforce corporate values ■ Enhance the store proposition of being number one locally ■ Drive traffic in-store ■ Provide added value
Cadbury Ltd and Save the Children	■ Enhance corporate image ■ Reinforce corporate values

Case studies (UK)	Business objectives
Norwich Union and St. John Ambulance	■ Raise awareness of Norwich Union and cut through the clutter of insurance advertising noise ■ Align Norwich Union more closely with their corporate brand positioning of 'better protection' ■ Generate warmth towards Norwich Union and transform the image of insurance companies ■ Encourage people to be more likely to choose Norwich Union products
Centrica plc and Help the Aged	■ Enhance brand image ■ Provide competitive edge ■ Position British Gas as taking a lead and making a tangible difference to the community ■ Involve customers and enhance loyalty ■ Align community relations activity more closely to business objectives ■ Initiate and focus employee fundraising and volunteering
BT's Cause Related Marketing strategy	■ Promote Cause Related Marketing across BT ■ Establish best practice principles for BT people contemplating undertaking Cause Related Marketing activity ■ Unlock marketing budgets for the benefit of the community, building links between BT and the community ■ Make a quantifiable difference to core business, e.g. through sales figures, etc. ■ There are specific objectives for each of these case studies profiled which include partnerships with Whizz-Kidz, RNIB and WWF.
Adams Childrenswear and Save the Children	■ To support brand values ■ To provide a key point of differentiation ■ To reinforce corporate support of Save the Children with staff and customers ■ To raise funds for Save the Children and support their UK programme work

Case studies (UK)	*Business objectives*
Nambarrie Tea Company Ltd and Action Cancer	■ Enhance corporate and brand values ■ To demonstrate corporate social responsibility by making a positive impact on the local community ■ To maximize the marketing budget
Persil and Go Red for Comic Relief	■ Build the total Persil brand image ■ Increase awareness of the Colour Care variant ■ Communicate benefits of Colour Care in an innovative and interesting way ■ Increase sales of Persil standard powders
New Covent Garden Soup Company	■ Reflect the company's key values ■ To build on the long-term association between the company and Crisis and the National Trust ■ To provide retailers with an interesting Cause Related Marketing product ■ To provide a key platform from which to launch new products

Case studies (International)	*Business objectives*
Sears Roebuck's Cause Related Marketing strategy and programmes USA	■ A core method of doing business for Sears Roebuck ■ To reinforce and communicate Sears Roebuck's corporate values ■ To build customer relationships ■ To drive in-store traffic ■ Examples each have specific objectives and include partnerships with Gilda's Club; Big Brothers Big Sisters; Get Back, Give Back Schools programme
Kellogg's Kids Help Line Australia	■ To enhance consumer perceptions of Kellogg's as a company committed to supporting Australian kids and families ■ Assume a leadership position in the corporate sector in terms of social responsibility ■ To reinforce the organization's core values

Case studies (International)	Business objectives
Visa Read Me a Story USA	■ To encourage usage of the Visa card ■ To build relationships with cardholders, merchants and other stakeholders ■ To reinforce the organization's values
Target Stores Cause Related Marketing strategy and programmes USA	■ A core plank of the way Target Stores does business ■ To enhance corporate reputation and provide differentiation ■ To reinforce the brand proposition: Expect more – pay less ■ Examples each have specific objectives and include partnerships with St Jude Children's Research Hospital in Memphis Tennessee which began in 1995; Helping Hugs; Support of the Washington Monument Restoration; Guest Credit Card supporting Education: School Fundraising Made Simple
Avon Crusade Against Breast Cancer USA/UK	■ To create an opportunity for Representatives – or 'Avon Ladies' – to create relationships with their customers ■ To improve consumer perceptions and to differentiate Avon from its competitors ■ To make a real and sustainable difference to a cause their customers care about
Tanqueray AIDS Rides USA	■ Increase sales of Tanqueray gin ■ Engage the target market through the support of a cause ■ Recruit new 21–34 year old African-American and general market consumers by creating an emotional and powerful connection to the Tanqueray brand ■ Create a new brand value for the Tanqueray brand ■ Raise significant funds for AIDS charities in the USA ■ Raise awareness of AIDS education and prevention

Case study I: TESCO Computers for Schools

Background

In the UK Cause Related Marketing cannot be discussed without mentioning TESCO PLC and the TESCO Computers for Schools programme which is arguably the most successful programme in the UK. Having been created from an idea in the USA and launched in the UK in 1992 as a one-off sales promotion, it has developed significantly since then. By 1998, the TESCO Computers for Schools programme had put the equivalent of more than one computer in every school in England, Scotland and Wales.

In 1991 a large number of promotional schemes giving direct benefit to the individual customer were being run by supermarkets. TESCO PLC were keen to develop a loyalty programme that would help them develop relationships with their consumers and a scheme that would benefit the community, reinforcing the TESCO PLC mission to be number one in the community. At the same time in the USA, a supermarket scheme which provided schools with computer equipment was being hailed as a success.

Following research, computers were identified as the key requirement in schools in the UK. Research also indicated that investing in education was an important issue for consumers. The rationale was that if TESCO PLC could tap into the emotional motivations of the consumer this had great potential benefits for the business. TESCO Computers for Schools provided just that. Based on refining the mechanics of the American model, the development of Computers for Schools has provided TESCO PLC with a loyalty programme that provides customers with the opportunity to contribute to their local community at no extra cost to themselves and to help ensure IT literacy for all school leavers. The scheme is a good example of a nationally run programme implemented locally.

Extensive market research was conducted amongst customers, schools and education bodies. It was clearly identified that schools needed computing equipment in order to deliver the National Curriculum but that they did not have sufficient funds. Research indicated that parents and consumers generally agreed and supported the cause but they could not afford to make a donation straight to the school. They were however happy if through the course of going about their daily lives and shopping they were able to generate support for schools and thus the mechanic was developed.

Objectives

The key objectives of the programme were and are to:

■ Reinforce corporate values;
■ give added benefit to the community in which the stores are located;

- make a real impact on IT literacy in schools;
- drive traffic in store;
- improve TESCO PLC's positioning as a caring company reinforcing its 'Every Little Helps' philosophy.

Mechanic

The programme is based on a voucher redemption scheme. TESCO PLC customers collect vouchers for every £10 spent in-store or on petrol. In 1998 vouchers were also included on special promotional packs of Coca-Cola. In 1999 Ariel, Coca-Cola, Febreze, Nestle Ice Cream, Pringles, Shape, Sunny Delight and Utterly Butterly joined the scheme as sponsors. Customers donate these vouchers to local schools who can then exchange the vouchers for computers and IT related equipment. As with so many successful Cause Related Marketing programmes, the idea is simple, the mechanic straightforward.

In partnership with Xemplar (previously called Acorn) who are the brand leaders in educational computing hardware in the UK, an extensive catalogue of equipment to suit children of all ages and schools with varying budgets was developed, from which schools could select their equipment. Over the years the range of options within the catalogue has developed in line with schools' and pupils' needs. Anything from a PC and special needs computing equipment to palm top equipment is available for schools through the scheme.

First launched in 1992, the programme runs annually for a 10 week promotional period during the Spring term. A database of schools was originally bought by TESCO PLC and only schools within store catchment areas were mailed, thus aiming to avoid raising expectations in areas outside a TESCO PLC catchment area. Orders from schools are processed over the summer holidays and presentations of equipment take place during September at the beginning of the Autumn term.

Clearly this is a huge programme which invests in the region of £6 million a year and requires substantial support. In 1998 alone £1.5 million was spent on advertising support and a further £8.5 million was allocated to administration, printing and equipment costs.

The programme is effectively run through a partnership between originally the marketing department and now community affairs, supported by the PR agency, and a team at Xemplar, the mailing house and store staff. Whilst the programme is only live in store for 10 weeks a year, the processing of orders and presentation and delivery continue year round.

Support

A programme of this size requires and demands substantial support. TESCO Computers for Schools, whilst being a nationally created programme, is delivered locally by store staff. As such, large scale support and communications are provided to customers, stores and schools. Above and below the line advertising supports the programme but this package of support includes much more. It has evolved over the years and it now includes:

- Free half-day audit of computer systems by Xemplar Education specialists for schools to assist them in selecting the appropriate equipment.
- Cheese and wine evenings at local stores for teachers where teachers can receive information on the scheme and basic training. This also provides TESCO PLC with another communications channel to key target audiences.
- Store training rooms are used to accommodate free IT training for teachers.
- Dedicated TESCO Computers for Schools helpline and press office is available for schools to assist them with any computing, technical queries, PR and media advice.
- Clubcard and in-house magazine support, i.e. feature/consumer offer every quarter.
- National advertising via television, radio and press.
- National and local PR, press, radio, television and trade/customer press.
- Direct mail to schools with support material, catalogues and posters to assist them in communication to parents and the local press.
- A detailed brief is sent to stores as well as heavyweight in-store point of sale guides and materials.
- TESCO PLC sponsor educational conferences and attend educational IT exhibitions with Xemplar.
- Through an internal system, stores communicate ideas and tips to each other.
- TESCO Computers for Schools 'Business Links' initiative encourages local businesses to adopt a local school and set up a collection point for staff to collect vouchers.

Monitoring and evaluation

The point has been made through the Business in the Community Cause Related Marketing Guidelines and in Chapter 26 in this book that it is essential to measure the effectiveness of the Cause Related Marketing programmes if those involved are to be able to make informed decisions about the future. In the case of TESCO Computers for Schools, all the elements in the programme are measured and evaluated from a variety of sources including the TESCO PLC loyalty card 'Clubcard' and AGB customer research. This includes researching:

- voucher redemption levels;
- equipment orders;
- turnover;
- customer expenditure;
- frequency of visits.

Data is also gathered via:

- image-tracking surveys;
- measurement of PR generated;
- teachers who take part in IT training sessions.

Results

For the cause

In 1998 alone, 19,000 schools placed orders for equipment (half of all UK schools) and claimed £10 million worth of computing equipment including:

- over 5,000 computers;
- over 53,000 additional items of computer related equipment;
- over £18,000 worth of IT training for teachers.

Total impact from 1992–98:

- over £44 million worth of equipment nationwide (1992–98);
- 34,000 computers and over 200,000 additional items of related equipment delivered to schools – equivalent of one computer for every school in the UK;
- approximately £100,000 worth of IT training for teachers.

Business results

Clearly beyond the first year, the impact of the programme is increasingly difficult to measure in terms of sales and performance against the competition. This is particularly the case as now most of the competition have developed their own variation of the TESCO Computers for Schools scheme. However, by utilizing the variety of research measures that TESCO PLC do, TESCO PLC are clear about the programme's effectiveness.

Key results have been:

- high levels of consumer awareness;
- voucher redemption remains exceedingly high at 75 per cent;
- enhanced corporate profile in the community;
- customer loyalty;
- recognition as an innovative retailer;
- increased sales;
- press coverage has gone from strength to strength over the years.

The success of the TESCO Computers for Schools programme was, according to Tim Mason, TESCO PLC Marketing Director, the precursor to the highly acclaimed Clubcard which was the first supermarket loyalty card in the UK.

Lessons learned/future plans

The results of this programme have not only been impressive for the cause of IT literacy in schools but have also been extremely successful for TESCO PLC. So much so that the TESCO PLC Millennium initiative is founded in the area of Computers for Schools. Called TESCO SchoolNet 2000, the objective is for all schools throughout the UK to participate in creating a 'domesday book' on line. From September 1998 until the Millennium, pupils will be working on a range of stimulating projects based around the school curriculum. Pupils will go out into the community to investigate facts about their neighbourhood and the people who live there and for each project investigation create their own web page and enter the data they have collected on to the TESCO SchoolNet 2000 website. For those schools who do not have the facilities, TESCO PLC have kitted out more than 340 stores with IT equipment available as a free resource to schools and have funded some 40 advisory teachers as a resource for schools. Tesco clearly have a long-term commitment to education and IT literacy.

The planning and preparation that went into the creation of this scheme at the outset has paid off. Cause Related Marketing programmes like so many successful activities are based on 10 per cent inspiration and 90 per cent perspiration. The continual monitoring, review, research and analysis of the programme has meant that TESCO PLC and the programme has continued to add value. The programme is updated every year to refresh and improve it. This has enabled TESCO PLC to adapt and expand the details of the programme in light of lessons learned each year and from conducting primary research. This led to the introduction of free in-store IT training in 1997 and a reduction in the amount consumers were required to spend in order to receive a voucher. Consumers now have to spend just £10.00.

TESCO Computers for Schools is also an exemplary programme in terms of the full use of the marketing mix. Few programmes in the UK have actually used above the line advertising to promote and support their Cause Related Marketing programmes despite television advertising being a core part of their standard marketing mix. Direct mail and other below the line techniques have also been utilized in delivery of this programme.

TESCO PLC have also appreciated the fundamental role of employees both as stakeholders and in bringing a Cause Related Marketing programme to life. TESCO Computers for Schools is a nationally led programme delivered locally in and by store staff. It is the stores that are central to the community and it is the store staff with whom the relationships between schools, parents and consumers are nurtured and developed.

Why should you be interested in Cause Related Marketing over and above any other form of marketing? The answer to that is the effectiveness of Cause Related

Marketing. If I think about TESCO, Computers for Schools is a more cost effective driver of sales than other activities.

Tim Mason, Marketing Director, TESCO PLC

TESCO Computers for Schools has shown a real commitment to education for the last six years and with its many new initiatives introduced this year, including free IT training for teachers, it continues to evolve to help schools move towards the millennium with a relevant IT package and teacher confidence.

The Rt Hon. David Blunkett MP, Secretary of State for Education and Employment

As Official Education Sponsor for the Millennium and through our Computers for Schools scheme, education remains a high priority at TESCO. TESCO believes that one of the most important contributions it can make to the community is to help equip schools with resources that will give children the skills they need for the future.

Terry Leahy, Chief Executive, TESCO PLC

Case study II: Cadbury Ltd and Save the Children

Background

Cadbury Schweppes plc has a tradition of investing in the community in which it operates, having been founded by a Quaker family – the underlying philosophy of the Quakers being 'to do well by doing good'. This is still done today, primarily through the Cadbury Schweppes Foundation.

In the early 1990s apart from its philanthropy and its leading role as a socially responsible organization, Cadbury Ltd also ran various marketing driven initiatives which tended to reflect the short-term needs of individual brands, often as a result of promotional activity. Whilst high profile, these promotions tended not to follow any consistent policy. Against this background the marketing and corporate affairs team at Cadbury Ltd carried out a review with a view to consolidating their diverse charity involvement into one major 'driving force' initiative which was more aligned with their marketing activity.

Cadbury Ltd wanted to develop this activity to bring together the marketing demands for a clear single focus primarily related to the Cadbury Ltd masterbrand, although accessible to individual brands, combined with Cadbury Ltd's commitment to the wider community. The brief required that the solution be high profile, image enhancing (specifically caring, fun, contemporary) and communicated to family audiences.

Cadbury Ltd took a very structured and thorough approach to developing the strategy. Planning and preparing carefully, a brief was issued against which five charities were asked to pitch. Cadbury Ltd were one of the first to use the tendering process in this way. The charities were judged against a number of criteria including the four Cs:

- **compatibility** with Cadbury Ltd and its objectives;
- **capability** to work with a large company;
- **commitment** to develop an effective and active partnership;
- whether the link or the partner was **controversial.**

From the outset, Cadbury Ltd regarded this as a Cause Related Marketing opportunity which would provide mutual benefit and make a positive impact on the wider community.

Following the tendering process, Save the Children, the UK's leading international children's charity, was selected as the partners. Cadbury Ltd became a Corporate Member of Save the Children in January 1992 under which banner a number of Cause Related Marketing activities took place. Originally the relationship was planned to last for two years but was extended to a six year partnership which ended in December 1997.

Objectives

The overall objective of the relationship was to create a unified, structured and effective Cause Related Marketing corporate charity association that would bring mutual benefits to Cadbury Ltd and Save the Children. Specifically, some of the individual elements of the programme have worked towards:

- enhancing the Cadbury Ltd image of fun, contemporary and a caring company;
- reinforcing Cadbury Ltd corporate values, especially to children;
- raising funds for Save the Children;
- raising awareness of the work of Save the Children.

Mechanics

During the partnership with Save the Children the programme included a number of Cause Related Marketing initiatives including Cadbury's Strollerthon and Cadbury's Pantomime Season.

Cadbury's Strollerthon

This was a major aspect of the partnership between Save the Children and Cadbury Ltd. Essentially via the Cadbury Strollerthon, consumers were encouraged to participate in a 10 mile sponsored walk around London. This took place annually from 1992 to 1996, and in Birmingham in 1993. Through the Cadbury's Strollerthon on average 15,000–18,000 strolled to raise money for Save the Children and One Small Step. In other words thousands of people got up and walked because Cadbury Ltd had asked them to for two children's charities.

In terms of the reinforcement of the Cadbury Ltd core values one could not envisage a more powerful demonstration. In terms of projecting the fun and caring side of Cadbury Ltd this programme was highly successful. It also provided Cadbury Ltd with the opportunity to sample tens of thousands of products.

A huge fundraising success, in 1996 for instance in the region of £400,000 was raised through the Strollerthon for the two charities. Cadbury's Strollerthon therefore not only delivered against the business objectives but provided significant funds for charity each time it was run over the five years.

Cadbury's Pantomime Season

This was the second major aspect of Cadbury Ltd's support of Save the Children. Over 30 Christmas pantomimes were sponsored by Cadbury Ltd across the UK each year, promoting and raising funds for Save the Children until 1997 whilst Cadbury Ltd reinforced its corporate and brand values, and benefited from the halo effect of the association. Not only did Save the Children benefit through awareness on millions of pieces of print material and advertisements but collections held at the pantomimes were also in aid of the charity.

Other activities

In addition to the PR/sponsorship based activity, there were also a number of other smaller Cause Related Marketing activities to support the relationship. In celebration of Save the Children's 75th birthday, Cadbury Ltd produced a 75th birthday chocolate coin, featuring the Save the Children logo. Through the merchandising and sale of the coins, money and awareness were raised for Save the Children. There were also a number of PR initiatives linked to this promotion including a birthday party. Cadbury Ltd's support also included sponsorship of Save the Children's 75th birthday television advertisement featuring HRH the Princess Royal, the charity's president, the first time a member of the Royal family had starred in a commercial.

Support

Both Cadbury's Strollerthon and Cadbury's Pantomime Season have been supported through:

- dedicated support teams from all partners;
- specifically designed event charity logos for both sponsorships;
- significant editorial coverage in national, regional and consumer press;
- direct advertising;

- celebrity participation and endorsement;
- branded print material;
- branded advertising in programmes and brochures;
- sales promotional activity;
- direct mail;
- Cadbury Ltd employee participation;
- Cadbury Ltd internal communication.

In addition to this common support, each of the activities benefited from some unique and specific support; the Cadbury's Strollerthon from:

- thousands of Strollerthon branded tube cards for the underground;
- Strollerthon advertising on bus sides;
- product sampling and gifts at the Strollerthon sponsored walks;

and the Cadbury's Pantomime Season from:

- pantomime press launches/regional photocalls;
- use of pantomime horse and cow for PR and collection purposes;
- national phoneline set up to offer information on all pantomimes;
- goody bags and treat size throwouts distributed at pantomimes;
- branded collection boxes in the pantomime theatre foyers;
- audio tape promoting Save the Children, welcoming and reminding the audience of the collection boxes was played at the beginning, in the interval and at the end of pantomimes.

Monitoring and evaluation

Publicly it was clear that this relationship was a great success judging from the number of people involved or attending events and funds raised. As one would expect however, Cadbury Ltd monitored and researched the effectiveness of the relationships using media research, omnibus and audience research to gauge levels of awareness and qualitative response to the event. Separate media evaluations were also carried out to determine exact levels of media exposure. Clearly in order to make informed decisions about the future, Cadbury Ltd had to have clear evidence. The success of the relationship led to the extension of what was planned to be a two year relationship to a six year partnership.

Results

Each of the Cause Related Marketing activities undertaken in partnership with Save the Children raised significant funds, exposure and awareness for the charity. In total over £1.5 million was raised. These funds contributed to enabling the charity to continue its work in the UK and overseas. In the UK specific projects were identified, including Birmingham based activity close to the Cadbury Ltd headquarters in Bournville.

A key part of Cadbury Ltd's strategic marketing is to communicate the masterbrand values. As a result of the partnership with Save the Children, Cadbury Ltd saw measurable and quantifiable shifts in attitudes to the brand. Thus the relationship reinforced and enhanced the Cadbury Ltd image. In addition to these shared benefits each of the activities also resulted in significant media coverage for the partners, as well as having some unique and specific results for each of the programmes.

Specific results for the Cadbury's Strollerthon

- The Cadbury's Strollerthon sponsored walk attracted around 15,000 people each year with 18,000 walkers taking part in 1996.
- The Strollerthon raised £1 million for Save the Children over the five years it took place.
- Substantial media coverage was received.
- Significant celebrity participation and endorsements were obtained.
- Cadbury Ltd also sampled over 85,000 chocolate bars and drinks at the sponsored walks.

Specific results for the Cadbury's Pantomime Season

- The pantomime season raised over £260,000 for Save the Children in total.
- High profile exposure to an annual audience of 1.75 million people.
- In addition to the significant advertising and editorial media coverage, Cadbury Ltd has benefited through direct advertising on branded posters, product sampling and favourable image shifts in key areas.

Budget

Programmes of this size require investment, and, as has been said, that investment needs to be managed. During 1992–97, Cadbury Ltd invested over £4 million in the partnership with Save the Children.

Lessons learned/future plans

Cadbury Ltd are currently in the process of reviewing their corporate charity link. The link with Save the Children was highly successful, particularly in the Cause Related Marketing PR and sponsorship based activity. The process of identifying Save the Children worked well and the importance of measurement and evaluation was reinforced as it enabled Cadbury Ltd and Save the Children to identify and develop the programme from the initial two year partnership to the resulting six year partnership.

The partnership between Cadbury and Save the Children worked extremely well for three key reasons. Both parties shared common and positive brand associations. Both parties developed the relationship through their joint and separate marketing activities. Both parties were committed to regular planning and evaluation. In Cadbury, Save the Children found a corporate partner investing in Cause Related Marketing for the right reasons and with conscious business planning.

Alison Pavier, former Head of Corporate Development, Save the Children

The Cadbury Ltd–Save the Children partnership clearly highlights the strengths of planning and preparation, affinity and alignment of objectives, so much so that the two year relationship was extended to six years. Finding a partner through desk research followed by a tendering process[1] is something that I believe we will see increasingly as Cause Related Marketing partnerships increase. Its strengths are clearly that it forces the initiator to clearly think through its objectives and needs, and provides the potential partners with a thorough outline of the opportunity. It suggests that there is a very real opportunity and therefore that time invested in responding to the brief is not wasted.

Since Cadbury Ltd used this approach a number of other relationships have been initiated using the tendering approach, and to great effect. A key lesson for another organization that used this approach was the importance of defining what is expected for the pitch presentation, to avoid unnecessary outlay and expense on either side. Secondly the business, if it is the initiator, needs to consider covering the charity's pitch costs as they should consider the appropriateness of a charity using its limited resources to develop elaborate pitches.

The Cadbury Ltd Save the Children example also shows how a core relationship can be demonstrated in a number of ways. Whilst the partnership was led by the two key aspects of the Cadbury's Strollerthon and the Cadbury Pantomime Season, other Cause Related Marketing promotions also supported the campaign. If the partnership is working well it is in the interest of all those involved to identify and develop additional opportunities to leverage the relationship. Cadbury Ltd and Save the Children did this to great effect.

Cause Related Marketing should become a natural part of successful business practice because it is an effective way of enhancing corporate image, differentiating product and increasing both customer loyalty and sales. The challenge is for businesses, charities and causes to identify the appropriate partnerships, and then plan, implement and communicate them well. Cause Related Marketing is a potential potent force that can provide benefits for all.

Sir Dominic Cadbury, Chairman, Cadbury Schweppes plc

Case study III: Norwich Union and St. John Ambulance First Aid

Background

The financial services market in the UK is becoming increasingly overcrowded. Newer brands such as Virgin and Marks & Spencer are threatening traditional brands such as Norwich Union. As such, brand is an increasingly important differentiator. Norwich Union was therefore keen to reinforce its brand message 'No-one Protects More' and was looking for a vehicle to communicate this message in a memorable and lasting way.

Objectives

Norwich Union was clear what it wanted this partnership to deliver. The primary target market or stakeholder group for the reinforcement of the Norwich Union branding was ABC1 adults who influence or make the decision to buy financial services. The objectives of the programme were to:

■ raise awareness of Norwich Union and cut through the clutter of insurance advertising noise;
■ align Norwich Union more closely with their corporate brand positioning of 'better protection';
■ generate warmth towards Norwich Union and transform the image of insurance companies being distant and remote which had emerged as a consequence of dealing through intermediaries, and pensions being a once in a lifetime purchase;
■ encourage people to be more likely to choose Norwich Union products.

Process

Norwich Union set a challenge to all staff and agencies to provide their thoughts on how this might be achieved. This challenge resulted in 123 ideas being submitted and reviewed. Shortlisted ideas were researched. Through this process Norwich Union identified first aid as a real need that had resonance with their target market.

As the Business in the Community Cause Related Marketing Guidelines state, having clearly identified the objectives, like any successful marketing activity, Cause Related Marketing programmes depend on a good idea, thoroughly researched and planned. A national omnibus survey confirmed alarming levels of ignorance of basic first aid procedure. First aid was therefore seen as a genuinely impressive sponsorship that created interest and goodwill; was relevant to almost everyone and was of national importance. In addition to this, focus group research showed that the offer of first aid courses was seen to have considerable value, and importantly did not carry an obligation between the target audience and Norwich Union.

Concept

In response to the findings of the stakeholder research, Norwich Union launched the First Aid in the Home campaign in partnership with St. John Ambulance. The charity was chosen, as the country's leading first aid trainer, for its high public recognition and for its good regional infrastructure.

Mechanics and timing

Launched in 1996, Norwich Union funded a series of free first aid courses for the general public run by St. John Ambulance. The programme was communicated through a television advertising campaign which carried a hotline telephone number for inquiries and bookings. The advertisements show a child at home drinking a harmful liquid. Viewers are asked what first aid they would apply in this situation and then told what would have been appropriate in the situation to save the child's life.

Advertising and courses were piloted in the Granada TV region before expanding to other areas. Participants received a free place on a St. John's Ambulance three-and-a-half hour first aid courses and all those completing the course received a certificate jointly branded by Norwich Union and St. John Ambulance. A branded first aid booklet was sent out to all callers responding to the advertisement who were not able to attend a course.

Communications support

Norwich Union clearly identified their stakeholder groups from the outset and therefore leveraged the programme accordingly. The communication message was compelling and the communications strategy was well planned and implemented.

By taking the partnership above the line Norwich Union was able to maximize exposure to consumers. By so doing, not only was the impact of the programme leveraged but Norwich Union avoided a recurring consumer concern[2] that Cause Related Marketing activities should be made more visible.

The main purpose of the PR during the programme was to highlight and extend the life of the campaign. In accordance with the Cause Related Marketing Guidelines, communication was well balanced between the partners, providing joint branding in all cases. The core message promoted the relationship and its purpose, explaining and encouraging people to participate. Once underway the communications kept stakeholders up to date and celebrated their crucial role in improving the first aid capabilities for themselves, their families and their communities. The publicity campaign was organized by:

■ coordinating PR centrally between Norwich Union and St. John Ambulance;
■ training regional St. John Ambulance representatives as spokespeople;
■ offering free places to the media and running quizzes and competitions around the courses.

Internal communication, a key component for any Cause Related Marketing programme, was thorough from its development to its implementation. It included:

■ putting information on the company's e-mail bulletin board and in the internal newsletter;
■ giving each member of Norwich Union staff a First Aid in the Home booklet;
■ running a video of the TV advertisements at each of the main head office staff entrances;
■ offering free first aid training for all members of staff, and those that were trainers for St. John Ambulance were given the opportunity to carry out the training in their local regions.

Monitoring, measurement and evaluation

Monitoring, measuring and evaluating programmes and partnerships is a clearly understood discipline and a requirement of effective business management today. Cause Related Marketing is no different. With clear objectives from the outset and the measurement and evaluation plan developed from the start, the process is straightforward. The Norwich Union first aid programme was evaluated from a number of perspectives during its different stages including:

Pre-campaign measurement

■ focus groups discussing and helping to rationalize initial concepts
■ omnibus questions assessing levels of ignorance about first aid and therefore assessing the level of need
■ focus groups to develop and confirm the advertising concepts
■ national face to face omnibus awareness/attitude towards Norwich Union.

During campaign monitoring

■ self-completion questionnaires for delegates on courses on quality of training and attitude toward Norwich Union.

Post-campaign evaluation

- repeat of awareness/attitude omnibus to compare campaign regions with national findings.

This process of tracking and measurement provided both Norwich Union and St. John Ambulance with vital feedback from the general public, people who specifically had seen the advertisements, and from first aid course participants. It enabled both parties to assess the impact and effectiveness of the programme in achieving their objectives.

Impact on society

This programme enabled Norwich Union to expand its community activity outside its home towns and make public its association with the charity. It touched people on a personal level giving them the opportunity to acquire valuable skills.

- 25,000 free first aid places were offered to members of the public;
- over 13,000 people from across Britain trained to date.

Benefit to St. John Ambulance

Norwich Union paid St. John Ambulance a consultancy fee and fee per person trained. The partnership also gave St. John Ambulance their first ever television presence, new equipment and an increase in interest from the public wanting to attend further, paid courses. The ongoing PR campaign complemented their existing activity and the new activity developed a new valuable aspect to the St. John Ambulance database.

Research showed that of those who had seen the advertisement, 87 per cent said it made them think more about the need to know first aid, the core mission of St. John Ambulance. Of those who attended the pilot course 84 per cent rated the learning value and teaching methods as 'very good' therefore highlighting, reinforcing and recognizing the quality of the St. John Ambulance service and role.

Business results

Research revealed that recognition of this TV advertising was higher than *ever* recorded in the insurance sector. The usual score would be 42 per cent versus the 80 per cent achieved by the Norwich Union and St. John Ambulance first aid campaign. Awareness of Norwich Union increased significantly in a market where shifts are hard to come by.

Norwich Union scored on precisely the objectives it set out to address:

- 'offers insurance that gives better protection';
- 'is a caring company';
- 'has a good reputation';
- 'does more for good causes';
- 'warmth'.

One in five consumers said they would be more likely to consider Norwich Union as a result of having seen the TV advertising.

- 60 per cent of participants on the pilot courses felt more positive about the company after the session.
- 94 per cent approved of Norwich Union offering the course.
- 80 per cent awareness of TV advertisement, compared to 42 per cent average for insurance company advertisements.

Of those 80 per cent:

- 30 per cent agreed Norwich Union offers insurance that gives better protection – compared to 19 per cent before the campaign.
- 25 per cent were more likely to consider Norwich Union for insurance policy.

Lessons learned

The partnership with St. John Ambulance resulted in four key lessons for Norwich Union:

- The need for honesty and openness about commercial interests.
- The importance of a comprehensive contract between partners.
- Having centralized PR, but using local charity experts as spokespeople for the programme.
- Being realistic about the time involved when tailor-making a Cause Related Marketing partnership.

Norwich Union First Aid was a huge success for both Norwich Union and St. John Ambulance. This was largely down to the research carried out in developing the project and the very open way in which our two organizations worked together. We made our commercial objectives clear from the outset, and were impressed by the business-like response from the charity. The project was a long time in the planning but the results were well worth it.

Thomas Cowper Johnson, Group Brand Manager, Norwich Union

Case study IV: Centrica plc's Cause Related Marketing strategy

Background

Centrica plc is the holding company for British Gas and operates under two main brands, British Gas/Scottish Gas and Goldfish. The primary market is providing energy and services in Britain to more than 16 million customers. Privatization in 1986 and more recently deregulation of the gas and electricity markets has provided Centrica plc with an entirely different operating market, one that is now fully competitive and with increased stakeholder accountability.

In the past, Centrica plc have been actively involved in Cause Related Marketing and corporate community investment through programmes including the British Gas Handyperson Scheme with Age Concern, Centrica Caring for Carers and a partnership with Mencap.

Rationale

Operating under these changed circumstances, Centrica plc were keen to develop and maintain competitive advantage. Based on external research Centrica plc appreciated that an increasing number of consumers would not only act more positively towards an organization considered to be socially responsible but also a growing number have boycotted products on ethical grounds. A Cause Related Marketing strategy would therefore be highly appropriate.

British Gas provides gas to 16 million homes; electricity to 1 million; has 400 million customer contacts each year; employes 5000 service engineers; visits 7 million homes each year; has 240 high street shops; and 900,000 Goldfish card holders, the fastest growing credit card in the UK. By the nature of its core business, Centrica plc has a huge impact on society and understands and embraces its obligation to act in a socially responsible manner.

Despite a significant corporate community investment programme, customer research had indicated a low awareness of Centrica plc's existing community relations activity, although company perceptions were high amongst those who had benefited from individual projects.

Concept

Against this background, Centrica plc have embarked on a long term partnership with Help the Aged, which is a national charity which works to improve the quality of life of older people in the UK. The partnership is designed to provide a number of commercial opportunities whilst delivering demonstrable benefits to society. It has been developed to enable a solutions based approach to the issues facing the most vulnerable older people, moving on from awareness building campaigns successfully run by Help the Aged in earlier years. The core of the Cause Related Marketing partnership essentially focuses on the development of a home insulation programme providing long term solutions to fuel poverty, allied to practical shorter term measures.

Objective

Whilst aiming to make a real impact on improving the life of vulnerable older people through the provision of energy efficiency measures, heating vouchers and funding for advice lines, day centres and maintenance people, the objective of the Cause Related Marketing partnership is to:

- enhance brand image;
- involve customers and enhance loyalty;
- provide competitive edge;
- position British Gas as taking a lead and making a tangible difference to the community;
- align community relations activity more closely to business objectives;
- initiate and focus employee fundraising and volunteering.

Timing

The partnership will run for at least two years and this duration has been agreed up front in a contract, in line with the Business in the Community Cause Related Marketing Guidelines which highlight the need to agree in advance the duration of the agreement.

Process

Identifying the cause

The Business in the Community Cause Related Marketing Guidelines also outline a number of different methods for organizations to use in finding a Cause Related Marketing partner. The Centrica plc case study demonstrates how a combination of these methods can be applied to ensure a thorough consultative process. Centrica plc carried out focus group research amongst consumers looked at a range of potential themes including safety in the home, the environment, education and sports sponsorship. Older people and the related issues of warmth and comfort were consistently identified as an area where British Gas involvement would be positively received by consumers.

After a selection process involving other charities, a partnership with Help the Aged was developed based on the quality of their proposition and their effective delivery mechanisms.

Exclusivity

In the context of any Cause Related Marketing programme it is essential to consider the relevance and extent of exclusivity between the partners involved. The Business in the Community Cause Related Marketing Guidelines outline the different elements that should be considered for exclusivity as part of the formal agreement. In this case, Centrica plc will be the only corporate supporter of Help the Aged's main fundraising campaign which aims to reduce fuel poverty amongst older people and subsequently make their lives warmer and more comfortable.

Mechanics

The strategic partnership will be delivered through a variety of mutually beneficial mechanics. These include:

- Centrica plc core funding to deliver additional support to a number of existing Help the Aged projects;
- customer fundraising via gas bill enclosures and other product mailing mechanisms;
- donations and sale of lapel badges via British Gas Energy Centres and Help the Aged shops;
- Centrica plc will provide use of donation telephone lines and a premium rate line with specific fundraising messages in exchange for a set donation;
- corporate fundraising events.

Support

The campaign will be leveraged through holistic group support from Centrica plc. This will involve exploring the opportunities that exist to involve a range of supplier partners and product opportunities. A number of marketing channels will also be used to communicate the campaign and encourage customer involvement. Employee involvement will also leverage the partnership and a target of £250,000 has been set to be raised through fundraising activities for Help the Aged over the two year period.

Monitoring and evaluation

Critical success factors for the partnership have been set to facilitate definition and measurement of success. These include:

- positive media coverage, column inches and opportunities to see the key message;

- funds raised, targets have been set of £800,000 for customers and £100,000 for employees during 1999 (£250,000 over two years);
- corporate image and brand enhancement which will be measured through ongoing MORI surveys;
- targeted employee involvement of 50 per cent for fundraising activities during 1999;
- employee satisfaction through ongoing audits;
- other stakeholder satisfaction;
- number of older people receiving direct help through the campaign;
- customer loyalty which will be measured through active loyalty, i.e. customer retention.

Results

The partnership was launched in January 1999 and is currently gaining momentum. The funds generated will be distributed through a number of existing Help the Aged distribution channels:

- heating vouchers to provide emergency fuel payments to the most vulnerable elderly people;
- funding for day centres and lunch clubs to address the issues of isolation and loneliness and provide hot meals;
- funding for SeniorLine, Help the Aged's support and advice helpline for elderly people and carers;
- a HandyVan project where safety jobs are carried out free in the homes of the elderly to help them retain their independence within communities;
- Centrica plc support will also allow a significant proportion of funds to be allocated to install energy efficiency measures into thousands of homes, reducing fuel bills and providing longer term solutions to the issue of fuel poverty. This new area of funding will be delivered with energy efficiency group partners.

We have pledged to put our heart and soul into this partnership. As well as direct funding, we want to bring our 20,000 employees, our business partners and 16 million customers with us into the alliance to create long term change.

Charles Naylor, Director of Corporate Affairs, British Gas

The combined strength of Help the Aged and British Gas will be a force of direct action to bring warmth to vulnerable older people – to save lives now and in the future.

Michael Lake, Director General, Help the Aged

Case study V: BT's Cause Related Marketing strategy

BT, a multi million pound telecommunications business, operates across the full spectrum of communications technology and is in so many product markets with such diverse groups of customers and stakeholders that the challenge is to develop appropriate partnerships for appropriate markets. This case study highlights some of the diverse range of partnerships operated under the overall commitment to Cause Related Marketing and the process by which these partnerships are identified and developed.

Background

In December 1996 a position was established within the Community Partnership Programme (CPP) at BT specifically to promote Cause Related Marketing activity within BT. The CPP at BT is committed to increasing the number of Cause Related Marketing initiatives run in operational marketing divisions as part of its commitment to the community and to Cause Related Marketing. This commitment to Cause Related Marketing was in recognition of the benefits Cause Related Marketing can provide for the business and the community. With regards to Cause Related Marketing the key objectives are to:

- promote Cause Related Marketing across BT;
- establish best practice principles for BT people contemplating undertaking Cause Related Marketing activity;
- unlock marketing budgets for the benefit of the community, building links between BT and the community;
- make a quantifiable difference to core business, e.g. through sales figures, etc.

Rationale

Through the CPP, BT supports a programme of investment in and partnership with external organizations which are intended to demonstrably improve the quality of life and well being of the communities in which BT operate; build and maintain the companies reputation; provide a source of pride in the company for its employees; and enhance BT's business. Cause Related Marketing fits naturally into this programme as any one Cause Related Marketing activity has the potential to achieve all of these objectives.

Process

Community partners are identified and selected, and programmes are planned using a structured process. Market research about the causes BT consumers wish BT to support and identification of real areas of need in the wider community are reviewed. A shortlist of potential community partners is compiled. Shortlisted community partners are then selected on a number of different factors:

- fit with products/services;
- ability to deliver appropriate PR support;
- appropriate national and/or regional coverage;
- quality of proposal and performance in tender situation;
- where appropriate, historical and current relationship with charity.

A contract is then drawn up between the charity and BT and a BT project manager is designated to manage the programme.

Objectives

The key business objectives to date have been to:

- benefit the wider community;
- raise awareness both internally and externally of BT's contribution to the wider community;
- increase sales of a product or service;
- enhance BT's reputation.

Mechanics

A number of Cause Related Marketing programmes have been established to date including the following:

BT Big Button Phone and The Royal National Institute for the Blind (RNIB)

Objectives

- to support the launch of the Big Button telephone, the first product of the 'In Touch' product range;
- to increase sales of the Big Button telephone;
- to create an interesting in-store theme in BT shops in the post Christmas period;
- to extend BT's Cause Related Marketing to consumer products;
- to raise £100,000 for the RNIB, to support their new Helpline.

Mechanic
BT donated £1.50 to the RNIB for every Big Button telephone sold or rented, up to a maximum of £100,000. The Big Button telephone is on sale at £24.99 or can be rented for £4.99 per quarter.

Results

- product launch was hugely successful, providing an interesting in-store promotion in the post Christmas period;
- achieved 12 month volume sales target in 2 months;
- product/campaign awareness very high;
- raised profile of the aged/disabled market, its customers and BT products and services which target their needs;
- provided good visibility for RNIB brand to a wide customer audience, through BT shops and marketing promotions.

Whizz-Kidz/BT Mobile

Objectives

- to increase connections to BT Mobile within *BT* **Business***connections*;
- to raise a target of £50,000 to fund 20 specialist wheelchairs for Whizz-Kidz;
- to develop the Cause Related Marketing activities as part of BT's ongoing programme.

Mechanics

- BT donated £4 to Whizz-Kidz for every new connection made during quarter four of 1997/98 financial year (January–March 1998).
- This was promoted through a direct mail campaign distributed to approximately 175,000 business customers as well as press releases and staff briefings.
- All the marketing and promotional activities were funded by BT's Business Division.

Results

- The target of £50,000 has been raised for Whizz-Kidz which enabled the charity to buy 20 specialist wheelchairs.
- The campaign achieved a 5 per cent inbound response rate versus a 1.5 per cent target.

WWF/Call Diversion

Objectives

- To increase sales of Call Diversion to *BT* **Business***connections* customers with between 1 and 5 lines.
- To motivate *BT* **Business***connections* sales people.
- To raise up to £25,000 for WWF.

Mechanics

■ For every business customer with 1–5 lines who signed up to Call Diversion in quarter three of 1997/98 financial year (October–December 1997), £1 was donated to WWF up to a ceiling of £25,000.
■ The initiative was promoted via a direct mail campaign to approximately 200,000 business customers.
■ In addition, sales staff at BT call centres across the UK were briefed through team briefings, videos and posters and staff incentives were put in place.
■ CCP provided all the funds for WWF.
■ BT **Business**connections funded all the marketing and promotional activities.

Results

■ £24,394 raised for WWF.
■ 26.72 per cent increase on sales during the campaign.
■ The campaign has encouraged other parts of the BT Business Division to consider Cause Related Marketing projects.
■ Sales staff were motivated with a 99 per cent positive feedback on BT participating in future similar projects.
■ Press coverage achieved in marketing, WWF and BT publications.

Support

As can be seen from these examples, the mechanics and target market of each Cause Related Marketing programme are different but the same internal and external communication channels are available for use, as appropriate, in each programme, including:

■ telephone sales;
■ direct mail;
■ staff briefings;
■ videos;
■ posters;
■ BT staff newsletter.

In promoting Cause Related Marketing activity across BT, articles have been written for the staff newsletter, presentations have been made at team meetings and marketing managers have been targeted via e-mail and telephone. One article in the BT staff newspaper resulted in a number of BT people wishing to discuss their ideas for Cause Related Marketing programmes.

Monitoring and evaluation

All Cause Related Marketing projects undertaken require a business case, a contract, regular updates on the take up of the activity, regular reviews and thorough post evaluation. Specifically the following monitoring and evaluation takes place for each activity:

- Regular reviews are held with the partner charity throughout the course of the Cause Related Marketing programme.
- All projects are monitored in terms of press coverage through Impacon and in sales figures through BT's financial reporting mechanisms.
- The opinions of BT staff are captured in post event evaluation forms as well as BT wide research vehicles.
- An end of project report details actual results against targets in terms of monies raised, products sold, media coverage, people satisfaction and other measures, as appropriate.
- Post evaluation forms are also given to the charity, which measure their satisfaction with the campaign and the relationship with BT.

Results

Individually the projects impact upon their chosen activity area. For example, as was illustrated earlier, the Whizz-Kidz initiative raised enough money to buy 20 mobility aids for young people. The money raised from the WWF/Call Diversion initiative will contribute towards WWF's mission to raise awareness and understanding of environmental and sustainability issues amongst UK business people. For both BT and the charity partner, there are always the joint results achieved through enhanced reputation and media coverage.

Budget

Potential monies to the partner charities from these Cause Related Marketing activities could be in excess of £150,000. This does not include the resources spent on communicating and promoting the activity.

Lessons learned/future plans

These projects have already provided valuable learning including the importance of clear communication and recognizing the potential of strategically involving more elements of the business. In addition to this, the importance of dedicated PR and greater employee involvement with the charity could be utilized.

Of BT Big Button Phone and RNIB:

I was thrilled when I heard of the BT Big Button Phone initiative. The money raised from the partnership will enable RNIB Helpline staff to answer over 200 calls a day from people who need information, support and advice about sight loss. BT's support will truly make a difference to the lives of people with serious sight problems, their families, friends and carers.

Jean Harding, Helpline Manager, RNIB

Of BT Mobile and Whizz Kidz:

This (Whizz-Kidz) partnership programme has been a resounding success. We are extremely pleased to have reached our target of £50,000 and look forward to seeing the money go towards giving the Whizz-Kidz children the confidence and freedom to become more mobile.

Stephen Serpell, Head of Community Partnership Programme, BT

We are very grateful to both BT and its business mobile customers for helping to raise these much needed funds, which will go towards our £45 million goal.

Michael Dickson, Chief Executive, Whizz-Kidz

Of BT Call Diversion and WWF:

Throughout the partnership the relationship between BT and WWF continued to get better. The highlights of the campaign were the amount of funds raised, the feedback on employee motivation and more evidence that Cause Related Marketing works.

Paul King, Manager of Corporate Partners, WWF

Case study VI: Adams Childrenswear and Save the Children

This example demonstrates the benefits of a seamless partnership, where it becomes difficult to see where one organization begins and the other ends.

Background

Adams Childrenswear (Adams), part of the Sears Group, is a childrenswear retailer for girls and boys aged 0–10. Adams has a very clear brand proposition based around personality and character, being mischievous, having fun and being trendy. This fits perfectly with Save the Children, a child focused charity with a strong brand. The two organizations have similar values, the same target market, strong brands and keeping the fun in fundraising is key to the relationship.

Having been successfully working together since 1988, Adams stepped up the profile of its partnership with Save the Children in 1995, making the charity an integral part of their new brand proposition and child focused concept stores. In 1997 Adams further cemented this brand relationship by joining the charity's corporate membership scheme, committing to raise £100,000 a year for three years.

Objectives

The main commercial objective of Adams' support for Save the Children is the promotion of Adams' brand values through an association with the charity and the generation of positive local PR to create a motivating point of difference in a crowded retail market.

Supplementary objectives include increased customer traffic and loyalty, through in-store competitions and point of sale merchandise in aid of Save the Children; and staff motivation and improved internal communications, through Adams' staff fundraising campaigns, both with and independent to Sears Group staff fundraising. Adams is also concerned to ensure that their core business activity is run ethically.

Mechanics

Adams has established the on-going nature of the Cause Related Marketing partnership by building the Save the Children's 'FunRaiser' imagery into Adams new concept stores through a range of merchandise, point of sale material and fundraising vehicles including:

- a range of unique Adams Save the Children pin-badges featuring the FunRaiser characters which are promoted in all 330 stores for a donation to Save the Children;
- Save the Children merchandise, T-shirts, posters, balloons and transfers;
- tailor-made 3-foot high collection boxes;
- fundraising carol concerts held every December, with each store inviting their adopted local school to hold a concert outside their store.

Support

Mobilizing the workforce

Critical to the success of this relationship has been the top level support of Adams senior management for the relationship, including the ambassadorial role of Michael Hobbs, Adams' Managing Director. This has enabled Adams to involve everybody within the organization in the partnership, making it an integral part of their jobs. Adams have made it fun and easy for people within the organization to get involved, reviewing and communicating results through the organization, gaining employee support by recognizing individual contributions and rewarding them.

Staff participation is central to Adams' support for Save the Children; staff fundraising and the staff promotion of merchandise raises the majority of funds.

Leveraging the programme

The emphasis is on true partnership.

- Save the Children attend Adams' monthly planning meetings and workshop development days, so are always part of their marketing process. Regular review meetings are held which are all about driving new ideas and these often extend beyond the Cause Related Marketing aspect of the relationship, with purely commercial ideas for Adams or other ventures for Save the Children.
- Adams' conferences contain sections on Save the Children, they run competitions and have included Save the Children and their charity crest in some of their PR events.
- Save the Children have produced staff fundraising packs for all Adams stores, covering the generation of fundraising ideas, legal advice and guidelines on publicity and incentives such as information and nomination forms for the best staff fundraisers prize.
- Updates on the partnership are regularly communicated through Adams' weekly staff newsletter, 'Talking Shop', as well as being communicated through specific internal mailings to staff.
- Save the Children gives presentations on the UK programme work, which Adams funds, at regional staff conferences and project visits are organized for staff when possible. In addition at Adams' monthly head office meetings, or 'school assemblies', senior staff present a section on Adams current work with Save the Children.
- Adams is committed to socially responsible business practice within themselves and down their supply chain and Save the Children have introduced Adams to the ethical trading initiative which is an alliance of companies and non-governmental organizations who are developing in this area.

Through the supply chain

Adams have been able to further leverage the partnership with Save the Children through engaging supplier involvement, recognizing this as a valuable source of additional support and income.

When you start getting into the other areas that you touch from your organization you find even more opportunities to raise money and develop the partnership and there is nothing more pleasing to me than when I went to our recent supplier conference in Hong Kong; before I'd even had a chance to start I was presented with a cheque for £45,000 from our local Chinese factory owners who wanted to contribute to what was a very good cause.

Michael Hobbs, Managing Director, Adams Childrenswear

Results

Every year Adams raise more money for Save the Children and Adams has now raised over £1 million for Save the Children over the 10 years of the partnership. The relationship has worked so well, because the two organizations are a great match with similar values, sharing the same target market and both are strong brands.

Save the Children's FunRaiser imagery has been effectively incorporated into Adams' stores, creating an appropriate child focused and very positive high street image, and providing an effective competitive edge for the brand. It has also increased Save the Children's brand awareness through Adams' high street positioning. In-store activities and the promotion of merchandise in aid of Save the Children has motivated and mobilized Adams' workforce, and assisted in developing strong relationships with Adams' customer base, encouraging customer loyalty.

Staff morale and internal communications at Adams have improved. In addition to this, Adams' relations with suppliers have also benefited, as Adams' partnership with Save the Children involves them in joint activities, for example through supplying free print, artwork and design for fundraising products and publicity materials.

Considerable local publicity has been generated by the relationship, including £50,000 worth of local press coverage from the Christmas Carol Concert. Seven per cent prompted awareness of the partnership was reported in the 1998 Mintel Marketing Intelligence Report and the partnership was commended in the 1998 Business in the Community Awards for Excellence.

Adams' target market is children under ten, mothers and families, and all funds raised by Adams are earmarked to Save the Children's UK programme work with children of a similar age group, and their families, helping communities to be sustainable.

Monitoring and evaluation

Adams use a variety of ways to measure the success of the programme from tracking awareness, consumer perceptions, sales and funds raised. Save the

Children are seen almost as an extension of the Adams team and as such the programme is monitored constantly. New ideas are generated as a matter of course, some of which are then implemented, others of which are then used by Save the Children for other activities. As Michael Hobbs, Managing Director of Adams, explains:

> You've got to have regular review meetings, you've got to make them easy and you've got to focus on fund-raising. You must always question what is your performance like? From a PR point of view – how much are we getting?, what more can we do to drive it ... most importantly it's about driving our new ideas that we use on a purely commercial basis and Save the Children likewise in terms of some of the campaigns that they might follow up with. But don't forget when measuring success to reward it, it helps to maintain the momentum, so finally, the partnership we have is so strong it's difficult to tell where we start and they begin.

Michael Hobbs, Managing Director, Adams Childrenswear

As the partnership is fully integrated into all business plans and through regular meetings with all the external marketing partners, Adams and Save the Children are able to gauge the successes of the partnership. Internally within Adams, feedback from the partnership is understood through staff focus groups and employee attitude surveys.

An element of this measurement is the calculation of the equivalent advertising value of the space that Adams achieves in PR through their fundraising activities which is monitored and measured by Adams' PR agency on a monthly basis.

Save the Children, as part of its own internal auditing process, also evaluates the success of this work and this is communicated back to staff at Adams.

> In addition to the fantastic amount of money that Adams has raised, the PR, high street profile in 330 stores, local press, links to the schools and the time and expertise of Adams staff and volunteers ... we think the shared learning that we've gone through by maintaining and evolving this relationship is really valuable. We take that learning to our new corporate relationships, it's a very motivating account for the staff, it's very motivating for me, it's good fun, we've got an ambassador for Save the Children making introductions for us to some of the other companies that they know. The most important thing is the social impact and the difference that Adams makes to thousands of children in the UK and increasingly overseas.

Clare Mulley, Corporate Fundraiser, Save the Children

Case study VII: Nambarrie Tea Company Ltd and Action Cancer's Breast Cancer Awareness Month Campaign

This pioneering example demonstrates that no matter how small the company, a real and significant difference can be made. It illustrates how having audited the assets potentially available to the partnership, these assets are fully leveraged. For instance the production line being halted for the day in order to pack 100,000 fundraising ribbons into display boxes. This example highlights the power of synergy, energy and commitment.

Background

Nambarrie Tea Company Ltd (Nambarrie) is Northern Ireland's leading tea supplier. The Nambarrie brand is the number one selling tea in Northern Ireland and one of the most successful indigenous brands. It is a small company with 35 employees based over three sites.

Rationale

Northern Ireland has the highest incidence of breast cancer in the world and it is therefore a prominent social issue. Awareness has been heightened over the past three years by the work of Action Cancer, a leading Northern Ireland charity, using the pink ribbon as a symbol of the international fight against breast cancer. Action Cancer distributes 100,000 ribbons each October with advice cards on breast self-examination and early detection. Funds raised from the campaign support the charity's early detection clinics, support and counselling service and also its research into a cure for the disease.

Concept

Nambarrie and Action Cancer were natural partners from a Cause Related Marketing perspective. As well as being a local charity, Action Cancer, like Nambarrrie, were also dynamic and marketing orientated, targeting the same key audiences. The marketing expertise of both teams was complementary. Nambarrie's experience in communicating with this audience using techniques from the fast moving consumer goods industry, enabled them to apply this knowledge and approach to the challenge facing Action Cancer; namely to increase awareness of the issues, encourage breast self-examination and fund-raise.

In April 1998, Nambarrie signed a contract with Action Cancer which developed into a large scale Cause Related Marketing programme integrated across all areas of Nambarrie's marketing communications.

Objectives

After consultation between the partners, Nambarrie and Action Cancer's objectives for the partnership were set:

Partnership objectives

There were a number of objectives that this partnership hoped to achieve which included:

- Developing a programme for Nambarrie which would maximize the public relations budget and could be integrated across other marketing activity.
- Finding a solution that reflected corporate values which were based on commitment to the local community, dynamism and social responsibility.
- Reflecting the brand values of warmth, comfort, relaxation and reward.
- Finding a strong strategic fit with Nambarrie's target audience which was 'housewives' from 16 to 60 years old and a sub-target group of 20 to 35 years.
- Rationalizing charitable giving into one main focus which could achieve a return on investment rather than ad-hoc patronage.
- Finding a partner with a dynamic and effective PR capability – taking pressure off the limited in-house Nambarrie public relations resource.
- Having the benefits felt locally. It was stipulated that all proceeds had to stay in Northern Ireland.

Communications objectives

Again there were several communications objectives which included:

- Fully integrating the campaign across all of Nambarrie's marketing activities employing a range of media.
- Securing coverage of Nambarrie's involvement prior to and in addition to the launch of Breast Cancer Awareness Month.
- Communicating the reasons for and breadth of Nambarrie's support for the campaign to potentially cynical audiences.
- Ensuring that all communications were mutually beneficial to both Nambarrie and Action Cancer.

Mechanics

A number of solutions were created through the partnership offering benefits for both parties. These included 100,000 specially designed packs of Nambarrie's best selling tea with 5p from each pack being donated to the charity.

Support

After an asset audit, Action Cancer and Nambarrie were able to clearly identify the many mutually beneficial communications and branding opportunities that the partnership presented. For instance beyond the 'sales promotion approach':

- Nambarrie paid the media costs to create a TV advertising campaign, a first for Breast Cancer Awareness Month in Northern Ireland.
- Specially designed packs of Nambarrie tea acted as a direct marketing tool for the charity by carrying information on the campaign and how to make a donation.
- Nambarrie hosted the launch at a prestigious local venue. In addition to this they also provided tea to sponsored walk participants and to volunteers at Action Cancer and organized volunteers to assist with events.

Staff involvement

Led by Nambarrie's Operation Manager, the production line staff stopped production for a day, to devote it to packing campaign boxes for Action Cancer. This is a fantastic demonstration of the business' total commitment to the partnership and the cause. This was achieved with the hands-on involvement of management staff and involved the packing of 100,000 ribbons into 2000 display boxes. Not only was it a true demonstration of the corporate values but it was an extremely valuable contribution for Action Cancer whose staff and volunteers would normally take weeks to achieve what was done in hours. The day also provided the opportunity for Action Cancer staff and all levels of Nambarrie staff to communicate face to face.

Involvement along the distribution and supply chain

Again looking at how the organizations could support each other, Nambarrie were able to relieve Action Cancer of the problem of storing and distributing the 2000 packed boxes province wide. Nambarrie used their warehouse for storage, providing an accessible area with enough space to prepare them for distribution. Nambarrie integrated the box distribution into its existing province wide distribution network and allocated a van and driver to ensure that the process was completed on time.

Monitoring and evaluation

In addition to media monitoring and quantitative analysis of coverage, Nambarrie is monitoring awareness and the attitude towards the partnership through an on-going brand-tracking programme. In addition, an independent survey carried out by MRBI measured a 57 per cent prompted recall of Action Cancer's Breast Cancer Awareness Month Campaign among 300 people surveyed in the greater Belfast area.

Results

In some respects the results of the partnership are still to be seen through on-going tracking studies. But at this stage both partners are absolutely clear about its success and benefit and are currently planning next year's programme.

For the business

- This partnership was a brilliant demonstration of corporate and brand values.
- It raised awareness of the company in its markets and amongst its key stakeholders.
- It helped to improve perceptions of the company through the association.
- Staff attitudes towards the business were enhanced, as were the relationships with suppliers.
- In terms of brand tracking, respondents to the brand choice statement 'Brands that appeal to me' indicated a sample average was 29 per cent for Nambarrie – in line with market share. However, of the sample surveyed who were aware of the Breast Cancer campaign, the response was 61 per cent – more than a 100 per cent increased brand appeal.

For the cause

- This first year of partnership with Nambarrie raised over £200,000, doubling their funds and far exceeding expectations.
- As a result of the partnership and the use of new marketing techniques, awareness of Action Cancer and its work increased.
- 949 telephone enquiries were received at the Action Cancer support service between 1 October and 31 December, an increase of 24 per cent on the previous year's statistics. In addition to this 393 personal visits were made to the centre during this period.
- Due to the increase in awareness, Action Cancer provided additional evening and double clinics which were filled to capacity. Compared to the previous year attendance at clinics steadily rose as a result of the work of the partnership with a 2.5 per cent increase in attendance in October, an 18 per cent increase in November, a 19 per cent increase in December and an 18 per cent increase in January.
- Through Nambarrie's support in production and distribution, Action Cancer saved over £1000 and three weeks packing work and had much lower distribution costs. In addition to this cost per display box was reduced by being able to purchase a greater number.

For both

- The affinity between the partners was crucial to the success of the campaign. The partnership exceeded expectations in terms of marketing benefits to the company and fundraising and awareness for the charity. The key to this mutually beneficial success was 'synergy' and 'energy'.

- In February 1999, Nambarrie and Action Cancer were presented with the NICVA Link Award which is awarded on the basis of commitment shown by the company; impact and benefits to the community and originality and level of innovation.
- The advertisement, funded by Nambarrie and which was a first for Action Cancer, reached 82 per cent of the housewife market in Northern Ireland. The average frequency of the viewing of the advertisement was four times per person.
- The partnership received substantial media coverage.
- Both parties benefited from shared learning.
- Employees of both organizations were able to take pride in what was achieved during the campaign.

This is the most comprehensive marketing initiative that the company has ever undertaken. The return on investment has been enormous in terms of corporate, brand and internal communications. Most importantly it has directly benefited our community and our customers, the women in Northern Ireland who buy our tea.

Brian Davis, Managing Director, Nambarrie Tea Company Ltd

We have been truly inspired by Nambarrie and its employees, not only by the commitment financially and in kind but by their personal receptiveness, interest and compassion in playing a part in the fight against breast cancer in Northern Ireland. The campaign was a resounding success . . . Their support has put the campaign on a new level and we look forward to building on this partnership in years to come.

Janet Stevenson, Deputy Chief Executive, Action Cancer

Case study VIII: Persil Go Red for Comic Relief

This case study demonstrates the tactical use of Cause Related Marketing and the significant contribution it can make for both the brand, employees and the cause when committed totally and leveraged thoroughly. It also shows how existing communications strategies and executions can be adapted and leveraged for the Cause Related Marketing partnership.

Background

Persil is seen by consumers as a safe and trusted brand with a strong heritage. Lever Brothers Ltd has been involved with a number of Cause Related Marketing initiatives, including Persil Funfit, the Comfort Health Visitor of the Year Awards and the Jif Community Challenge, and wanted to build on this.

Rationale

Persil is a high profile, market leading consumer brand. A high profile Cause Related Marketing promotion was recognized as an appropriate opportunity for Persil to reinforce its position as a leader whilst engaging stakeholders and benefiting a charity.

As a trusted, well-known charity with strong branding and a heritage of raising significant funds for good causes, Comic Relief was chosen as an appropriate partner which supported the brand positioning of Persil. Comic Relief also provided a synergistic brand fit with Persil's emotional values ('Because it matters, nothing cares like Persil') and brand attributes – happy/ cheerful, caring, confident, mainstream.

Persil Colour Care was chosen as the lead variant to support the partnership. As a product that is designed to look after coloured clothes there was another natural link with the colour red and the 'Go Red with Comic Relief, Stay Red with Persil Colour Care' theme was developed.

Concept

Persil packs were developed to incorporate the Comic Relief Red Nose branding to convey the partnership and to give the packaging increased prominence on the shelf.

Objectives

- Build total Persil brand image.
- Increase awareness of Persil Colour Care variant.
- Communicate benefits of Persil Colour Care in an innovative and interesting way.
- Raise at least £250,000 for Comic Relief.
- Increase sales of Persil standard powders.

Timing

This programme was developed for Comic Relief 1999. Promotional packs were available in store from 15 February 1999 in the run up to Comic Relief day on 12 March.

The first meetings between Lever Brothers Ltd and Comic Relief were at the beginning of 1998. The theme was developed from this point onwards and work on implementing the campaign commenced in October 1998.

Mechanics

On pack donation scheme

A donation from Lever Brothers Ltd was made to Comic Relief from every special edition 'Red Nose' box of Persil sold, the amount of the donation depending on the size of the pack bought: 1.35kg pack, 5p; 2.7kg pack, 10p; 4.5kg pack, 25p; and for a 6.75kg pack, 40p.

Sponsorship

- Lever Brothers Ltd produced 'Go Red' information packs full of red-themed ideas for people to raise money which contained a money-off voucher redeemable for Persil products.
- Persil funded the telephone line which consumers called to obtain the 'Go Red' fundraising packs. This line was promoted on the back of Persil standard powder packs.

Support

Above the line

- TV advertisements promoting the partnership between Lever Brothers Ltd and Comic Relief and highlighting the donation made from special packs were shown. As Persil regularly advertises on television this was an important aspect of the communications process, leveraging the promotion through balanced communications with stakeholders.
- Advertisements were also placed in magazines, encouraging people to 'Go Red for Comic Relief' and promoting the message to 'Stay Red with Persil Colour Care'.
- A radio campaign also ran from February up until Red Nose Day on independent radio stations around the country. There were two variations, both promoting the fundraising initiative.

On pack

- As well as heavily promoting the association on-pack, the back of the special edition packs also provided details on how to obtain fundraising packs with ideas on how to organize 'Go Red' events.

Internal communications

- Lever Brothers Ltd organized a number of activities around its three sites for Red Nose Day to enable staff to join in and raise money for Comic Relief. These included red menus in staff restaurants, red quizzes, red nail makeovers, red-rub massages, and reception areas and restaurants decorated in red.
- The activities were advertised on posters and noticeboards and a feature was included in the in-house newspaper with competitions to win prizes, including tickets to the televised Comic Relief event on 12 March.
- A round-up of all activities and details of the money raised was included in a subsequent issue of the in-house newspaper and on the in-house radio tape.

Public relations

There was a significant PR campaign to support Persil's link with Comic Relief including:

- attendance at the launch of the 1999 Red Nose campaign;
- 'Red Room' briefing for journalists;
- reader offers in women's magazines and regional press;
- live radio interviews with celebrities on 14 stations;
- 'Paint the Town Red' radio campaign and competition to win a trip to the Red Sea;
- 'Go Red Ed' campaign inviting editors to wear red and feature a picture of themselves in the paper for which a donation was made by Persil Colour Care;
- coverage within the televised event on Red Nose Day with the amount of money raised by Persil.

Retailer specific activity

- Sainsbury's 'Washing Machine Red Nose' offer;
- Roadshow in top 50 stores.

Monitoring and evaluation

The Business in the Community Cause Related Marketing Guidelines emphasize the importance of monitoring, measuring and evaluating Cause Related Marketing programmes with comparable rigour to that applied to other marketing programmes. This process enabled Persil to assess the success of the programme in terms of the objectives set and to compare it with other marketing mechanics.

The Persil programme was evaluated against the following:

- tracking of Persil and Persil Colour Care sales, share and penetration;
- Comic Relief feedback on satisfaction with campaign;
- Persil brand awareness tracking changes;
- PR coverage evaluation;
- coupon redemption from Information Pack;
- response to phone line;
- the delivery of activity on time and within budget.

Results

- 25 per cent uplift on sales;
- £260,000 raised for Comic Relief;
- high recall of TV advertisements;
- great PR coverage;

- enhanced brand profile through the association;
- improved relations with Sainsbury who represent a key retail customer for Persil and Lever Brothers Ltd;
- created a 'feel good factor' within Lever Brothers Ltd.

Budget

Total budget for activity around £1.5 million, including:

- donation to Comic Relief;
- fees to Comic Relief;
- media space;
- PR programme;
- production of all materials;
- phone line costs.

Lessons learned

Managing the programme is one of the key elements of a Cause Related Marketing programme. Understanding how to work together to get optimum results is key to all marketing and fundraising activities involving a number of parties, otherwise even the most fitting Cause Related Marketing partnership can fail. Lever Brothers Ltd's key learnings from the Comic Relief promotion involved the importance of knowing each other's objectives, understanding the issues of managing two brand images together and the need for a realistic timing plan.

> The Persil 'Go Red' campaign with Comic Relief was a great success for Lever. The link was a particularly relevant one as Persil's attributes and values fitted so well with those of Comic Relief. . . . The activity not only helped to build Persil's image and increase sales, it raised much needed funds and engaged Lever's employees, giving them an opportunity to become involved and creating a 'feel good factor' within the company.
>
> **John Ballington, Corporate and Consumer Affairs Director, Lever Brothers Ltd**

> Comic Relief was delighted to work with Persil as part of our Red Nose Day 1999 campaign. The fit between Persil and Comic Relief as two well known, popular, UK brands was perfect and Lever Brothers created a really fantastic Red Nose Day promotion. . . . The on-pack activity was combined with sponsorship of the 'Go Red' fundraising initiative to reach both their customer base and Comic Relief supporters. This integrated approach created a coherent message both in the High

Street and in the home which fully embraced the spirit of the campaign and raised a staggering amount of money for the projects we fund in the UK and Africa.

Amanda Horton-Mastin, Marketing Director, Comic Relief

Case study IX: New Covent Garden Soup Company, the National Trust and Crisis

This is a case study which illustrates the many levels on which a Cause Related Marketing partnership can work from the consumer through to the supplier, all providing benefits to the cause. It also demonstrates the use of communications at the end of the partnership.

Background

New Covent Garden Soup Company, the company that pioneered the fresh soup sector in the UK in 1988, is a relatively small company employing about 160 people. The core values of the product are fresh natural ingredients and home-made style.

Ever since New Covent Garden Soup Company first formed, it had a philanthropic relationship with Crisis, the national charity for homeless people in the UK, providing them with surplus soup. In addition to this New Covent Garden Soup Company discussed the concept of sponsorship with the National Trust, the environmental charity which looks after 600,000 acres of coast and countryside in England, Wales and Northern Ireland, together with hundreds of country houses and gardens, working farms, mills and mines.

The issues for the brand at the time of developing its Cause Related Marketing relationships focused on the relatively limited brand awareness and a need to stimulate trial and purchase. New Covent Garden Soup Company was clear that any affinity had to reinforce the brand values and establish mutual benefit.

New Covent Garden Soup Company and the National Trust

Following the discussions of sponsorship, New Covent Garden Soup Company and the National Trust developed a mutually beneficial on-pack Cause Related Marketing promotion. New Covent Garden Soup Company's first experience of Cause Related Marketing was thus with the National Trust.

A new promotional 'Wild Mushroom' soup was developed which carried on-pack details of the National Trust garden restoration project at Fenton House, which New Covent Garden Soup Company supported. The affinity with Fenton House, a National Trust property built in 1693, is that it is adjacent to Hampstead Heath, where a wide variety of wild mushrooms thrive. Through the partnership with the National Trust, New Covent Garden Soup Company had differentiation and were able to reinforce the brand values. It was also a very effective way of testing or piloting a new product in the market before launching it as a core product line. At the same time funds were raised for the National Trust and the relationship between the two partners was developed on an additional and new level.

Mechanics

The proposition was that for every carton of soup sold over the three-month promotional period, a donation would be made to the National Trust with a £40,000 donation guaranteed. The promotional message was communicated on one full facing of the soup packaging as well as the National Trust's name being clearly featured on the front and back of the pack. For the press launch New Covent Garden Soup Company sent their media contacts a sample of soup, a packet of wild mushrooms and a mushroom cookery book together with a guide book to Fenton House in a specially produced gift box in the shape of Fenton House.

Results

The soup had distribution with all the major grocery retailers. The Cause Related Marketing promotion was featured on many thousands of cartons and well exceeded the planned quota, with the soup subsequently becoming the number two best selling soup in the range.

The activity outstripped expectations. £40,000 was raised for the National Trust whose name and mission was exposed to new audiences in an innovative way. 'Wild Mushroom' soup became one of the New Covent Garden Soup Company core lines indicating the overwhelming success of the product. Indeed the soup won the best new vegetarian product at the prestigious Good Food Awards that year.

Importantly, following the achievement of the goal, New Covent Garden Soup Company continued to promote the Fenton House project and the National Trust by again using the side of the pack to inform consumers of the achievement and thanking the customers for their support. So often this aspect of the communications loop is overlooked, as is the importance of recognizing and appreciating the consumer and or other stakeholders' support[1].

Using Cause Related Marketing provided New Covent Garden Soup Company with an additional marketing edge. It reinforced the brand values and attributes; it provided a point of difference in a highly competitive market place, it provided substantial media coverage and PR. It generated both trial and sales. The relationships between New Covent Garden Soup Company and the National Trust was developed on a new and additional level and significant funds were raised, as was awareness. Marketing, sales and fundraising benefit were therefore all convincingly achieved.

We were delighted with the success of the relationship with New Covent Garden Soup. The association with a dynamic, pioneering company and the resulting exposure in supermarkets was of tremendous benefit to us as it gave the National Trust a new, innovative image while at the same time reinforcing our core message of conservation.

Margaret Hopper, Corporate Development Manager, the National Trust

New Covent Garden Soup Company and Crisis

Based on this success, New Covent Garden Soup Company went on to develop the use of Cause Related Marketing, this time with another long-term charity partner, Crisis. Crisis is the national charity for single homeless people. Established in 1967, it develops schemes in partnership with others to provide help where it is most needed, from emergency assistance on the streets through to permanent housing and resettlement support.

Having already been involved through gifts in kind, in terms of providing products and sponsorship of the Crisis vans, the relationship was developed on a new platform. Timed for Christmas, the first Cause Related Marketing relationship with Crisis focused on communicating Crisis' message and featured a donation hotline for Crisis with the objective of raising £10,000 to enable Crisis to install kitchens in their 'open houses' around the country.

Once again using the platform of the launch of a promotional soup, New Covent Garden Soup Company allocated a full facing of the packaging of the new soup to be launched on the market providing Crisis with the opportunity to communicate their message prominently on 200,000 cartons over four months and sold to retailers nation-wide.

For the cause, in this case homeless people, the objective was clear: to raise awareness, communicate the Crisis message, to build a deeper relationships with New Covent Garden Soup Company and to raise funds. For New Covent Garden Soup Company it was about not only raising funds for a cause they had long been associated with but also to reinforce the brand values of the organization, to provide differentiation and a newsworthy launch platform.

The importance of brand fit is crucial. As with the National Trust, the affinity between Crisis and New Covent Garden Soup Company was very strong. In this case the message of using fresh vegetables to make nutritious food and providing a nutritious diet for homeless people was highly appropriate.

The success of the relationship between Crisis and New Covent Garden Soup Company was such that it led to a second year of activity. This was over a four-month period just after Christmas and based on the launch of another new soup. A very emotive message about the work of Crisis and its Winter Watch programme was featured on the pack. A donation was given to cover the cost of over 10,000 meals in winter shelters and as with the previous programme it was supported by a preplanned public relations campaign.

Whilst largely the same mechanic was used with the National Trust, there were a few new developments that are worthy of note. In the first programme, beyond the New Covent Garden Soup Company donation, new money was generated for Crisis through the support of customer contributions by the innovative use of the hotline, featured on the pack. The profile of Crisis, the cause and the fact that they are nation-wide and that this is a year round issue were well communicated on the pack once again using a whole facing and also featuring Crisis' logo on the front and back of the pack.

Importantly New Covent Garden Soup Company with their partner Crisis identified an opportunity which so many others miss: this Cause Related Marketing programme was used for and succeeded in leveraging business to business relationships both for the benefit of the business and for the charity. For New Covent Garden Soup Company, relationships with retailers are vital. If one is able to find an affinity with the retailer that works on a number of levels the better that relationship.

> Crisis worked with New Covent Garden Soup in a fresh and innovative way to come up with a campaign which made a significant difference to sales, image and corporate involvement with a cause that is high in the list of concerns with customers, staff and the business community.

> #### Angie Turner, Corporate Partnership Executive, Crisis

> One of the key reasons and benefits as regards retailers was the concept of adding value. In 1996/7 TESCO stocked the soup as an extra line because it recognized that the promotion was adding value to the shelf. In addition to pledging a contribution of 10p per carton sold, TESCO also carried a promotional shelf strip to highlight support. Crisis' relationship with Sainsbury led to their involvement too. In 1998 both TESCO and Sainsbury renewed support with the donation and the shelf strip, and New Covent Garden Soup achieved new listings. Through Crisis homeless people have benefited, the retailers have benefited, the consumers have benefited and so have we. Cause Related Marketing really is a win:win:win:win.

> #### Kate Raison, Marketing Director, New Covent Garden Soup Company

In this case New Covent Garden Soup Company's relationship with TESCO PLC benefited as a result of the link with Crisis. TESCO PLC was also a supporter of Crisis and with the efforts of all three parties, the relationship between them was enhanced. TESCO PLC's involvement was encouraged through the supplier-buyer relationships with New Covent Garden Soup Company. TESCO PLC agreed to donate 10p for every carton of soup sold in addition to the New Covent Garden Soup Company donation and the customer hotline donations.

Leverage is an often untapped opportunity in Cause Related Marketing. If it is a sales promotion type approach there can be a tendency not to think beyond the product itself and the charity. The other stakeholders in the potential equation can often be overlooked, undervalued and underutilized. By involving TESCO PLC, what was originally developed as a partnership of two became a very successful relationship of three providing wins for the supplier, the retailer and for the charity.

This case study indicates just what can be achieved if further angles and opportunities are considered and utilized. It also illustrates that Cause Related Marketing does not only apply to large businesses and causes or charities. New Covent Garden Soup Company employs just 160 people with a turnover of £18 million and Crisis employs 30 people with an income of £4.69 million. Complementary objectives, a clear affinity and long-term commitment have been key success factors in this relationship. The management of the programme, the innovation and the leverage have all meant that commitment and modest budgets have achieved significant results.

> Cause Related Marketing has become an integral part of our marketing strategy and we have further activity planned.

> **Kate Raison, Marketing Director, New Covent Garden Soup Company**

Notes

1 Please refer to The Cause Related Marketing Guidelines – Towards Excellence (1998), Business in the Community.
2 The Game Plan (1997), Business in the Community qualitative consumer research into Cause Related Marketing conducted by Research International (UK) Ltd.

Chapter 17

International case studies

Case study I: Sears Roebuck's Cause Related Marketing strategy

Background and rationale

Sears Roebuck, the second largest retailer in the world, with sales over £11 billion, is the biggest retail advertiser in the world reaching over 200 million people each week. Sears Roebuck has 1000 full department stores across the USA and Canada and 21,000 other outlets which employ more than 300,000 people.

Five years ago Sears Roebuck under the new leadership of Arthur Martinez began to turnaround its recent performance. Sweeping changes were made, new divisions created, old programmes discontinued and today as Bob Thacker, Senior Vice President Marketing, said 'The company is one of the proudest and strongest in retailing.' Much of the reason why Sears Roebuck was able to effect such a dramatic turnaround was because of the place Sears Roebuck held in the American heart. Bob Thacker very much sees his role as 'to develop our strategic marketing and promotion activities in a way that allows us to clearly communicate our mission to our customers.' Apart from communicating that Sears Roebuck is the place to shop, work and invest, 'We want them (customers) to know that Sears Roebuck cares deeply about community and about families.'

The argument that you 'cannot have a healthy high street without a healthy back street' is very familiar and deeply rooted in the Sears Roebuck consciousness. Sears Roebuck take their corporate social responsibility very seriously and are clear this has business benefits, as Bob Thacker says: 'Our bottom line directly relates to the responsibility we have to every community in which we do business. We know that as our communities thrive, we thrive.'

For Sears Roebuck, Cause Related Marketing is a new strategy but lies at the very heart of the strategy on how to communicate these values and how to develop their corporate giving. Bob Thacker explained: 'Cause marketing is a strategy that ties a merchandising plan with a focused corporate giving effort.' It provides corporations with a new dynamic, highly effective way to respond to community needs: 'We recognize that it (Cause Related Marketing) is going to play an important role in our growth, and we're prepared to take giant steps to make a difference to our communities.'

Sears Roebuck's focus

Sears Roebuck's primary target audience are women aged between 25 and 54 representing all ethnic backgrounds, who own their homes and/or have children at home. The Sears Roebuck Cause Related Marketing programmes are being developed with this target audience in mind.

'Cause marketing is about strengthening the ties that bind,' according to Bob Thacker, and therefore Sears Roebuck chooses to support grassroots efforts based in the community.

Sears Roebuck's objectives

Clearly each programme has a particular set of objectives but the overarching aim is that the programmes help the customers and their communities and aim to solidify families, serve women and promote cultural diversity. In developing the new strategy, each opportunity was carefully considered and evaluated.

Sears Roebuck's Cause Related Marketing programmes

Sears Roebuck's partnership with Gilda's Club

Gilda Radner was a popular American television comedian who died of ovarian cancer in 1989. Before she passed away she developed the idea of a place where people living with cancer could come together with family and friends for emotional support, social events and laughter. The idea became a reality with the help of Radner's husband, actor Gene Wilder, and Radner's cancer psychotherapist Joanna Bull. The Gilda's Club is a non profit organization that provides a network of local meeting places for people for all ages. Each club offers networking groups, lectures and workshops, all free of charge.

Objective
Sears Roebuck began its partnership with Gilda's Club in 1990, and in the first three years, generated $3 million to help build new clubhouses all over the country.

Mechanics
Apart from the cash donations there are product donations, volunteer time and Cause Related Marketing programmes to help raise awareness. These Cause Related Marketing programmes included:

- a percentage of the sales price from designs of ties and scarves donated by national celebrities recruited by Sears Roebuck;
- a link up with Levi's on the 550 jeans in Gilda's Club cities;
- the DieHard Racing Team donated $1 per lap for every truck race in the Craftsman Super Truck Race in Nashville ($15,000);
- a Home Fashions golf outing was sponsored for Gilda's Club that raised over £61,000 in one afternoon in 1997 and $100,000 in 1998.
- a 98 holiday compact disc generated $237,000 in one month.

Additional support

In 1998 further merchandise lines, sporting events, magazine advertisements and a dramatic increase in the in-store visibility for the programme took place. Sears Roebuck also sponsors the national training centre for Gilda's Club designed to help other people learn how to establish Gilda's Clubs in their own communities.

The results for the business

- Apart from reinforcing and communicating Sears Roebuck's corporate values and building relationships with their customers, Sears Roebuck benefited from the sales of 100,000 ties and 30,000 scarves sold in just a few months bringing customer traffic, interest and excitement.
- The Levi link up saw sales of 550 jeans increased in-store by 56 per cent compared to 16 per cent in non-Gilda cities, providing benefits to both Sears and Levi as well as Gilda's Clubs.
- Generates pride among employees, especially in Gilda's Club markets and developing markets.

The results for the cause

The proceeds from the sales of the designer ties and scarves; the Levi's 550 jeans; US$15,000 from the DieHard Truck team, the awareness generated by the advertising and other support plus the proceeds from numerous events including US$100,000 in one afternoon through the sponsored golf outing and the sponsorship of the national training centre. Visibility for a virtually unknown non-profit is also a major benefit. Other benefits included in-store signing, Sunday circular reaching 50 million homes each week and a one-page advertisement which ran between November 25 and December 24.

> Making Gilda's Club a 'nonprofit of choice' for Sears has truly been a win-win-win for all parties involved. Gilda's Club receives substantial donations and visibility, Sears gets a sense of pride and accomplishment among our associates plus goodwill among our customers, and our local communities get access to much needed social and emotional support as they, their friends and family members live with cancer.

> **John Connolly, Community Relations Manager, Sears Roebuck**

Sears Roebuck's Get Back Give Back Programme

Background

Sears Roebuck regard this as the biggest Cause Related Marketing initiative in the company's 112 year history. It is a programme that takes place during the back-to-school marketing season (September). In the USA many children wear school uniform and therefore the back-to-school period for Sears Roebuck is second only to the Christmas period in terms of sales; it is also potentially a stressful time for some parents who can't afford to properly clothe their children at the start of the school year.

Objective

Sears Roebuck believes that every child deserves decent clothing and therefore this programme aims to address this. It takes place during the back-to-school season.

Concept

With the Get Back Give Back programme, Sears Roebuck and its vendors used the important back-to-school season to help clothe up to 1 million needy children by supporting Kids In Distressed Situations (KIDS), a non-profit organization that specializes in matching corporate merchandise donations with local non-profits that assist children living in crisis.

Mechanic

Every time a children's clothing purchase was made at Sears Roebuck from July 26 through September 6 1998, a percentage of the sale was donated to the programme. Merchandise donations by Sears Roebuck and its vendors took place throughout 1998, with half of the donated apparel items from Sears Roebuck and the other half a combined total from their vendor partners.

The results for the business

This programme enabled Sears Roebuck to make the company's largest single donation. The programme also provided Sears Roebuck the opportunity to enhance their corporate image and build relationships with vendor partners and non-profit organizations who were also involved in the scheme.

The results for the cause

The Get Back Give Back programme provided real tangible benefits as, throughout 1998, needy children received approximately 1 million articles of clothing donated by Sears Roebuck and their vendor partners.

> This programme will drive the single largest donation in Sears 112 year history. It supports our image as a company that's concerned with America's families and helps to further position Sears as the 'kids' store.

> **John Connolly, Community Relations Manager, Sears Roebuck**

An organization our size has a unique opportunity to make a tremendous impact in terms of clothing needy children. The entire children's team has come together to make this effort a reality. Because of their determination to make this programme work, Sears is now viewed as a leader in our industry.

Greg Sandfort, Vice President of Children's Apparel, Sears Roebuck and Director, KIDS

We had been slowly building a programme where we help to outfit children for school. Partnering with Sears means the magnification of our dream. With our new facility, we have a dedicated 'Sears Room' where all Sears tags are removed and it's where clients come to shop for new clothes.

Lieutenant Colonel Bettie Love, Salvation Army

Case study II: Kellogg's Kids Help Line

Background and rationale

Kids Help Line is Australia's only free, 24-hour, confidential and anonymous telephone counselling service for 5–18 year olds. There are 3.6 million young people in Australia between the ages of 5 and 18. Every year they make 1.5 million phone calls to Kids Help Line. Only one in two calls could be answered due to lack of funds. The key issue was therefore to raise funds to ensure that more than half the calls were answered.

Although well known amongst children, Kids Help Line did not have a high profile amongst the general giving public. Kids Help Line identified a need to raise the awareness of the service and its need for funds as part of a strategy for building community funding support.

Corporate support through Cause Related Marketing was seen as a key element in future funding for Kids Help Line. It was a key way to raise awareness of the service and of the problem, as well as to raise money to fund it.

From Kellogg's point of view, rather than simply choosing a well-known 'household name' charity such as the Salvation Army, research was conducted to find a charity that was not only responding to a real and urgent social need and was pro-active and preventive, but which also was a close fit to the company's own values.

In 1998 a sponsorship arrangement was formed with Kellogg Australia that delivered significant funds to answer more calls, raised the profile of Kids Help Line substantially and laid the foundation for building a donor base for the service. The Kellogg's Kids Help Line sponsorship is a fully integrated campaign which through Kellogg's Cause Related Marketing support encompasses advertising, PR and sales promotion. It was a landmark in Cause Related Marketing in Australia that was far more extensive than the typical product promotions conducted in the past.

Objectives

Key objectives were established for the fundraising programme developed around the Kellogg's sponsorship.

Kids Help Line objectives

- Raise significant funds to increase the number of calls Kids Help Line could respond to.
- Raise awareness of the service amongst the general community and giving public, as well as awareness of the need for funds.
- Raise awareness of the service amongst kids.
- Raise awareness of issues related to childhood and parenting.
- Develop opportunities for a licensing and merchandising programme.
- Develop opportunities for other major corporate partnerships.
- Establish a donor database for Kids Help Line.

Kellogg's objectives

- Support Kids Help Line in generating donations to fund calls.
- Enhance consumer perceptions of Kellogg's as a company committed to supporting Australian kids and families.
- Assume a leadership position in the corporate sector in terms of social responsibility.

Mechanics

This programme is multifaceted and fully integrated, showing the value of leveraging a programme through the full marketing mix. Key aspects of the programme include:

- sponsorship contract with cash contribution to Kids Help Line;
- national television, newspaper and magazine advertising campaign promoting Kids Help Line and soliciting donations;
- national fundraising campaign involving 1 million donation bookmarks available through supermarkets;
- promotion of Kids Help Line on 7 million cereal boxes;
- national public relations launches resulting in extensive print and electronic media coverage;
- creation of a special event – the Kellogg's Beating The Blues Celebrity Photographic Auction – to raise funds and profile;
- recruitment of Kylie Minogue as Official Ambassador for Kids Help Line.

Strategies

Advertising strategy

- An extensive advertising strategy was put in place to meet both partners' public relations and promotional objectives.
- Kellogg's commissioned the creation of two television advertisements. One was a 30-second advertisement promoting the sponsorship by Kellogg's and aimed at raising consumers' awareness of the specially marked packs. The second advertisement was a 30-second fundraising community service announcement aimed at generating donations for Kids Help Line from the community.
- Kids Help Line produced a 30-second radio fundraising community service announcement which was distributed to all radio stations nationally.
- Kids Help Line produced sheets of newspaper filler advertisements with a fundraising focus which were distributed to all newspapers nationally with a request for free space.
- Kellogg's commissioned the production of a full page magazine advertisement and used their media leverage to secure *pro bono* spots in major magazine titles.
- Kellogg's commissioned the production of a paid newspaper advertisement promoting their sponsorship and to raise donation funds for Kids Help Line which was run in national newspapers.
- Kellogg's produced 7 million cereal boxes to raise awareness of Kids Help Line and featuring an entire back panel devoted to educating kids about the service and how it could help, as well as a special side panel targeting adults and soliciting donations for Kids Help Line.
- Kellogg's in conjunction with a major retail supermarket produced point-of-sale posters promoting Kids Help Line. They also commissioned the production of 1 million Kids Help Line bookmarks in Aus $2 and $5 denominations which were available in supermarkets to raise additional funds for Kids Help Line.

Media and public relations strategy for sponsorship launch

- Kellogg's sponsorship of Kids Help Line was launched using high profile celebrities on the 5th anniversary of the Kids Help Line using hard hitting key research to heighten awareness of the issues facing kids and the increase in calls to the line.
- The launch was supported by a *Kids Help Line Week July 13–19* and the Kellogg's Beating The Blues Celebrity Photographic Auction supported by 20 leading Australian celebrities including Kylie Minogue, who as a result became the official ambassador for Kids Help Line.

Fundraising strategy

Income for Kids Help Line was generated through the above activities including:

- Kellogg's Aus $500,000 commitment to Kids Help Line in year one of the sponsorship;
- Kellogg's Beating The Blues Celebrity Photographic Auction;
- Corporate Breakfast;
- advertising campaign soliciting donations;
- sale of Kids Help Line bookmarks nationally.

Support

Internal commitment

Kellogg's internal commitment to its sponsorship has been enormous with Jean Louis Gourbin, Area President (Asia-Pacific) of Kellogg's, taking a position on Kids Help Line's board. Kellogg's Managing Director David Mackay has also taken a personal role in challenging the community and other companies to join Kellogg's in supporting Kids Help Line.

Extension of sponsorship programme

Beyond its own commitment to Kids Help Line, Kellogg's has taken an active role in recruiting other corporate partners to the programme such as retailers, media and business partners.

Results

Results of the advertising

- The television, radio, magazine and newspaper community service announcements received extended airplay during the promotional period.
- Kellogg's magazine ads were given an extraordinary run over weeks in high-circulation magazine titles which even featured the ad on the inside cover.

Results of the media and public relations strategy

- Using the twin strategies of celebrity interest as well as topical youth issues was extremely successful in generating extensive media coverage.
- The launch generated 13 newspaper articles nationally, including page 3 of the major Sydney newspaper. It was also covered by national and local television news, and 28 radio interviews were conducted, including national radio networks.
- A major magazine for the supermarket trade and suppliers featured the sponsorship launch as their cover story.
- The announcement of Kylie Minogue's ambassadorship and the launch of Kids Help Line week generated an enormous media response.
- Television coverage included all commercial networks news, entertainment programmes and cable television programmes.

- In the 24 hours following the Depression media release, 91 radio interviews and news items went to air nationally.
- Regional papers are continuing to run the Depression issue and the Kylie Minogue announcement.

Fundraising results

- Fundraising income from the sponsorship and related events is in excess of Aus $550,000 and continuing to rise, which will allow Kids Help Line to answer more than 156,000 additional phone calls over the coming year.
- As a result of the promotion and the involvement of Kylie Minogue, Kids Help Line is now in negotiation with two other major companies interested in a significant sponsorship of the service.

Community response

- Kellogg's have received a stream of congratulations from customers, the trade and staff for their involvement with Kids Help Line. Feedback has been overwhelmingly positive.
- Since the launch of the cereal packs on-shelf, 12 per cent of new callers to Kids Help Line have told counsellors that they first heard of the service from the Kellogg's cereal boxes. Around 40 per cent of callers during the promotional period cited television as their source of referral, generated from the Kellogg's ads.
- Kellogg's commissioned market research into community awareness of Kids Help Line and perceptions towards both organizations prior to the launch of the campaign. Follow-up research indicated not only a shift in Kids Help Line as the number one charity of importance amongst adults but also saw consumers' perceptions of Kellogg's community involvement strengthen.

Future plans

Educational campaign

Beyond its financial commitment to Kids Help Line, Kellogg's will play a leading role in promoting the service to young people in Australia, and in disseminating useful information to parents nationally. Information about Kids Help Line aimed at young people will be printed on 5 million cereal boxes in the initial months of the campaign.

In coming months a panel of experts on family issues will produce a range of helpful information for parents which will be promoted on-pack. With Kellogg's brands reaching 40 per cent of households nationally this will provide invaluable support to families and achieve an important educational aim for Kids Help Line.

Case study III: Visa USA and Read Me A Story

Background

Since 1996, Visa USA have run a Cause Related Marketing programme aimed at literacy in partnership with Reading is Fundamental (RIF). Visa had agreed with the findings that when price and quality are equal, linking with a cause can make the difference. Exploring that argument Visa carried out some cardholder research which identified that over 70 per cent of cardholders felt reading was important and that if Visa were to support such a cause it would make a difference to their card usage. Visa therefore sought to develop a strategy based on this.

Like the American Express programmes, this is a fourth quarter promotion taking place in October–December. Reading as an issue was known to be a key issue with 38 per cent of American children never having been read to and over 30 per cent of American families 'live without books'[1]. RIF was identified as the charity partner as they were not only one of the most credible charities according to a report at the time by *Parenting Magazine*, but they were also rated as one of the ten charities that really help kids, according to the *Chronicle of Philanthropy*, and with more than 219,000 volunteers and nationwide community based projects since 1996 the potential of the organization was formidable. Following the first year of the programme in 1996, Visa developed some of its aspects with the key objective being to increase visibility.

Mechanic

Basically each time the Visa card is used, a donation is made to Reading is Fundamental. This core mechanic was enhanced at selected merchant locations by Visa doubling the donation, and RIF could earn free books themselves by posting signage relating to the partnership at their various sites, thus not only benefiting themselves but increasing the venues where the Visa logo could be seen. The minimum guaranteed donation was $1 million, with additional funding if Visa's volume goal was achieved.

Clearly apart from the primary business objective of encouraging usage of the card, Visa was building relationships with its merchants whilst at the same time reinforcing the organization values and forming relationships with its customers and other stakeholders on a new and different level, tapping into an issue that is known to be important amongst just about everyone.

Support

The campaign has been supported by TV advertising, local radio, shopping mall media and has had a $20 million advertising budget with more than $4 million in co-operative merchant marketing, indicating the strength of these relationships, the merchants being the key route to market for Visa and any other credit card company. The campaign has further been supported by communications with card holders – more than 50 million flyers were distributed in cardholder statements – and has benefited from in-branch material, customer service information and community involvement kits not to mention a wide rage of member activities. These have included story reader events and appearances by some of the book characters to support the programme. There have also been mailings to 1 million small merchants, which included free promotional signage, mailings to encourage usage from dormant and less active card holders in partnership with Visa-issuing financial institutions. The merchant partners have included ACE Hardware, Applebee's Restaurants, Kmart, Target, Toys R Us, United Airlines, Waldenbooks, Winn-Dixie and many more, illustrating well the opportunity that Cause Related Marketing presents in building and cementing business-to-business relationships. These merchant partnerships in themselves developed unique ways to leverage the partnerships and promote the message ranging from additional advertising including inflight video and radio advertising, to signage, point-of-sale and support material. A theatrical performance was also created in support of the 'Read me a Story' campaign and was performed in the top 24 cities of America which naturally led to further local media tie-ins and relationships. Shopping malls were used as sites for reading events and there was co-operative advertising to build traffic to the centre, again cementing the business relationships and promoting the message of the cause of literacy. The conclusion is that the programme was pretty well leveraged.

Results for the cause

Clearly with this level of core and leveraged support, the issue of reading amongst young people was promoted by many organizations beyond Visa with whom the relationships had been created and the message was communicated amongst vast audiences. Visa was in fact not only the key partner and communicator of the issues, but a fundamental multiplier and facilitator, increasing the size of its impact through its partners and thereby providing RIF with incredible reach for its vital message.

Results for Visa

The programme had significant impact on the Visa brand image with an increase of 7 per cent and an all-time high of 62 per cent for Best Overall Card in Visa's on-going image tracking study. Visa's bankcard share of market was up to 66.3 per cent from 65.9 per cent in the same quarter of 1996. Indeed in November 1997, sales volume was up 16.9 per cent over 1996 and transaction volume was up 18.9 per cent. In 1997, 20 per cent consumer awareness of the promotion was achieved, an increase of over 82 per cent on 1996, and 64 per cent of those aware of the promotion perceived value from it. Importantly from a communications point of view the advertising was judged through the research as clearly communicating a balanced message of cause and usage. Seventy-three per cent of those exposed to the advertising understood that using the Visa card helps. Seven per cent of cardholders aware of the promotion indicated an increase in perceived card usage and 34 per cent of those exposed to the advertising reported an increased Visa card usage.

The benefits of this partnership for the business, the cause and the wider community speak for themselves.

> The Visa 'Read Me a Story' promotional programme was so very gratifying because it was good for Visa's business, good for our communities, and good for the hearts and souls of those who participated in the programme.
>
> **Bob Pifke, Senior Vice President, Marketing Services**

Case study IV: Target Stores' Cause Related Marketing strategy

Target Stores in the USA has over 850 stores. Arguably it has one of the most impressive records in charitable giving and community investment, its use of Cause Related Marketing currently in the USA having contributed over $1 million a week in the last decade through one campaign or another.

Bob Thacker, previously Senior Vice President of Marketing of Target Stores, explained at a presentation made in the UK in July 1998 that Target Stores had a strong history of charitable giving, 'but for 25 years those contributions were largely anonymous. The average consumer had no idea just how much of its profits Target Stores gave to the community. The competition on the other hand was giving far less and getting far more credit.'[2] This issue of awareness has been discussed earlier in this book. Bob Thacker is clear that Cause Related Marketing helped Target Stores change that perception.

The original strategy at Target Stores was to identify the particular charity and then identify logical vendor partners. This led for example to baby products being paired with the prevention of child abuse; crayons and stationery products with education; publishers with reading and literacy, etc. Bob Thacker states: 'What we found was that Cause Related Marketing increased sales of our vendor partners and gained them more publicity than they could have gotten alone.'[2]

Rod Eaton, Director Sales Promotion, Target Stores has very much seen Cause Related Marketing as a way to reinforce the core values, the Target Stores proposition and to further build the Target Stores brand. The Target Stores proposition as Rod Eaton described it is 'Expect more – pay less'. The business issue is how to bring that proposition to life and therefore Target Stores considers Cause Related Marketing within that context.

Rod Eaton is clear that what Target Stores are looking for in the development of their strategies including their Cause Related Marketing strategies is the opportunity to be unique and to make a unique difference. Whilst others may support a cause or issues that Target Stores are involved with, the conclusion that Target Stores want its stakeholders to reach is that 'no one does it, or can do it quite like Target'.

Having identified the cause or issues, the key questions for Rod and his team at Target Stores are: 'Who else is involved; what can Target Stores bring besides money; can it be cross promoted; in short can it be leveraged?'

To date Target Stores' Cause Related Marketing partnerships have included:

- St Jude Children's Research Hospital in Memphis Tennessee which began in 1995;
- Helping Hugs which brings Hershey Chocolate together with a charity to provide teddy bears to traumatized children;
- Target Support of the Washington Monument Restoration;
- Guest credit card supporting education: School Fundraising Made Simple[SM].

Target Stores and St Jude Children's Research Hospital

Background
This children's hospital in Memphis, Tennessee, has received world-wide recognition for its research in the treatment of children's cancer and other life-threatening illnesses. It treats all of its patients without charge and provides transportation and housing for the patient's family. Based on this background, Target Stores brought several health and pharmaceutical vendors together and created a Cause Related Marketing programme to help St Jude.

Objective
From a business point of view it was important to increase the awareness of pharmacies and health and beauty departments in store whilst at the same time as investing in this vital community resource.

Mechanic
The mechanic was straightforward. Target Stores and the pharmaceutical vendors promised a percentage of all sales in the health and beauty department to be contributed to St Jude. Target Stores at the same time also started a programme to build Target House, a special place for the families of children undergoing long-term treatment. The relationship was supported in-store with pamphlets and signage and supported by well known celebrities including Amy Grant, Marlo Thomas, Skaters Scott Hamilton and Ekaterina Gorderra who also contributed a percentage of the sales of tickets to her show to the cause. The Amy Grant Music room will be a central feature to the house.

Results

In less than three months over £3 million was raised for St Jude and they had a key celebrity raising awareness of their cause as well as the power and the spread of this major retail brand. The benefits to Target Stores were also significant. The objectives of reinforcing the brand values and awareness of the pharmacy, health and beauty areas were achieved, vendors' sales and awareness benefited and the support of Amy Grant was perfect and beneficial for everyone. And the consumers were the heroes as through purchasing products at Target Stores they were making the funding for the project possible.

Target Stores and Helping Hugs

Background

This is a programme designed to support traumatized children, by accident and emergency technicians simply providing them with a teddy bear – a gesture which though simple is known to relieve the stress in these terrifying situations. The request originally came from a local charity who asked Target Stores to donate some bears. Realizing there was no national initiative, Target Stores set about to create one and so Helping Hugs was born in partnership with Hershey chocolate and a Valentine's Day promotion was developed.

Mechanic

Again a simple mechanic was used with a donation being triggered by customer purchase of a Hershey product.

Support

As part of the Valentine's promotion, Helping Hugs is supported by in-store signing, Target Stores' weekly circular (which reaches 40 million households) and press releases. The signing is positioned in the candy department due to Hershey's partnership and at cash registers.

Results

Since the programme's creation, Target Stores has donated hundreds of thousands of teddy bears to paramedics who have given them to children in need of comfort. The benefits to the Target Stores brand, the reinforcement of Target Stores core values and the relationships developed with their customers, suppliers and the wider community are obvious. Hershey too would have significant benefits in these areas and also saw sales increase substantially every year.

> Because many of our guests are women with young children, Helping Hugs is a charitable program that they can easily relate to. The other advantages of Helping Hugs is that it's a national program that each of our stores can be part of at a local level; the store employees personally deliver the bears to emergency medical technicians.
>
> **Eric Erickson, Director, Creative Services, Target Stores**

Target Stores and The Washington Monument

Background

The Washington Monument is America's oldest and one of its most visible patriotic shrines. Over a century old, it is in need of extensive restoration of its marble exterior, as well as its interior observation levels and elevator. In partnership with the National Park Foundation and National Park Service, Target Stores helped to raise the $5 million needed to restore the monument. In addition, it has donated additional funds to restore the interior observation levels. Target Stores brought internationally known architect Michael Graves to the project to design the scaffolding that will surround the monument during restoration and to design the interior observation levels. The project will be completed by 4 July 2000.

Mechanic

Target Stores acted as a lead sponsor and sought out other companies to join it in raising funds for the restoration. It first turned to companies that do business with Target Stores, including VISA, Kodak, 3M, EMI-Capitol Music Group to name a few. Funds were raised both through purchase behaviour (VISA, Kodak) and also through straight donations from the Target Stores Community Relations department.

Support

Support for the Washington Monument Restoration Project has been broad and wide-ranging. Over the past three years, it has included: in-store signing; national advertising in *USA Today, Time* magazine and the *New York Times*; a TV commercial; sponsorship of the 4th of July fireworks in Washington, D.C.; a school-based curriculum developed by *Scholastic Magazine*; a contest to send teachers to Washington, D.C.; a website; an exclusive CD; and outdoor advertising in Minneapolis and Los Angeles.

Results

Target Stores successfully raised the funds needed to start and complete the restoration. Press recognition of Target Stores' sponsorship has been extensive and has helped to give Target Stores' giving programme national prominence and recognition. As a by-product of bringing Michael Graves to the monument project, Mr Graves was introduced to Target Stores and has recently completed designs for over 100 home products sold exclusively at Target Stores.

This marks the beginning of a tradition of partnership that is really going to take off ... [It's] a model of what advertising can be, because Target is talking up to the American people.

Bruce Babbitt, U.S. Secretary of the Interior, commenting on the national advertising that Target Stores ran in support of the restoration project

Target Take Charge of Education Program

Background

Guest Surveys have shown that education is an important topic to Target Stores' customers and an area in which they would like to see concentration of charitable dollars. At the same time as the decision was made to have an educational focus to community giving, Target Stores launched its own credit card, called Target Guest Card. Under the concept of 'School Fundraising Made Simple'SM Target's Guest Card holders can benefit schools across the USA.

Objectives

■ To differentiate the Target Stores credit card from other store cards and bank cards.
■ To bring together Target Stores' educational initiatives into an impactful, cohesive campaign.

Mechanics

Cardholders can designate any kindergarten through 12th grade school. When they use their Target Guest Card, 1 per cent of the amount of their purchase will be donated to the school they have chosen. In some cases an additional 3 per cent donation is also made by the participating vendor. School Fundraising Made SimpleSM is available to any public, private or parochial school, K-12, that has a 501(C)(3) or 509(A)(1) tax-exempt status. Target Stores tracks purchases charged to participating accounts and distributes the donations to designated schools each March and November.

Schools can allocate their School Fundraising Made SimpleSM dollars wherever they are needed most. Several schools have used their fundraising dollars to update computer software, purchase playground equipment or classroom materials.

Support

The programme has been supported through TV commercials, in-store signing, magazine ads in educational journals, press releases, newspaper advertising, appearances at trade shows, website, direct mail, special events.

The child actor featured in the TV commercial has become something of an icon of the programme and has even appeared on 'The Tonight Show with Jay Leno' as a result of the Target Stores commercial.

Vendor bonus buys on select merchandise allow guests to earn additional funds for the school designated. Bonus offers change monthly and apply to purchases made on the Target Guest Card.

Results

More than 86,000 K-12 schools across the USA are actively participating in School Fundraising Made Simple^{SM}. To date, over 2 million cardholders are enrolled in the programme. In 1998, of Target Stores' $9 million contribution to education, $3 million have come from the credit card programme.

> The Target Take Charge of Education program is an example of how Target continues to look for ways to differentiate its products and services – even in the highly competitive credit card business.
>
> **Eric Erickson, Director, Creative Services, Target Stores**

Case study V: Avon's Crusade Against Breast Cancer

Background

Avon was established in 1886 in New York and was one of the first companies to offer American women an opportunity to work in business, 34 years before they won the right to vote. Avon is the world's leading direct seller of beauty and related products, marketing to women in more than 135 countries through 2.8 million independent sales representatives, the internationally renowned 'Avon ladies'.

In the 1980s, Avon struggled for survival as an independent public company, fending off numerous take-over attempts. After emerging unchanged, the company renewed one of its founding principles, to give back to the citizens who support it. Avon clarified and strengthened its vision: 'To be the company that best understands and satisfies the product, service and self-fulfilment needs of women globally.'

In the United Kingdom in 1992, Avon conducted a comprehensive research study amongst its customers and representatives to better understand women's needs, interests, and motivations. The results showed clearly that breast cancer was the issue of leading concern to these women. This led Avon UK to create the Avon Crusade Against Breast Cancer later that same year, and led Avon in the United States to create Avon's Breast Cancer Awareness Crusade in 1993. The mission of both initiatives is to raise awareness of the breast cancer cause, and to help Avon sales representatives raise money for breast cancer organizations through the sale of special fundraising products.

The Cause Related Marketing model that was first created in Avon UK seven years ago has now been successfully exported to 26 other countries around the world where Avon has programmes that support women's health. Collectively, these 28 programmes are known as the Avon Worldwide Fund for Women's Health, and together they have raised and distributed over $50 million. Avon Products, Inc. has announced plans to raise and distribute another $50 million by the year 2000, bringing its expected total contribution to women's health to $100 million.

Initial Avon UK programme

A new charity called Breakthrough Breast Cancer was formed in the UK in 1992 and was identified as an appropriate partner for the Avon Crusade. At the time the charity was seeking a major corporate or private partner who could raise the first £1 million of a £15 million campaign.

In the beginning, Avon raised funds for Breakthrough Breast Cancer through the sale of £1 pin badges and £2 pens, using the Avon Crusade for Breast Cancer as the rallying headline in promotional literature. These items were sold through the 160,000 sales representatives in the UK and were advertised through the Avon catalogue, 3 million of which are printed with each run, 18 times a year. In the first year £1 million was raised and publicity coverage was extensive. Avon sales representatives were so engaged by the programme that a relationship was formed with a second beneficiary, Macmillan Cancer Relief, to fund three Breast Cancer Nurses who provided special care to women who had undergone surgery and other treatments for breast cancer. A market research study, conducted just six months after the launch of the Crusade, showed that one in ten UK consumers could cite the amount of money Avon had raised for the cause.

Expansion of Avon UK programme

Six years later Avon UK had raised £5.3 million for breast cancer. The programme was a philanthropic success, but public awareness of Avon's support for the cause had diminished and Avon's competitors were becoming involved with Cause Related Marketing and deriving much more commercial benefit from the programmes, such as positive changes in consumer perceptions, improving brand loyalty and gaining market share.

Avon UK decided to transform its strategy so that the Crusade would serve its business needs while continuing to raise funds for the cause. It marketed the Crusade in a new way that would focus attention on the company's contemporary image, and reach new customers. To meet these objectives, Avon UK became a sponsor of Fashion Targets Breast Cancer, an organization started by Fashion Designers in America, which raises funds for US breast cancer research programmes. By 1997, Fashion Targets Breast Cancer had expanded internationally and it was then that Avon UK became a sponsor, designating Breakthrough Breast Cancer as the beneficiary.

Sponsorship of Fashion Targets Breast Cancer

As part of its sponsorship of Fashion Targets Breast Cancer, Avon UK redesigned the fundraising pin and paid for T-shirts bearing the Avon name that were sold as fundraisers in high street fashion stores. It sponsored fashion shows that were held in ten shopping centres and other public venues across the UK. Avon makeovers were performed at these shows and free sample cards featuring a shower gel and instructions for how to perform a breast self-examination were distributed. It offered a *Freefone* telephone hotline for women to call for information about breast cancer, the Fashion Targets Breast Cancer campaign, and to order T-shirts. Avon promoted Fashion Targets Breast Cancer and celebrity model Yasmin Le Bon appeared on the front cover of the Avon catalogue which generated extensive media coverage and was received so positively that 125,000 extra catalogues had to be added to the usual print run of 3 million.

Results of Fashion Targets Breast Cancer sponsorship

Through this new approach, both the Avon brand and the breast cancer cause received a tremendous boost. As the President and General Manager of Avon UK Sandy Mountford said: 'With Fashion Targets Breast Cancer, we really got it right. We continued to raise money and awareness for this leading women's health issue, and we benefited our business in important ways. It's what an effective cause campaign should do.'

As a result of Avon UK's sponsorship of Fashion Targets Breast Cancer, it received an estimated £200,000 of complimentary advertising in print publications, and an estimated £300,000 of complimentary advertising through 1000 London Underground posters and 3000 bus shelter posters. Over 1196 calls were made to the telephone hotline and many callers expressed an interest in purchasing from Avon, who had never done so before. Avon was mentioned in three-quarters of all print and television publicity for Fashion Targets Breast Cancer, and experienced an increase in sales versus the same period in the previous year. The impact of the sponsorship was further quantified in a consumer research study, which showed a significant increase in consumer awareness of Avon as a major supporter of the breast cancer cause. Finally, a donation in excess of £400,000 was made to Avon's UK beneficiary, Breakthrough Breast Cancer.

Avon US programme mission

Avon's Breast Cancer Awareness Crusade in the United States is the largest programme of the Avon Worldwide Fund for Women's Health. It supports non-profit, community-based organizations across the country that provide women, particularly those who are medically under served, with information about breast cancer and with direct access to low-cost or free early detection screening services. By January 1999, the American aspect of the Crusade had raised over $32 million for more than 300 of these organizations through the sale of pink ribbon fund-raising products by Avon's independent sales representatives.

Avon US programme partnerships

Avon's Breast Cancer Awareness Crusade in the US has formed partnerships with the National Alliance of Breast Cancer Organizations (NABCO), the National Cancer Institute (NCI), and the Centers for Disease Control and Prevention (CDC) to deliver education and early detection services.

Avon's Crusade formed a partnership with NABCO in 1993 which has a network of 375 member organizations to administer The Avon Breast Health Access Fund, through which Crusade grants are awarded that support a variety of services ranging from health advisors to organizations that monitor women who have received screening mammograms.

The NCI is the US government's leading agency on cancer research, education, diagnosis, early detection and treatment. The partnership with Avon which began in 1993 includes the distribution of breast cancer educational materials and support of the NCI's Cancer Information Service (CIS) hotline which operates across the country in regional centres dedicated to providing cancer information.

Avon's partnership with The Centers for Disease Control and Prevention (CDC), an agency of the US Department of Health and Human Services, began in 1993. The Crusade supports community-based breast health programmes and co-sponsored a teleconference on community outreach in April 1996 to highlight key lessons learned from five breast health programmes funded by the Crusade.

Initial Avon US programme

Avon's Breast Cancer Awareness Crusade in the US introduced its first fundraising product from October to December 1993, the Avon Pink Ribbon Pin for $2.00. All pins were delivered with an educational flyer about breast cancer early detection and Avon's Crusade. Sales of the pins throughout these months generated $5.7 million in net proceeds. The Crusade has since introduced a new pink ribbon fundraising product each year, and has continued to offer the best-sellers, the pins and a pen (introduced in 1995).

During its first year Avon underwrote a television special, *The Breast Care Test*, that aired on most public broadcasting stations throughout the US on October 15 in 1993. The Crusade also cosponsored a commercial television programme, *The Other Epidemic*, a powerful one-hour special that aired on 14 September 1993. The show featured breast cancer facts every woman should know and the moving testimonials of survivors. *The Other Epidemic* also marked the first broadcast of Avon's 30-second commercial, which introduced Avon's Breast Cancer Awareness Crusade and urged women to obtain more information about breast cancer.

Avon US programme 1998 special events

In 1998 Avon in the US were involved in a number of special events. First, in October the Crusade sponsored an outdoor fundraising walk, *Avon's Breast Cancer 3-Day*. There were 2400 participants who each walked 60 miles over three days, along the coast of southern California and in total raised $5 million. The funds will be awarded to non-profit, community-based breast cancer early detection organizations throughout the US. Over 70 million people were reached through print, radio, and television publicity. Due to the success of the event, four more *3-Days* are planned for 1999.

Secondly, to promote breast cancer early detection throughout the Internet during October, National Breast Cancer Awareness Month, in 1997 and 1998, Avon's Crusade sponsored an on-line event, 'Wear the Pink Ribbon For Women on Your Web Page'. As a result, more than a dozen leading websites, and hundreds of others, have 'worn' Avon's pink ribbon prominently on their web pages, generating over 3.2 million impressions of the symbol on-line each October.

Thirdly in 1997–98, Avon's Crusade targeted a new population of supporters for breast cancer early detection: kids. In the 'Avon Kids Care' Essay Contest, America's young people were invited by Avon's sales representatives to submit an original essay about how they would encourage a favourite adult female to take good care of her health. The 16 winners each received a $1000 savings bond. On their behalf the Crusade awarded a $50,000 'Avon Kids Care' grant to 16 non-profit breast health organizations that were matched geographically to the contest winners. Winners, grant recipients, and the sponsoring Avon sales representatives were honoured at awards ceremonies held on National Avon Representative Day, 19 March 1998. Additionally, a contest winner was featured on one of the most popular television talk shows in the US, 'The Rosie O'Donnell Show' (seen by 5 million viewers each weekday), in October 1998.

Avon US programme results

In a recent national survey, The Cone Breast Cancer Awareness Trend Tracker, conducted to test American consumers' awareness of companies that support breast cancer, showed that Avon's Crusade was the number one programme identified by survey respondents without prompting.

The Avon Worldwide Fund for Women's Health

According to Joanne Mazurki, Director, Global Cause Related Marketing:

> The success of Avon's 28 international cause marketing programmes and the Avon Worldwide Fund for Women's Health is the direct result of leveraging our unique strengths as a company, the direct selling system, and the dedication of our sales representatives around the globe. No other company could have delivered the magnitude of support for women's health that Avon has because no other company has our particular resources. Because we have focused on what is unique about us, our key constituents – consumers, not-for-profit partners, the government, and the media – trust that our efforts have integrity and commitment. Other companies interested in cause marketing should leverage what is unique about their ways of doing business.

Case study VI: The Tanqueray AIDS Rides

Background

The Tanqueray brand owned by DIAGEO, is a brand of gin which is imported and marketed by Schieffelin & Somerset Co. in the USA, a unit of DIAGEO. The Tanqueray brand was looking for ways to develop a key niche market, to establish and create stronger more meaningful relationships with their target audience.

Rationale

The Tanqueray brand needed to use an innovative, targeted marketing campaign to establish the brand as a leader in causes of concern to the target market, thereby increasing its relevance to consumers. Having researched the target market, a number of issues were identified as having particular relevance. Coincidentally at the same time the producers of the AIDS Rides in the USA mailed 200 companies looking for sponsorship support for the first AIDS Ride in 1994. Only Tanqueray replied! The brand and cause objectives matched and together they developed a Cause Related Marketing partnership.

Concept

The concept was based on sponsorship of a high profile series of bicycle rides which would raise funds for AIDS charities in the USA and attract the support and participation of the Tanqueray brand's target market.

Objectives

The key objectives of the programme were to:

- increase sales of Tanqueray gin through an innovative targeted campaign;
- engage the target market through the support of a cause close to their hearts;
- recruit new 21–34 year old African-American and general market consumers by creating an emotional and powerful connection to the Tanqueray brand. For the 25–44 age group in the USA, AIDS is the number 2 killer which for this group is a bigger killer than cancer in the USA;
- create a new brand value for the Tanqueray brand, establishing it as a leader in causes of concern to all brand targets, thereby increasing its relevance to consumers;
- raise significant funds for AIDS charities in the USA;
- raise awareness of AIDS education and prevention.

Timing

Tanqueray began their support of the AIDS Rides in 1994 as the presenting sponsor of the first AIDS Ride, which was held in California, and they have supported the AIDS Rides annually ever since.

Mechanic

The AIDS Rides are fully supported long distance bicycle rides in ten cities in the USA. They are not races and the emphasis is on participation and the raising of funds for AIDS charities. The AIDS Rides started with one ride in California in 1994 and by 1997 there were five AIDS Rides across the USA.

The AIDS Rides are fully supported with the provision of accommodation, catering, medical and mechanical back-up for the thousands of cyclists and hundreds of volunteers involved.

Support

A number of activities take place around the AIDS Rides. These include:

- local distributor incentive programmes and various involvement opportunities;
- welcoming and encouraging trade representatives to either volunteer or register and ride;
- numerous AIDS Rides parties with sampling of Tanqueray;

- 'Team Tanqueray', a group of Tanqueray representatives who are sponsored and supported by Tanqueray;
- 600 AIDS Ride awareness nights in all Tanqueray markets.

As presenting sponsor Tanqueray's logo is featured on all AIDS Ride produced events, advertising and collateral materials. The following promotional support was provided for the AIDS Rides as a value-added part of Tanqueray's sponsorship:

- AIDS Ride web site;
- AIDS Ride retail window displays;
- AIDS Ride photo contest;
- AIDS Ride recruitment videos;
- AIDS Ride celebrity public service announcements;
- AIDS Ride community street pole banners;
- AIDS Ride celebrity committee;
- AIDS Ride welcome home pendants.

An aggressive Tanqueray advertising campaign supported the AIDS Rides. This advertising campaign used Tanqueray's advertising 'spokesperson', Mr Jenkins, as the AIDS Ride mascot. The Mr Jenkins AIDS Ride print and outdoor advertisements ran nationally covering all Tanqueray markets. Additionally the AIDS Rides placed 200 national and local print advertisements to recruit and support riders. After the rides, Tanqueray thanked 365,000 people directly who participated in the AIDS Rides as riders, crew, volunteers or donors.

Monitoring and evaluation

Both quantitative and qualitative research conducted by Tanqueray since 1994 amongst those participating in the rides and target audiences in ride markets have shown a number of extremely positive indicators including:

- a strong emotional bond between the brand and those that participate;
- significant growth in awareness of the brand's involvement over the years;
- significantly stronger propensity to purchase, consume, consume more frequently and recommend to others amongst consumers aware of Tanqueray's sponsorship (each of these factors has also increased steadily since 1994);
- strong majority of positive feelings towards the company for their sponsorship of the AIDS Rides.

Results

Tanqueray's American AIDS Rides are widely recognised as the most significant Cause Related Marketing AIDS fundraising programme in the USA.

The rides have enabled non-profit organizations in all ten cities to raise record breaking amounts of money for people living with AIDS and HIV as well as generating great awareness for AIDS education and prevention.

Since 1994, more than 30,000 cyclists, many thousands of crew members and volunteers and hundreds of thousands of donors have participated in the AIDS Rides. Since the first ride, Tanqueray's American AIDS Rides have raised over $100 million for more than 60 HIV/AIDS service organizations in the USA.

Annually the results have included:

- In 1994 California AIDS Ride 1, over 450 cyclists raised $1.5 million for AIDS related services in Los Angeles.
- In 1995, California AIDS Ride 2 raised $5.5 million.
- In 1995, Boston–New York AIDS Ride attracted 3800 cyclists from across the USA and five other countries raising $6.5 million.
- In 1996, California AIDS Ride 3 raised $8.5 million dollars and 2183 cyclists took part.
- In 1996, three additional AIDS Rides were held. In total Tanqueray's 1996 American AIDS Rides attracted over 10,000 participants and raised over $25 million dollars.
- In both 1997 and 1998, the five Tanqueray's American AIDS Rides raised over $30 million each year.
- As of March 1999, the AIDS Rides' 'lifetime total' has surpassed $100 million.
- There will again be five rides in 1999.

Massive public relations and high profile media coverage was achieved for a product in a sector which often experiences difficulty in advertising. More than 275 million media impressions were generated through print and electronic publicity on Tanqueray's American AIDS Rides in 1997 alone. From the front page of *USA Today* to CBS Evening News, media coverage of Tanqueray's American AIDS Rides was seen nationally as well as in each of the top 50 media markets.

Tanqueray's sponsorship of the 1995 AIDS Rides was honoured in 1996 by *Brandweek Magazine* and *Inside PR Magazine* as the gold medal winner for 'Cause Related Marketing' during their annual marketing and publicity awards. Tanqueray's recognition and involvement with the AIDS Rides was further enhanced with more than 600 AIDS Ride awareness nights in all Tanqueray markets. In addition to this, increased consumption of gin with a movement towards Tanqueray is reflected in increased sales of the Tanqueray brand.

Budget

Annually, Tanqueray provides approximately $900,000 in cash directly to the beneficiaries to offset the Ride expenses. This is supported by nearly $3 million in marketing support in the form of advertising, public relations, materials and events to generate additional awareness and help recruit more riders.

Lessons learned/future plans

Valuable lessons have been learned, including how a programme can expand successfully, how to leverage all appropriate elements of the marketing mix and the importance of allocating adequate resources to administer and support the programme.

> Although our greatest hope is that there will soon no longer be a need for the AIDS Rides, we are extremely proud of our sponsorship and honoured to have helped make possible the most successful AIDS fundraisers in history.
>
> **J. Penn Kavanagh, CEO and President, Schieffelin & Somerset Co.**

> The AIDS Rides have made a big difference in our organization. The Ride helps us to feed our clients and provide people living with AIDS proper nutrition, essential for sustaining life and health. There is no substitute for what we do at Food & Friends – and there is no way to do this without the AIDS Ride.
>
> **Craig Shniderman, Executive Director, Food & Friends**

Notes

1 US Department of Education (1996).
2 Bob Thacker speech; Institute of Fund Raising Managers UK annual conference July 1998.

Chapter 18

Lessons to learn

One day a company will go ahead with a Cause Related Marketing partnership so ill-conceived that it could be ruinous to the image of both the company and the charity. However it develops in the future, Cause Related Marketing must be done right.

Robert Gray, Freelance Journalist

As will have been understood from Part Two, Cause Related Marketing can build corporate and brand reputation, increase customer loyalty and build relationships and sales; it can provide differential and significant awareness and PR but things can go wrong.

Joint marketing ventures can be extremely lucrative, but they can also backfire if charities do not adequately assess the core values of their partners – not to mention their own.

Chronicle of Philanthropy, 30 October 1998

Benefiting from hindsight and the developments in the American market, the Business in the Community Cause Related Marketing campaign in the UK has been striving to build, maintain and protect the integrity of Cause Related Marketing in the UK, as an effective way of both building business and benefiting the wider community. As such Business in the Community is trying to set standards and put ground rules in place to try to avoid such issues.

A key part of this work and an intrinsic part of the campaign has been the development of the first ever Cause Related Marketing Guidelines. Based in a UK context, the principles of these guidelines are applicable worldwide. Indeed probably the only aspects which need local interpretation are those dealing with the formal agreement and the tax implications where clearly the rules, regulations, codes and laws of the particular country in question will prevail. The principles however are the same everywhere and therefore the Business in the Community Guidelines remain a highly relevant start point.

As Cause Related Marketing has been used in the USA for longer, what can happen if things go wrong is best illustrated with examples from the USA. For example recently the Sunbeam Corporation and the American Medical Association have been involved in a soured relationship which is estimated at costing $9.9 million, whilst The Arthritis Foundation and McNeil Consumer Products have suffered criticism due to their relationship. Relationships between business and education have also caused concern on both sides of the Atlantic and headlines in the *Financial Times* in the UK like '"Pester Power" gets bad marks' (27 October 1998) are becoming more frequent.

Sunbeam Corporation and the American Medical Association (AMA)

The recent union – and now ugly divorce proceedings – between the American Medical Association an the Sunbeam Corporation should serve as a cautionary tale for charities looking to forge income producing ties to business world.

The Chronicle of Philanthropy, 30 October 1997

This five-year exclusive relationship was launched in August 1997. Essentially the programme was planned to be a licensing or co-branding programme whereby the AMA name and logo would appear as an endorsement on a range of nine categories of Sunbeam Corporation Home Health products. In return the Sunbeam Corporation would include educational materials for the AMA with its products and give AMA a portion of the profits to pursue its work under the agreement which perhaps had the potential to raise millions; the AMA would not only gain from this enormous potential income but could also increase its awareness significantly. Clearly the Sunbeam Corporation stood to gain endorsement, benefit from the halo effect and implied approval from this well respected high profile and influential not-for-profit.

Within days of the announcement according to press reports, there was a public outcry from consumer activists, advocates, physicians and editorialists, members of the AMA and others, accusing the AMA of selling off its logo. According to reports, in less than two weeks of the original announcement the Executive Vice President of AMA, John Seward, MD, declared that:

The Sunbeam deal would not move forward without significant revision, including changes to the product packaging to avoid any suggestion of AMA endorsement and cancellation of the contracts royalty.

American Medical News, 17 August 1998

As *Philanthropy Journal* wrote (6 August 1998), 'After taking the heat for entering the deal without planning to test the products, the association decided to break the pact.'

By the first week in September, just three weeks after the launch announcement, the AMA board of trustees voted to withdraw completely from the Sunbeam Corporation deal. Within a few days, Sunbeam filed a $20 million lawsuit against the AMA, charging breech of contract, but this was later revised to seek unspecified damages.

In the aftermath of the events, an internal review was held by the AMA. A Task Force was set up on the Association's Corporate Relations, to set standards for future business arrangements. A set of principles has been developed and three top AMA executives resigned including the Chief Operating Officer. In July 1998, just under a year since the partnership was launched, the AMA announced that it would pay the Sunbeam Corporation $9.9 million from its reserves to settle the lawsuit.

In summary, a charity and business formed a Cause Related Marketing relationship, which within days of the public announcement, was revoked by the charity and led to accusations of breach of contract by the business which threatened to take the charity to court. The charity also dented its reputation significantly, alienated various stakeholder groups and cost itself $9.9 million of hard earned 'charity' money.

There are so many lessons to be drawn from this example that it is difficult to know where to start. Thanks to this incredible story, many others will be forearmed and therefore forewarned, benefiting from AMA's experience.

In terms of the lessons to be taken out of this case study, I have used the Business in the Community Cause Related Marketing Guidelines, 'Towards Excellence', as the structure against which I have drawn out the lessons.

The key principles of Cause Related Marketing are integrity, transparency, sincerity, mutual respect, partnership and mutual benefit. I am sure one can speculate for ever which or how many, if any, of these principles were transgressed. Those best able to answer the question will be those involved in the negotiations and discussions. One of course cannot legislate for inexperience, or lack of understanding or worse, but from an organization's point of view it is essential that those involved with any negotiations which could affect the reputation as well as the funding of an organization, be it business or not-for-profit, have able people representing them, who, if they are lacking in experience or knowledge, are able to ask and seek it out.

Planning and preparation

This is a prerequisite for any activity and that includes Cause Related Marketing. The old adage what you put in is what you get out is perfect for this. In terms of the planning and preparation, one has to question whether there was a clear understanding of the vision, values and objectives of the partner organization and the nature, implications and ramifications of the proposed deal.

As the *Chronicle of Philanthropy* reported in October 1997: 'A close examination of Sunbeam's policies . . . should immediately have raised a red flag for the association.' The article went on to question the company's employee strategies and their philanthropy programme.

The point is that those involved in the planning and preparation of a programme need to look at the values and performance of an organization. The role of desk research is to uncover and identify any issues, both positive and negative. Perhaps in this case the research for the AMA should have seriously questioned the potential of the relationship.

It would seem from the reporting that each side was clear what they wanted out of the relationship and were happy with the balance. Clearly AMA had not fully thought through or appreciated the implications of the deal. Charities should in every case question whether a relationship will have a positive or detrimental effect on its brand and reputation, which is, after all, sacred. The risk analysis and the media test[1] are as essential for the charity to conduct as the business. If a decision is made to endorse a product, programme or company it is essential to test the validity of it before putting the organization's name and therefore reputation on the line for it.

The *American Medical News* (5 January 1998) news report stated: 'When AMA signed a contract last August with the Sunbeam Corporation, the stated intention was hard to fault: Improve public health by providing health-related information with consumer products. The less-often-stated intention – to increase nondues revenue – also has merit, given the risks of ailing dues.' The report goes on: 'In exchange for royalties, the contract gave Sunbeam the stunningly inappropriate exclusive rights to use the AMA's logo on packaging.'

Mutual benefit, another key principle of Cause Related Marketing, is clearly for the potential partners to discuss and agree. One cannot legislate for all instances as all Cause Related Marketing partnerships and circumstances are unique. No one will know better than those involved, what the particular circumstances are, but as stated in the *American Medical News* report, in this case the balance of this relationship seemed 'stunningly inappropriate'.

It is imperative that those involved in negotiations understand the vision, values, and the objectives of the relationship from all parties' points of view, understand what is and is not negotiable and have the authority to negotiate on the organizations' behalf.

From the point of view of gaining senior internal commitment from within the organization as well as from the various stakeholder groups, in this case this appeared to fail abysmally judging from the reported train of events. Ann Marie Dunlap, MD of Illinois, endorsing her state's resolution calling for the ban on AMA product endorsement, argued that,[2] 'The beloved seal of the serpent on the staff was not sold – it belongs to the House of Delegates, and the House of Delegates did not sell it. The Board of trustees and senior staff acted without authority.'

In a further report by *American Medical News* (29 June 1998) it was reported, 'The report places most of the blame for the Sunbeam incident on AMA staff who "either ignored or failed to recognise that the Sunbeam contract . . . was clearly and directly contrary to AMA policy".'

Engaging the commitment of senior members of the organization as well as key stakeholder groups is a key factor in developing effective Cause Related Marketing partnerships; they will, after all, be key ambassadors for the programme, or not. With so much potentially at stake, their agreement, approval and endorsement is essential. Not only will it smooth the path of progress for the partnership and save time, but it will force key questions and issues to be asked, answered and resolved from the outset, rather than later under the intense spotlight of the media and public.

Negotiating the partnership

As has already been mentioned, it is vital that those doing the negotiating have done the planning and preparation and have the skills and authority to negotiate. Objectives have to be aligned and in deciding the value of the opportunity, it is important to take everything into account. In defining the nature of the activity not only should the creativity of the idea, the mechanics, the range of products be considered, but it is also fundamental to look at the balance of benefits and assess the risks.

It is crucial that a full risk assessment is carried out by each party individually prior to entering the partnership. Risk can include risk to reputation, logistical risks in terms of actually being able to deliver the agreement and financial risks. The AMA relationship with the Sunbeam corporation certainly failed completely in terms of appreciating the reputation and financial risks and never got as far as testing the logistical issues.

The formal agreement

Formal agreements are essential; indeed in the UK The Charities Act 1992 makes it clear that a written agreement in a prescribed form is required between the charity institution and the commercial participator. The purpose is to set down in writing the nature of the agreement. If a relationship is successful and going well there should be no reason to refer to the contract. When things go wrong however, the formal agreement comes into its own. Clearly in this case there was a formal agreement which, when breached, led to significant penalties.

Understanding roles, responsibilities and liabilities is a fundamental aspect of any contractual relationship. In the UK there are a number of basic documents to be aware of which include The Charities Act 1992 and 1993, The Charitable Institutions (Fund-Raising) Regulations 1994, The British Codes of Advertising and Sales Promotion, the Trades Description Act 1968 and the Control of Misleading Advertisements Regulations 1988. Other countries will have a similar series of codes, regulations and laws and it is up to the participants to be aware of their roles and responsibilities.

An organization's name is precious. It is the means by which an organization is known and by which its reputation is judged.

In the networked world you cannot and cannot expect to control your company's image; the best you can do is influence it.[3]

E. Dyson, 1997

Directors and trustees alike must therefore be careful how they allow the name to be used. Before they enter such a contract they must ensure that the relationship is appropriate and will not damage the organization or its good name; in the case of a charity that the money could not be raised by a more efficient means; the name will not be exploited, that there is a clear contract and that they have the right to prevent future use of the name if they are not satisfied that the original conditions are not being flouted. In this case, according to a report in *Philanthropy Journal* (August 6 1998), it appears that the charity had not tested the product it was intending to endorse. One has to question how this state of affairs could possibly have arisen.

Cause Related Marketing is just like any other contractual relationship which should not be entered lightly. If one side breaks the contract there are penalties to be paid. It is amazing that this particular relationship ever reached this stage. Had the desk research, planning and preparation been carried out thoroughly, if the risk analysis had been carried out, if the 'media test'[4] had been conducted then one wonders whether this disaster could have been averted.

McNeil Consumer Products Company and the Arthritis Foundation

The AMA and Sunbeam Corporation Cause Related Marketing relationship never really got off the ground. It sank before it left the dock and some of the reasons for these problems have been outlined. In another example of a relationship that suffered problems and finally was withdrawn, the reasons for the problems weren't quite so obvious from the outset.

In this case the relationship was between four over-the-counter arthritic pain relief products produced by McNeil Consumer Products Company and the

Arthritis Foundation. The consumer proposition was essentially that on purchase of the product, which was heavily branded with the charity's name, the purchaser would receive a discount. Money would be donated to the charity, and the consumer would receive free membership of the charity for a year. Retailers selling the brand were involved in a range of activities promoting the product thus the programme also leveraged through the distribution chain.

In this example, the charity not only apparently gained from the donation against sale, but also apparently gained through high profile awareness of the cause and presence of the product. The advertising together with other forms of communication support provided significant awareness and financial contribution. The retailer benefited from a range of exciting promotional activity. The consumer gained through money off and a value added offer of free membership to the charity. The business benefited through product differentiation, awareness and PR, association and increased sales.

In classic Cause Related Marketing terms, this relationship seemed to provide a win for the business, a win for the charity, a win for the retailer and a win for the consumer. With such a matrix of benefits across all partners, the question is what went wrong?

In the previous example the key principles[4] of integrity, transparency, sincerity, mutual respect partnership and mutual benefit have been referred to. And in this case it would seem, and both partners have argued, that they felt the relationship was very appropriate. The charity after all is about advice on relieving arthritic pain and the products were designed to do the very same.

The charity and the business were both criticized for the association for a number of reasons. It was argued by some that the charity, by tying themselves so closely to a particular form of arthritic pain relief, had compromised their ability to provide objective advice on all forms of pain relief. The question was raised how the charity could advise impartially about the strengths and weaknesses of another pain relief product or indeed an alternative medical approach if it was so tightly bound up with a particular manufacturer. The charity was accused by some, of selling its soul, an accusation that the charity vociferously denied. The charity and the business partner argued strongly that this was a legitimate relationship as it meets both their objectives. The question is, who is to judge?

Points made in the State's case against McNeil Consumer Products Company and Arthritis Foundation Inc.

- The advertisements for the 'Arthritis Foundation Pain Relievers', as they were known, represented directly or by implication that the products rather than the brand were new.

- The advertisements represented the charity as having 'helped to create' the products, when in fact this was not the case. The product had already been available and approved by the United States Food and Drug Administration for some time.
- The advertisements apparently suggested the products were effective because they had been created, produced or endorsed by the Arthritis Foundation. In fact they were no more effective than other over-the-counter products containing the same ingredients.
- The advertisements represented directly or by implication that with each purchase consumers will be supporting the charity or contributing to finding a cure for arthritis. Actually the charity would have received a guaranteed $1 million payment annually under a trademark licensing agreement anyway.
- The advertisements suggested the products were 'doctor recommended' when in fact it was specific ingredients that were recommended rather than the products themselves.

Source: State of Minnesota, County of Ramsey District Court, Court File, October 16 1996

From a process point of view in relation to planning and negotiating the partnership there appeared to be some oversights. Senior internal agreement of what is available for negotiation, its value, and endorsement of the programme, is vital. Perhaps however in this case whilst the internal commitment of both organizations strongly supported the relationship and showed themselves to be a strong partnership, with both parties arguing together the strengths of the partnership, the mutual respect and mutual benefit, a key group of stakeholders were not engaged, namely the beneficiaries of the charity in some cases, as well as the media and some parts of the general public.

A good rule of thumb when testing out the strength of an idea is to explain it to a young child or elderly person, basically someone who has nothing to do with any of the parties involved. If it takes more than a couple of minutes to explain and you find yourself justifying yourself with the verbal equivalent of small print, then there is something fundamentally wrong with the proposal.

If what is planned has the potential to be contentious, then the answer is to test the proposal with key stakeholder groups. This provides the opportunity to either tweak the proposal in terms of its balance or the communications or whatever, reject it altogether or indeed proceed but forearmed with the knowledge of what concerns constituent groups. This therefore provides the parties involved with the chance to address these issues in briefings, so that the Cause Related Marketing partnership is not forced into a defensive position from the start.

Communication – the way you communicate, the balance of the message and the transparency of the communication – is crucial for effective Cause Related Marketing. This is discussed in more detail in Chapter 25. In this particular case there were some issues to do with the way this relationship and the promotional message was communicated on-pack and in advertising. Firstly the packaging is emblazoned with the Arthritis Foundation name and with the words new, suggesting perhaps that the product itself is new. Some might even think that perhaps the Arthritis Foundation had something to do with the development of the product. This was in fact not the case.

In addition to these issues it was felt by some that the packaging was misleading. The packaging reads 'Each year, more than $1,000,000 from sales of this product will go to research to help find a cure for arthritis.' This seems to imply strongly that by buying the product a donation would be made to the Arthritis Foundation. There was not however a direct relationship between purchase and donation. Whether or not the product was purchased, a donation would be made, under a trademark licensing agreement anyway, to the Arthritis Foundation to the tune of $1 million, through this relationship. The act of purchase was not the trigger.

These concerns led to the media and public rejection of the partnership in some quarters and led to the withdrawal of the programme despite both sides in the partnership arguing that the programme was and is legitimate and appropriate. It also led to some 18 American states threatening to sue the company.

A settlement was reached with the courts, with Attorney General Hubert H. Humphrey III stating that 'ads for drugs carrying the Arthritis Foundation logo misled consumers into believing that the drugs were new medications created by the Foundation and that buying the products would provide additional funds to help find a cure for arthritis. The settlement filed today requires the company in any future ads to tell the whole truth about its product, provide refunds upon requests and pay almost $2 million for consumer education, arthritis research and fees.'[5]

Another key lesson to be drawn from this example is the importance of understanding and checking out the risk of a relationship. This can encompass reputation risk, logistical risk and financial risk and each element needs to be considered. Some organizations have a very sophisticated way of approaching such an analysis, but even a basic but thorough piece of risk analysis through desk research and research amongst stakeholder groups will serve to identify potential challenges, issues or problems and therefore give the opportunity for taking a preventative approach rather than dealing with the urgent and intense scrutiny under the public and media spotlight.

If, through analysing the risk, a potentially contentious issue is identified, it is important to clarify the position of the stakeholders. Indeed identifying the potential areas of contention internally with the partner organizations, and externally with stakeholders, and being clear on their position, is an essential aspect of the initial risk analysis process. Should there be a delicate area, and assuming there is endorsement and agreement to pursue the opportunity, then a strategy can be developed for engaging the groups who could potentially reject the partnership. At the same time investment can be made in planning and preparing a question and answer paper for these groups. Indeed identifying areas of concern can provide the very means to engage particular groups in active and constructive dialogue. The greater the dialogue and the more inclusive you can be, the better. After all, if you can persuade the problem to become part of the solution, then everyone wins.

Other programmes have come under fire from the legal authorities, the media and/or the public with products ranging from smoking cessation products and cancer charities to manufacturers and high street retailers across a wide range of sectors with education, children and schools. Criticisms have ranged from misleading advertising to inappropriate associations and poorly balanced benefits in the eyes of a particular stakeholder group.

In the UK for instance, as well as the USA, there has been a particular focus on the appropriateness of some of the business links with schools and children, with the debate focusing on what constitutes an appropriate relationship between businesses, schools and students.

In an attempt to address some of the issues before the problem escalated, the National Consumer Council with the involvement of Business in the Community, a number of educationists and businesses, developed the Business Sponsorship in Schools Guidelines which provide some useful guidance. Taken together with the Business in the Community Cause Related Marketing Guidelines, business and charities do have some useful information at their disposal to help guide them towards appropriate relationships. These guidelines and other information should help guide organizations away from situations where, for instance, teachers are forced to allow commercials to be shown in classrooms for so many minutes a day as part of the contract agreed for the loan or free provision of television and IT equipment, as happens in some parts of the USA.

There are clearly potentially contentious areas and pitfalls to watch out for in relation to all sorts of causes and issues. Programmes, relationships and partnerships have therefore to be developed professionally, methodically, thoroughly and appropriately, based on the key elements and principles of the Business in the Community Cause Related Marketing Guidelines already discussed.

As is argued throughout the Game Plan[6], consumers are at best indifferent and at worst cynical, sceptical and distrustful of business. If a Cause Related Marketing programme starts its life on the defensive it is doomed to a rough ride and potential failure. It is such a waste of effort to get into that negative spiral in the first place, particularly when through a simple, dispassionate but thorough process one can identify potential challenges and issues and address them upfront. Having identified them, one can decide what action to take, how to balance the nature of the offer or the message or the communication, for instance, and therefore deal with these challenges before they become problems.

There is no doubt that, when done well, the consumer wholeheartedly supports Cause Related Marketing. Consumers and other stakeholders are increasingly sophisticated and marketing aware. They have information at their fingertips and are prepared to act. We underestimate their concern, intelligence, perceptions and sense of justice at our peril. The challenge is therefore to engage all stakeholders positively in your plans, to ensure you respect them, their intelligence and their sense of balance, appropriateness and justice and to enable them to respect you and your intentions.

> If you manage to get the communication of a product and charity together to really move the psyche of the nation or the psyche of a specific group you can do anything, you can get them to give their world goods.[6]

Consumer quote from The Game Plan, 1997

Programmes that generate negative publicity because they appear to one or several stakeholder groups to be wanting do untold damage, not just to themselves corporately, and their brands, products or services and the organization's reputation, but also potentially curtail one of the few forms of relationship that bring together the business and the not-for-profit sectors for their mutual benefit and the benefit of the wider community.

There only needs to be a couple of mismanaged programmes to precipitate negative stakeholder reaction and perceptions leading to rejection and media backlash for all the partners involved. For Cause Related Marketing generally such a negative experience could set it back years. Not only does the misuse or abuse of Cause Related Marketing mean cutting off a potentially valuable resource and income stream for the wider community, but, looking at it selfishly from the organization point of view, it can have an incredibly negative impact on the reputation and values of the organization, on the trust that the various stakeholder groups have of it, and therefore affect the organization's business and ultimately the bottom line.

> A good company programme is good for our reputation and a good reputation is good for business.

Sir Iain Vallance, Chairman, BT

The failed American Medical Association and the Sunbeam Corporation Cause Related Marketing relationship and the Arthritis Foundation relationship with McNeil Consumer Products are not the only or the first Cause Related Marketing disasters, nor sadly will they be the last. Learning from others' experience and with guidance in the form of the Business in the Community

Cause Related Marketing Guidelines and other useful documents and experience it is hoped that fewer disasters will take place and that business, charities and causes will all benefit from the potential that Cause Related Marketing has for the good of the wider community.

Notes

1 Refer to 'The media test' in Chapter 25 and The Cause Related Marketing Guidelines – Towards Excellence (1998), Business in the Community.
2 American Medical News (29 June 1998).
3 Dyson, E. (1997) 'Looking Ahead: Implications of the Present' from Nelson, J. (1998) 'Building competitiveness and communities – How world class companies are creating shareholder value and societal value', The Prince of Wales Business Leaders Forum.
4 The Cause Related Marketing Guidelines - Towards Excellence (1998), Business in the Community
5 State of Minnesota, Office of the Attorney General Press Release, October 16 1996
6 The Game Plan (1997), Business in the Community qualitative consumer research into Cause Related Marketing conducted by Research International (UK) Ltd

Part Four

Towards Excellence – The Principles and the Processes

Chapter 19

A case study scenario

Cause Related Marketing remains a delicate flower, requiring unusual sensitivity of handling from client and good cause alike. Our common benefactor, the consumer, must be treated with complete integrity.

John Hooper CBE, Director General, Incorporated Society of British Advertisers (ISBA)

Cause Related Marketing is entirely based on integrity, ethics, openness, honesty, transparency, sincerity, mutual respect, partnership and mutual benefit. When planned, implemented and communicated well, Cause Related Marketing can provide huge rewards for both the business, the cause, the charity and the wider community. When done poorly it puts the business, the cause, the charity and ultimately the wider community at significant risk. As illustrated with the fictitious case study below, if Cause Related Marketing is planned, implemented or communicated poorly, there is a very real risk of ruining the potential opportunity that Cause Related Marketing has to address some of the social issues of the day through constructive, creative and mutually beneficial partnerships. Partners who enter Cause Related Marketing relationships therefore should do so in the knowledge of the enormous potential rewards and be mindful of the risks.

Cause Related Marketing can indeed pose some threat to the organizations involved. The fictitious case study that follows illustrates what the negative effects can be if a Cause Related Marketing campaign falls foul of the consumer, media or indeed the partner.

Aside from these clear threats, Cause Related Marketing can present other challenges if quality time is not invested in the planning, preparation, implementation and communication of a partnership.

Imagine a scenario where an organization decides that having read the arguments for and against Cause Related Marketing and knowing that they never seem to get any particularly good press they decide to create a Cause

Related Marketing partnership. For example, being a manufacturer who makes a product using a lot of natural resources as part of the process including water and wood, the organization decides to try and do something that will invest in the environment. One of the individuals involved in the discussion suggests a partnership with an environmental charity which operates globally through alliances throughout the world.

A potential partner is selected and during the next few months the business meets with the potential partner and develops a programme. This programme it is decided will be supported by TV advertising, will be communicated on the pack, will be part of the sales teams presentation, will be supported by a roadshow that will travel around the country and stop particularly in those areas where the company has plants, administrative offices and key customers. An education pack will also be available to schools and a page on the company's Internet site will promote the relationship. The CEO of both the business and the charity are going to the launch of the Cause Related Marketing partnership which will be held at a major national landmark.

The launch is a fantastic success with key media present. The story is taken up by the news agencies and is syndicated around the world. A few weeks into the programme, the results of an independent investigation into the organization's environmental performance are announced. The company has been accused of abuse and destruction of parts of virgin rainforest in South America and has caused the destruction of a local village and the relocation of a native tribe. Due to the pollutants in the environment caused by the manufacturing process, local families are suffering from serious skin irritations and respiratory problems.

One of the charity's affiliated members based in the country has been part of the investigative team and as part of the plans surrounding the launch of the investigation's findings, calls a meeting with representatives from the various environmental groups in the area. A plan of action is agreed to make an example of the company and bring them into line. The PR campaign for the launch of the investigation's findings uses all forms of media and other connections available including the resources and support of other affiliates around the world.

A press conference is held by the environmental group leading the investigation. Film evidence is shown of the devastation to the tribal village and its surroundings, the new village the people have been moved to and the standard of accommodation that they now live in. The evidence of the pollution is clear on the film and individuals are shown in makeshift hospital beds gasping for breath and covered in sores.

The final message of the press release is:

This company is destroying our environment, polluting the air we breathe, forcefully moving our peoples. At the same time they are investing in development of meadowlands in rural England. What a despicable con!

Visit our website – see the destruction for yourselves; register your protest; boycott their products. Act now.

Headlines in international papers around the world carry this message in their leaders the next day and within 24 hours hundreds and thousands of people have visited the website and registered their protest.

This fictitious scenario highlights two main points. First that the world is indeed becoming a global village. Pressure groups have the power and the organization, consumers have the sophistication, the will and the means to register their protest. An organization therefore has to be consistent and manage its actions and performance in every market in which it does business. An action in the Arctic will be known about in Zimbabwe within hours, even minutes.

Second, it highlights how essential it is to adhere to the key principles of Cause Related Marketing. This following section explores these key principles and elements that should be considered when striving towards excellence in Cause Related Marketing.

As Chris Marseden wrote[1]:

In this age of instant global communication, a multinational company's reputation precedes it as well as follows it – wherever it chooses to go.

Note

1 Global Corporate Citizenship – Rationale and Strategies, by David Logan, Delwin Roy and Laurie Regelbrugge for The Hittachi Foundation.

Chapter 20

The key principles and processes

Whilst Cause Related Marketing can be seen to have great strengths, it is not the panacea for all ills. It cannot compensate for fundamental corporate, product or service deficiencies. Those who see Cause Related Marketing as an opportunity to 'buy' or benefit from the halo of legitimacy or credibility when the business basics are profoundly wanton, should look again. Cause Related Marketing is not a fig leaf – rather it is a strategy that can support and enhance existing good business. It needs foundations, it does not of itself provide them. For effective Cause Related Marketing therefore it is essential to have the business basics right. The potential partnership must be based on the key principles and a logical thorough process needs to be followed. Then it is a question of vision, synergy, imagination, creativity, passion, energy, planning, implementation, management and commitment.

The key principles

Integrity, honesty, transparency, sincerity, mutual respect, partnership and mutual benefit are the founding principles on which effective Cause Related Marketing is based. Regardless of the initiative for the potential partnership, or the perspective – whether it is that of the business, the cause or charity partner and/or the agency – these key principles apply.

The key principles are just that. Before the relationship, partnership or programme goes any further it is essential that all involved consider whether or not the proposed partnership is based on integrity, transparency, sincerity, mutual respect, partnership and mutual benefit. If not, adjust it, change it or stop it!

In July 1998 Business in the Community published the first ever Cause Related Marketing Guidelines. The purpose of these guidelines is to help organizations develop excellence in effective, quality Cause Related Marketing programmes. The Cause Related Marketing Guidelines are designed to be a practical tool that assists existing or new entrants to develop sound partnerships.

In order to reach the point where the Cause Related Marketing Guidelines could be produced, more than 30 charities, more than 20 agencies and more than 15 businesses, all of whom have practical experience in Cause Related Marketing, were consulted through the Game Plan research[1].

These Cause Related Marketing Guidelines are not definitive and do not represent the end but the beginning of the process. It is the first time in the world that such guidelines have been attempted in this complex area and these guidelines have been distributed in the UK, throughout Europe, the USA and Australasia. Business in the Community fully anticipate developing these Cause Related Marketing Guidelines over time and positively ask everyone to give feedback and suggest additions to these guidelines so that they may be developed.

In practical terms these principles impact right from the very start of the process in considering Cause Related Marketing as a potential tool. From the outset it is essential to be honest with oneself and one's organization about why Cause Related Marketing is being considered how it fits with the overall strategy and mix of activity, and what one hopes to achieve. It is vital to be transparent about this personally, internally, and, when the time comes, with the potential partner and indeed all the other stakeholders. Stakeholders can range from opinion formers and consumers to the media. Integrity, honesty, transparency, sincerity, mutual respect, partnership and mutual benefit are the foundations of the whole relationship; Cause Related Marketing is not about exploiting an opportunity. Cause Related Marketing is about sincerity, long term sustainable relationships and making a real impact for both good causes and the social issues of the day as well as for the business.

These principles are the core to effective Cause Related Marketing. These essential principles should be kept at the front of the mind when negotiating partnerships. If they are, there is every likelihood that the partnership will be strong, of quality, will effectively address real issues and be to the benefit and satisfaction of all involved. In other words, keep these concepts at the heart of the relationship and it is likely an excellent Cause Related Marketing partnership will result.

Having established the key principles and the core of the motivation, a thorough process should be followed in order to ensure that the potential partnership is well planned, implemented, executed, evaluated and developed. Through the Business in the Community Cause Related Marketing Guidelines we identified six key elements in the process:

- **Planning and preparation:** this covers the process of finding a partner, defining the scope and duration of the partnership and gaining commitment.
- **Negotiating the partnership:** this includes aligning objectives, auditing assets, defining the nature of the activity, valuing the opportunity and assessing risks.
- **The formal agreement:** this covers some of the legal requirements and codes, and the responsibilities and liabilities.
- **Managing the programme:** this highlights the project management aspects.
- **Communicating the programme:** this covers the delicate balance that is required and the importance of the 'media test' (see Chapter 25).
- **Monitoring, measuring and evaluating the programme:** this suggests ways in which this can be addressed.

Note

1 The Game Plan research is the third piece of research conducted on a pro bono basis by Research International (UK) Ltd into the issues around Cause Related Marketing.

Chapter 21

Planning and preparation

The old maxim that failing to plan is planning to fail is as true of Cause Related Marketing as it is of any other discipline. Investment made here is invaluable. Unless the prospecting organization is clear in its objectives for the relationship; understands fully the mission, vision and values of the partner organization and therefore what is an appropriate requirement of this affinity and has senior internal commitment, the process will at best be tortuous and at worst be a waste of time or result in a poorly conceived programme which will fail to deliver the mutual benefits sought.

Principle objective

It is essential to clearly define the reasons and principle objectives for a potential Cause Related Marketing partnership. These may range from reinforcing values and reputation, be they those of the charity, cause, corporate or brand; developing relationships and loyalty amongst new or existing stakeholder and target groups; adding value and differentiation; to generating awareness, profile, trial sales and/or income for the cause, charity or business. These objectives are clearly relevant and applicable to charities, causes and businesses. Whatever the driving objective, or combination of objectives, these must be clear to the individual involved in the negotiations and to the organization on whose behalf they are negotiating. To be clear about the objectives simply makes good sense. It enables all involved to clearly understand what the aims of each party are and therefore in deciding whether to go ahead with the potential partnership, in developing and communicating it both internally and externally with all stakeholders, in setting the success criteria and in monitoring and evaluating the results of the partnership, the process will have much greater integrity, transparency, openness and honesty. By being clear and focused from the outset it is also less likely that unpleasant surprises will come to light during the course of the relationship and it will enable each party to understand whether the objectives have been met and indeed whether the relationship is worth continuing.

To shy away from the fact that all parties have clear objectives that they wish to achieve through the Cause Related Marketing partnership can simply cause muddled thinking and confused communication, both between the parties as well as with stakeholders internally and externally. It can lead to a consumer and media backlash, indeed rejection from all stakeholders. Investment in defining, refining, understanding and motivation is essential in order to provide clear guidance in the search for the potential partner/s and indeed provide a clear, open, honest and transparent base on which to progress and negotiate the potential partnership.

Integration into the business strategy

For Cause Related Marketing to be most effective it is important to ensure it is built into the overall business strategy and can be seen to be adding value not only to the marketing and corporate reputation strategies but also to the community investment and human resource strategies amongst others. This has many benefits not just from the profile and awareness perspective but from the resource and leverage point of view too.

Values match

Before you decide on a partner, make sure that you fully understand the other organization's objectives and values in broad terms and that they fully understand yours. Organizations whose values have no synergy are unlikely to be able to develop an effective partnership. It should not be taken for granted that an individual necessarily understands their organization's vision, mission and values. Nor should it be assumed that internal perceptions match external perceptions. It is important that time is taken to present the values and culture of each organization to each other, so that it is possible to identify and appreciate in what ways the organizations might match.

Sometimes, an apparent close synergy is in fact counter-productive. For example, a relationship between a particular medical product and a health charity that deals with all forms of treatment for a particular problem may arouse consumer concern. Questions may be asked about the ability of the charity to give objective advice if it is too tightly bound to one particular form of treatment or one particular organization. Concerns may also be raised about the balance of benefit to the cause and indeed the direct vested interest of the business and perhaps even anti-competitive behaviour.

The vital factors are therefore that having understood one's own organization that there is a values match with the potential partner. Without a match in principle, it is extremely unlikely that an effective sincere partnership can be developed as the values and belief systems which drive organizations should not be compromised.

Clear and appropriate affinity

Having established the objectives of the partnership and having identified that the values and belief systems of the two organizations match, it is essential that there is a clear affinity between the business and the cause generally, and/or between the project, product or service specifically. Clear affinity is not the same as an obvious affinity. Some obvious affinities are in some cases too close for comfort in other stakeholder minds. For example, a match between a charity that focuses on a particular medical issue which partners a company providing a specific form of pain relief may seem obvious, but may not be appropriate. There is a great deal of evidence showing that, for instance, the consumers and the beneficiaries of the charity may reject the affinity, as has happened in the USA (see Chapter 18). One of the reasons the partnership was rejected was because questions were raised about the charity's ability to provide independent objective advice about other sources of pain relief when it was so closely associated with one particular medical treatment. Hence the importance of an appropriate affinity and testing the concept with the target audiences and stakeholders.

Identifying an appropriate affinity is essential and is the responsibility of both sides in the potential partnership. It is vital that the negotiators of the potential partnership understand the views of their various stakeholders. This can be achieved through surveys, questionnaires, focus group research and indeed desk or telephone research of representative groups. To fail to take the views of stakeholders into consideration is to tempt failure of the potential partnership.

It should be clear from this that the quality of the fit is not about size or indeed cause but about appropriateness and clarity of communication.

Organizational structure

Having understood the organization's vision and values, and having identified one's objectives and identified organizations whose values and belief systems mirror one's own, it is vital that one invest time in understanding the organizational structure and methods of working.

Businesses and voluntary sector organizations often work in very different ways from each other therefore be sure you understand:

- the organizational structure;
- the geographical distribution;
- the relationship between the organization and its employees, volunteers, supporters and beneficiaries, as appropriate;
- the work ethos and decision-making processes;
- the planning and investment cycles.

Many of these aspects are basic but it is surprising the number of large businesses for instance in the UK who suddenly find that a major charity does in fact not operate in Scotland and Ireland. Clearly for a national programme this is a major flaw. It is also essential to understand the nature of the relationship between the organization and its employees, supporters, volunteers and beneficiaries; volunteers and supporters for instance have to be persuaded they will not be instructed.

It is absolutely essential to understand what is possible and what is probable given the nature of the organization's structure, and to be open and honest within the discussion. As with any effective partnership it is essential that one does not over-promise or under-deliver.

Senior and internal commitment

The potential rewards for both parties through Cause Related Marketing are significant. So are the risks. Reputations take decades to build and moments to destroy. It is therefore essential that from the outset integrity, ethics, openness, honesty, transparency, sincerity, mutual respect, partnership and mutual benefit remain at the forefront of discussions. By the nature of the potential impact – both positive and negative – of a Cause Related Marketing partnership, it is essential that senior management are committed to, aware of, buy in to and are championing the partnership throughout.

A common theme that is evidenced by many case studies is how much more effective Cause Related Marketing partnerships are when they secure top level and internal support for the concept. This tends to bring strong organizational support and sincerity. Indeed, in identifying the partners, senior and internal support can be intrinsic to the selection process.

Apart from smoothing the process generally, another key reason for senior management support is because they, amongst others, will after all be ambassadors for the partnership. These individuals are ultimately answerable for the relationship. It is essential therefore to engage them in the partnership and incorporate them into the plans from the outset.

The employees, supporters, volunteers and beneficiaries are also essential players in an effective programme as they also have a vital role to play. Indeed for the most encompassing and holistic programmes that are well leveraged throughout the organization, the employees' and/or supporters' role will have been carefully considered as part of the plan and the asset audit.

Defining the scope of the partnership

Defining the scope of the partnership includes being clear about anything from ownership of the idea, the duration of the relationship including an exit strategy through to the likely scale of contribution.

Problems have arisen where in the process of developing an idea, the business, the agency and the charity have all claimed that they 'invented' the idea. It is therefore worth being quite clear about this from the start, whether it be through stating this clearly in a proposal document or agreeing this in the terms of reference before a brainstorming session commences.

Regarding the duration of a relationship, there are no hard and fast rules about how long a Cause Related Marketing partnership should last. A short-term tactical campaign can be valuable. Generally, however quick 'in and out' initiatives should be avoided: you may not get a full return on the effort and resource invested in setting up the partnership in the first place and, more importantly, unless handled carefully, with honesty, openness and clear communication a short-term approach can lead to accusations of exploitation. Like many successful brand-building campaigns, some of the best Cause Related Marketing partnerships are based on long-term commitment.

It may seem contradictory but from the outset as considerations and plans develop for the launch of the partnership time and effort should also be given to considering how the programme will end. In other words the exit strategy should be attended to with as much rigour as the entry strategy. Partnerships do come to an end of their life cycle which is natural. Individual organizations and stakeholders therefore need to be aware that if the partnership is not planned to be lifelong, as it is for instance with the relationship between Dannon's Danimals and the National Wildlife Federation in the USA, that the exit strategy is kept in mind. To come to an abrupt end without any form of communication, indeed celebration, or report back to consumers and other stakeholders not only fails to leverage all the PR and communication opportunities for all parties, but also can lead to concern and cynicism from these same groups. All aspects of communication both at entry and exit need to be fully managed.

Defining the budget

Before identifying and engaging a partner, the business needs to be clear what budget is available for the partnerships from the point of view of the individuals and departments and what funds and support from other departments may be able to be leveraged (see Figure 21.1).

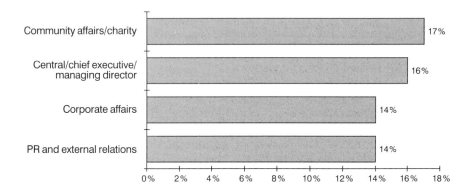

Figure 21.1 Budgets other than marketing used to co-fund cause related marketing. *Base:* 63 marketing directors. *Source:* The Corporate Survey II, Business in the Community/ Research International (UK) Ltd

From The Corporate Survey II it was clear that a number of budgets can contribute to Cause Related Marketing partnerships, ranging from marketing, community affairs to central or chief executives budgets.

Having a reasonable idea of the potential size of the organization's commitment both in donation and marketing support terms is an important aspect to be included in any brief.

Process for selection

Finding a partner

Increasingly organizations are applying particular methods of finding a partner which are appropriate to their organization. Recent UK research suggests that there a number of methods used (see Figure 23.3). According to this research there are therefore nine key ways that are currently being used by businesses to select potential partners:

■ previous experience;
■ formal policy;
■ contacts;
■ desk research;
■ recommendations;

- consumer/stakeholder research;
- external agency;
- tendering process;
- prospecting.

Previous experience

Clearly, as with business it takes many times more effort to establish a new customer than to continue to develop an existing one. If one applies that principle therefore, all these partnerships that exist already between businesses and charities or causes whether or not they are Cause Related Marketing relationships have a very good chance of continuing or leveraging the relationship provided the existing relationship is sound and providing mutual benefits. It makes a great deal of sense in terms of investment of time and resources, and provides a solid bank of credibility from the consumers' point of view whilst at the same time providing ideal substantiation for the communications platform.

To those who already have relationships which are perhaps not yet leveraging through Cause Related Marketing, the opportunity is there to develop. For those that are already in a Cause Related Marketing relationship the future is encouraging providing the relationship continues to be providing mutual benefits, and challenge. For those who are not in the enviable position, there are many other ways in which businesses are looking for partners.

Formal policy

It is not clear from the research conducted by Research International (UK) Ltd for Business in the Community which part of the organization is setting the formal policy. It could develop from previous Cause Related Marketing experience or from corporate and community affairs departments who have a key role to play in helping to create a partnership based on sound principles. Corporate and community affairs professionals are therefore a vital group for the marketing aspects of the business to engage and for the charity and the cause sector to woo.

Desk research

The brief for what type of partner is sought and what attributes are required needs to be clear. One then needs to use all manner of information and services to identify the partner/s ranging from the local library to paid-for, on-line information services. This is a clear process of elimination based on identifying potential partners that fit with the values and affinity match. Depending on how refined this understanding is and the ability of the potential partner to meet the criteria, a clear choice can sometimes be made through meetings and discussion with the potential partners or short-listed organizations.

Recommendations from contacts
Referral from one organization or recommendations from contacts to another can be the source of a new potential partner. Indeed it may be part of the agreement for the exit strategy that the business partner supports the cause in identifying the next potential partners. Clearly this is a strong route but perhaps less frequently employed.

Consumer/stakeholder surveys
Employees, supporters, beneficiaries, consumers and other stakeholders can be surveyed to identify the potential partner organizations. This can be very effective as this approach has the benefits of having stakeholder support from the outset and often can build on the organization's existing relationship with the partner, thus building credibility. Desk research or some other additional method of short-listing may still be required in order to make the final choice.

Prospecting
In some cases partner organizations, be they businesses, charities or causes, can be identified through targeted mailings following desk research. Carefully constructed, well targeted proposals that focus on mutual benefit and the key principles are likely to have stronger results, particularly bearing in mind the volume of the proposals being received by businesses for instance.

Respondents to the Business in the Community research were asked how many approaches they were receiving:

- 79 per cent of respondents receive at least one Cause Related Marketing proposal each month;
- 61 per cent of respondents receive between 1 and 10 proposals every month;
- 6 per cent of respondents receive over 20 Cause Related Marketing proposals a month;
- On average businesses are receiving seven Cause Related Marketing proposals a month. The figures are much the same across community affairs directors and marketing directors.

There are various methods of selecting a cause partner used by businesses, with slight variations between the methods preferred by marketing directors and community affairs directors.

Tendering process

A tendering process can be adopted as a consequence of desk research or from other ways of identifying a short-list of organizations. In order for a tender process to be effective a number of principles and protocols need to be borne in mind.

A clear brief should be provided to all short-listed organizations. Clarity from the outset is likely to help reduce conflict, ambiguity and misunderstanding, thereby aiding a smoother process. This should include:

- the background and nature of the organization and the vision, values and objectives;
- an introduction to the organization;
- details covering the background to the approach;
- what is being sought and whether or not a unique project or programme is required, etc.;
- what the constraints are;
- what the budgets, timescales and process are;
- key facts and figures;
- what experience, skills, commitments, roles and responsibilities are expected of each side;
- what the selection criteria are, etc.;
- who the other short-listed organizations are;
- whether and what costs of tendering will be reimbursed and to what extent;
- a confidentiality clause should be incorporated if necessary;
- a contact who can respond to questions relating to the brief;
- other relevant information.

The more detail you can include at this stage, the better. This serves not only to ensure that the prospective partner is clear on the objectives but by going through such a rigorous process it should clarify your own thoughts. As part of the selection process, consider what costs may be incurred and who will meet them. If you choose to follow a tendering process, you should follow existing guidelines and protocols. See 'Sources of Further Information'[1] for details.

Naturally to be involved in this process everyone needs to be absolutely clear on its vision, values, objectives and the criteria on which the potential partner, opportunity, or proposal is to be judged.

Once a decision has been made on which organization has been selected care should be taken in both informing the successful as well as the unsuccessful organizations, before the media or other third parties are informed.

The principles of integrity, transparency, sincerity and mutual respect run throughout this process.

Clearly this is a competitive market place. In order to stand out proposals therefore need to be clearly targeted and well thought through and there needs to be a clear process internally for dealing with such volume of proposals.

Regardless of the method of identifying the potential partners, the most successful partnerships will benefit from solid preparation, understanding of the potential partner and applying the key principles.

Note

1 Business in the Community (1998) *Cause Related Marketing Guidelines – Towards Excellence*, pp. 22–24.

Chapter 22

Negotiating the partnership

Having identified the chosen partner, the next stage is to negotiate and agree the details of the Cause Related Marketing programme. It is essential for this to be conducted in the spirit of the key principles of integrity, mutual respect, transparency, sincerity, partnership and mutual benefit. If these principles cannot be adhered to by either party, it is unlikely that a quality partnership will develop effectively or that the programme will achieve mutual benefit and excellence. If the negotiation and final agreement are managed well, all sides should be delighted by the partnership and the mutual benefits it hopes to provide. Neither side should feel exploited. In order for this to be achieved however, open, honest and frank discussions need to take place.

Identifying SMART, convergent objectives

As has already been said, it is essential to understand each other's objectives from the outset. It is important to identify where there is convergence and where there is not, and agree what the objectives of the partnership are and the mutual benefits that are aimed for as a result of the partnership. It cannot be stressed enough how essential the key principles are in striving towards solid foundations for potential partnerships. The beginning of this process is of course to be honest with yourself, your colleagues and then your potential partners, treating them each with the respect they deserve.

There are a number of useful acronyms that are applicable to setting objectives for Cause Related Marketing. The objectives that are agreed need to be SMART. That is objectives need to be simple, measurable, achievable, realistic and time limited.

As part of the process of agreeing objectives, both sides, through their planning, should be clear what is fixed and what is negotiable in terms of their own objectives and assets.

Asset and leverage audit

As part of the planning and preparation, and in the process of negotiating the partnership, auditing what assets and tools are available to be used as part of the partnership is important. This may include not only advertising (both in the media and on products or services), direct marketing, sales promotion, sponsorships, PR, etc., but also a wealth of other tools which may include for instance catalogues or sales literature, letterheads, notice boards, web sites, and intranets, e-mail, newsletters and internal briefings as well as the sales force, employees and the many other communication routes and tools.

Employees from the chief executive, chairman and members of the board to all other employees as well as supporters, volunteers and beneficiaries can be a vital source of communication and support.

Assets or potential resources could also include gifts in kind (for example, products and services); gifts in time in terms of expertise and volunteers; premises, retail outlets, warehouses and other sites or venues; the strength and influence of your organization and its connections and ability to attract other people, departments and organizations, as well as other resources and finance both internally and externally (see Chapter 6, p. 38). The important point is to identify the range of potential tools and resources or assets and to leverage them as part of the negotiation towards a mutually beneficial partnership.

Auditing assets

- other departments
- employees, volunteers, supporters, beneficiaries
- partner organizations
- suppliers
- other non-competitive organizations
- customers of all of the above
- government (local, national, European, international)
- other non-governmental agencies

By auditing all such assets, you and your partner can see how the programme might bring together and amplify the impact of your individual strengths. The audit also serves as a useful basis for the later stages of negotiations and programme implementation.

Defining the nature of the activity

Like any successful marketing activity, Cause Related Marketing programmes depend on a good idea, thoroughly researched and planned. Cause Related Marketing partnerships place extra demands on the partners by virtue of the absolute need to demonstrate integrity and a balance of real benefit between the cause, the business and the consumer. Creativity and innovation are welcomed by consumers. They also want targets to be achievable and the balance between effort and reward to be realistic. The most successful campaigns rely on a simple mechanic, a message which can be effectively communicated to everyone involved and appropriate benefit to all parties. When defining the nature of the activity therefore, you must consider:

- the creative idea;
- the balance of benefit between charity or cause, business and consumer;
- the range of products/services to be involved;
- the mechanics of delivery;
- whether the goals are achievable;
- appropriate donation value;
- the communications messages and strategy;
- the exit strategy.

Valuing the opportunity

Valuing how much a potential partnership is worth to the organization is extremely complex. There is no one answer.

'Value' can take on many forms including straightforward cash, other tangible resources, together with the value of the intangibles such as benefit of association. Valuing the opportunity should be carried out with the key principles in mind of integrity, transparency, sincerity, mutual respect, partnership and mutual benefit. The investment in the preparation phase and the asset audit will be crucial in helping to value the opportunity. At the conclusion of the negotiations, both sides should be pleased with the outcome and the potential mutual benefit.

Valuing the opportunity and the contribution should be established in terms of the total value all parties derive. In calculating the value, it is essential for each organization to know their value and therefore their worth to the other, in terms of profile, reputation, values, brands, awareness, distribution channels, routes to market and communications channels etc., not to mention the strength of the other networks. All sides need to be clear on their income and value ratios and balance this with the value of the future relationship. Within this it is important to understand your organization's unique value and contribution *vis à vis* the competition.

Judging the level of donation and valuing the opportunity are key and complex aspects of the process. It is difficult to give a simple answer or an equation to apply. Valuing the 'brand' is a core issue for all organizations, be they charity or businesses, but as they are increasingly factored into the balance sheet so this aspect will become easier.

In the meantime consideration should be given to the power of the brand with whom your organization wishes to be associated; the value of that association to you; the 'usual' level of marketing and promotional spend in that particular market on other third party relationships or incentives and similar activities linked to a charity or cause in this sector or at the price point.

The value of a potential partnership will be unique to it. There is no one answer: 'value' means many things beyond the purely financial. Increased awareness, enhanced reputation, product or service differentiation, added value and an exciting PR platform all contribute to the potential value of a partnership. When negotiating the details of the partnership, consider everything that will contribute to this value, by referring to the results of the audit of your assets. All of these elements add value to the relationship and help to achieve common objectives.

It can be interesting to identify how a relationship could further enhance other aspects of the organization. Not only does it gain attention, but it can potentially attract additional resources and support. Encouraging ownership and interest in the programme across a number of internal functions and within other organizations can develop the sustainability of the partnership and enhance the potential benefits.

It is also important to remember that valuing the opportunity applies to both the business and the charity or cause. As was reported in an article in *Corporate Citizen*, charities are clear about the value of their brand.

> Don't underestimate the value a charity places on its brand. A link with a household name may offer a welcome boost to your sales, increase customer loyalty and enhance your reputation, but association with any business also poses risks to the charity's integrity.

Ken Madine, Head of Corporate Partnerships, Age Concern[1]

Often a useful test is to explain what the intentions are to a lay person. If there is a tendency to start trying to justify the partnership, nature of the relationship, the amount you are investing or receiving, or the listener is questioning why, then it is likely that the balance is wrong. Researching it whilst researching the mechanic and the relationship as a whole is often a good source of guidance. Considering what is reasonable, understanding what the market expects and knowing what can be afforded as opposed to what one can get away with will be important guides.

Beware and don't kid yourself. Negotiating the partnership is an important area in which the key principles are fundamental. In a market where the consumer and indeed all stakeholders are increasingly sophisticated and have high expectations it is important to get this right.

Risk assessment

Risk assessment is about thinking the unthinkable, developing worst case scenarios and making sure that your relationship and programme holds up to scrutiny. It enables organizations to address and counter potential issues before they arise.

It is important to appreciate that there are potential risks for all parties and it is therefore strongly advised that you carry out your own risk assessment independent of your potential partner before setting up a Cause Related Marketing programme. Risk assessment covers three key considerations:

- reputation;
- logistics;
- finance.

Reputation

Could the partnership under extreme conditions undermine, compromise or even damage any aspect of the reputation of your organization, cause, project or brand? You should be looking for skeletons in your own cupboard as well as in your partner's. Conducting a 'media test' (see Chapter 25, p. 266) will be an important part of this risk assessment.

Consideration should be given as to whether and how far one wants to go in terms of endorsing the potential partner organization and the proposed programme of activity, as mentioned previously.

Logistics

It is important to go through in detail the roles and responsibilities of the partners involved, and to understand how failure to deliver any aspect of the plan could impact on the programme and indeed on your organization. Discuss and agree where the risk areas are and decide how to manage them. For example, is there any conflict between the shelf-life of the product and the timing of the campaign.

It is essential to understand all the parts of the process, the organizations involved and to understand how their role could impact on your organization, both from a reputation point of view as well as the delivery of the partnership.

Supplier and distribution issues for example can impact on the activity; their support and delivery is essential. For instance, if the business partner is a manufacturer and the partnership's programme depends on being delivered in a retail outlet, the programme relies on in-store presence and therefore the retailer is part of the relationship and must be engaged and audited appropriately. Details like the duration of the Cause Related Marketing programme *vis à vis* the product shelf-life and date of promotion are important. It is essential that all the details of the logistics are considered and factored in. Logistics are often budget driven and the mechanics of programmes and activities are based on understanding that risk.

Consideration needs to be given to participation and redemption levels (over and under) of the programme which can lead to the financial risks. As part of this assessment, agreement needs to be reached with regards to minimum guarantees and what will be done if these minimums are exceeded. The partners need to agree openly and transparently what will happen in such a case, working not only within the law but also with integrity, openness, honesty, transparency and sincerity with the goal of mutual benefit.

There are a number of points to consider regarding setting a minimum and maximum contribution. The important point in this respect is to understand how over- or under-achievement will be funded and managed. All parties need to be clear what happens if the programme exceeds expectation and bear in mind stakeholder responses to the agreed course of action.

In practical terms how one calculates the minimum guarantee is interesting. It could be calculated for instance on the very basic level of covering the charity's costs or matching the proposed communications spend. This issue needs to be considered, discussed and dealt with openly and in detail.

As part of the financial assessment, it important to understand the level of dependence the organization has on the particular partnership and discuss the exit strategy in terms of both the manner and the effect. As part of this, consideration should be given to how to identify the replacement for this relationship if appropriate. These details are essential to discuss and agree.

Once any areas of concern have been identified and the partnership is still considered viable, the partners will need to discuss in detail and agree how these risks should be managed.

Note

1 *Corporate Citizen* (1999) 'Companies do's and don'ts for working with charities,' Issue 25.

Chapter 23

The formal agreement

Before drafting any legal document it is essential to seek qualified legal advice. In this book I simply put forward the suggestion of some of the types of issues that should be considered. It is not definitive but purely illustrative. Legal advice should be taken in every case. The purpose of the formal agreement is to reflect the legal requirements and the deal that has been negotiated.

Broadly speaking it could be argued that there are essentially seven key steps in the process of concluding the formal agreement.

- understand your responsibilities and liabilities;
- understand the contractual model;
- highlight the key issues;
- identify the pitfalls;
- negotiate and agree the contract;
- re-read the contract;
- sign.

Understand your responsibilities and liabilities

It is essential to identify the legislation that pertains to the partnership. There are a number of basic documents you should be aware of when developing a Cause Related Marketing partnership and programme. In the UK these basic documents include: The Charities Act 1992 and 1993; The Charitable Institutions (Fund-Raising) Regulations 1994; The British Codes of Advertising and Sales Promotion; The Trades Description Act 1968; the Control of Misleading Advertisements Regulations 1988; and The Lotteries and Amusements Act 1976. It is important to understand your roles, responsibilities and liabilities.

The Acts and the Regulations explain for instance that:

- A written agreement in a prescribed form is required between the charity institution and the commercial participator.
- Commercial participators are required to make clear to the prospective customers which institutions are going to benefit and the way in which contributions will be calculated.
- Transfer of property to which the beneficiary institution becomes entitled must be transferred in accordance with article 6 of the Charitable Institutions (Fund-Raising) Regulations 1994.
- All records which are relevant to the venture must be made available to the beneficiary institutions.
- Where the venture does not involve a charitable institution but does involve making the representation by the promoter that funds will be applied for charitable, benevolent or philanthropic purposes, they have to make corresponding disclosure to their customers.
- Where the relationship is not conducted according to The Charities Act and The Charitable Institutions (Fund-Raising) Regulations 1994 stipulations, the commercial participator may be guilty of an offence.
- The controls are not considered to apply to promotional ventures involving a trading company owned by a charity, rather than a charity itself, but the promoter must make it clear that the contributions are going to the trading company.
- The charitable institution which is the intended beneficiary of a particular promotional venture can ask the court to terminate the venture in any case where there is no agreement with the promoter as mentioned in the first bullet point above.
- A 'commercial participator' is defined as: 'any person (other than a charity or its subsidiary) who carries on for gain a business other than fundraising business but in the course of that business engages in any promotional venture in which it is represented that charitable contributions are to be given to or applied for the benefit of a particular charity.'
- The promotional vehicle 'includes any advertising or sales campaign and any other venture undertaken for promotional purposes.'

The British Codes of Advertising and Sales Promotion also give important guidance for those involved with Cause Related Marketing. Section 42.1 of the Code explains that promotions should:

- Name each charity or good cause that will benefit and be able to show that they have consented.
- Specify exactly what will be gained by the named charity or cause and state the basis of the calculation.
- State whether the promoters have imposed any limitations on the contribution they will make out of their own pockets.

Moreover:

■ Consumers' contributions must not be limited and any extra money collected must go to the charity or cause.
■ The benefit to the charity must not be exaggerated.
■ If asked, the organizers must reveal their total financial contribution.
■ Care must be taken when speaking to children.

Communication should also be legal, decent, honest and truthful. All parties involved in a Cause Related Marketing partnership must operate within the law and as a matter of good practice all parties should work within the spirit of these Regulations and Codes.

Contractual models

Clearly your legal adviser will advise on what type of contract is appropriate depending on the circumstances of each partnership, and each particular partnership will be unique. The contractual models that are often used are the sponsorship contractual model, the on-pack promotion, product endorsement and licensing models.

Clearly as marketing and fundraising tools and techniques develop and as the range of relationships develop, as the partnership becomes increasingly creative so too will further contractual models develop. Professional legal advice is essential.

Heads of agreement

Legal advice should be sought before drafting any legal document. Below we have simply given some indications of the areas that should be considered. The formal agreement should include what you are going to give to whom and what you are going to get, over what period of time (please refer to the box at the end of this chapter). It should explain:

■ name and address of partners to the agreement;
■ date;
■ the prime purpose of the partnership;
■ intellectual property rights;
■ who is bound by the agreement, including suppliers, agencies and any other third parties;
■ their roles and responsibilities;

- the duration of the agreement;
- the activities and timing plan;
- details of the arrangements for funding and other resources;
- proportions of receipts by benefiting charities (if more than one);
- proportions of consideration of promotional proceeds of sale;
- sums to be donated in respect of the promotion;
- remuneration (if any) for the commercial participator;
- the payment schedule;
- the process for updating details;
- the process for approving copy, logos and press notices;
- the review plan;
- the terms relating to the termination of the agreement including the exit strategy.

You may also wish to include a goodwill clause, about respecting each other's values and attitudes and protecting the reputation and name of the partners and their assets.

Unless the partners agree otherwise in the UK, commercial participators must:

- at all reasonable times make all relevant records available to the charity;
- within 28 days of receipt remit all monies to the charity;
- pay monies to the persons having general control and management of the charity;
- comply with the charity's extensive powers to give instruction about how property in respect of which the charity expects to benefit is dealt with, handled and kept secure.

Unless the commercial participator and the charity negotiate appropriate variations these requirements are likely to form the basis of the arrangements. The onus is on the commercial participator.

If there is no lawful commercial participator agreement, this can lead to a number of serious consequences. It is a criminal offence in the UK for instance to fail to provide book and records or remit monies in accordance with the Charitable Institutions (Fund-Raising) Regulations 1994. If the agreement is not in line with the prescribed legal requirements, then it is unenforceable against the charity except by a court order. As has already been mentioned, without lawful agreement the charity can apply to restrain the commercial participator from continuing its fundraising participation.

Minimum guarantees

As part of the negotiation, partners should agree the minimum guarantee in terms of funding and delivery. This is intrinsically linked to valuing the opportunity and risk assessment. Each Cause Related Marketing partnership and programme is unique, but, at the very least, costs should be covered by the worst case scenario.

It is then essential to agree how over- or under-achievement will be funded and managed and how it will be communicated. All parties need to be clear what happens if the programme either fails or exceeds expectations. The reactions of all stakeholders should be taken into account before an agreement is reached and this agreement should be captured formally.

Exclusivity

Imagine the situation in which the same Cause Related Marketing programme is being run by your partner with another competitive organization, during the same time period, targeting the same audiences with the same message using the same mechanic. Unless this is deliberately conceived and co-ordinated as such, for instance in an international disaster appeal, it is highly unlikely that any of the partners in question have applied the key principles of Cause Related Marketing. Such a conflict would deflate the potential of either partnership. It could also lead to suspicions of exploitation. It is therefore important to consider whether exclusivity is relevant in relation to your proposed partnership and if so the details of the exclusivity arrangements need to be discussed, agreed, defined precisely and contained as part of the formal agreement. Exclusivity can cover a number of elements including:

- time;
- geography;
- environment, whether it be in a particular retail chain, branch network or type of media;
- competitive industry, cause sector or product category;
- type of mechanic.

Partners should identify areas of commonality in their aspirations for the exclusivity of the partnership and reconcile any differences. Being open about the concerns of both partners will be important. The key principles will feature strongly in this discussion, which should aim at achieving a balanced and mutually acceptable solution.

Tax and VAT

Tax and VAT issues are very important in this area. Each partner should understand what element of the finance is provided on a philanthropic basis and what is provided to achieve commercial benefits. Different tax and VAT rules apply, depending on the nature of the finance. Partners should be aware of their responsibilities and liabilities. They should refer to their own legal, tax and accounting experts and/or refer to Customs and Excise and the Inland Revenue for advice.

First Direct's Anorak Amnesty with Shelter

First Direct, the pioneering telephone banking business in the UK, created a Cause Related Marketing partnership to launch their web site. Building on the concept that customers expect the unexpected from First Direct, an innovative partnership was developed with Shelter. Traditionally the Internet had been linked with computer buffs, or 'anoraks', but with the Internet fast becoming part of everyday life for more and more people First Direct wanted to develop the premise that you don't need to be an 'anorak' to surf the web or indeed visit their web site.

The Anorak Amnesty, a national appeal supported by press, was launched as the First Direct web site went live. The web site detailed the 'amnesty', the work of the charity and encouraged visitors to the site to donate their old anoraks and other coats to Shelter. These would then be resold through Shelter's 84 national shops for between £4 and £30. Thousands of anoraks were donated including those from Hugh Grant, Elton John, Julian Clary, Helen Mirren, Tim Henman, Patsy Palmer and Mystic Meg which were auctioned on the Internet.

Before signing

Before finally signing a formal agreement, partners should consider the nature of the Cause Related Marketing partnership and programme once more and focus on any nagging doubts. The strengths, weaknesses, opportunities and threats of the potential programme should be reviewed one more time, to make sure that all issues have been addressed.

Some questions to consider in relation to the formal agreement

Before drafting a legal document it is important to seek qualified legal advice. This section simply serves to suggest some thoughts, ideas and issues that should be considered. Legal advice should be taken every time.

- Are the objectives aligned and clear?
- Is the partnership a prudent use of the charity's or the corporations assets?
- Has the brand or corporate been adequately protected?
- Have you taken qualified legal advice?
- Are you clear on what your roles and responsibilities are by law?

- Have you checked, understood and are you familiar with the other rules and regulations that impinge on this area?
- Does the programme comply with the law, codes and regulations, etc.?
- Is it clear and unambiguous?
- Do you have a formal agreement and does it cover all aspects?

Some specific questions to consider include:

- Have you defined a clear exit strategy?
- The terms relating to the termination of the agreement including the exit strategy
- The prime purpose of the partnership
- Intellectual property rights
- Who is bound by the agreement, including suppliers, agencies and any other third parties?
- Their roles and responsibilities
- The duration of the agreement
- The activities and timing plan
- Details of the arrangements for funding and other resources
- Proportions of receipts by benefiting charities (if more than one)
- Proportions of consideration of promotional proceeds of sale
- Sums to be donated in respect of the promotion
- Remuneration (if any) for the Commercial Participator
- The payment schedule
- The process for updating details
- The process for approving copy, logos and press notices
- Name and address of partners to the agreement
- If it is a licensing partnership have you defined stringent provision terms of use of the brand?
- Date
- The review plan
- Are you clear whether the charity is getting a donation, a royalty or payment for a supply of service?
- Is there a confidentiality clause?
- Have you covered the issues of exclusivity?
- Are you clear on all tax and VAT implications?
- Have you covered the issues of minimum guarantee?
- Are the Key Principles reflected in the agreement?
- Does it define project management processes?
- Will you both be winners as a result of the agreement?
- Have you agreed how to co-ordinate and communicate the messages to maximize mutual benefit?
- Is there a goodwill clause?
- Does it cover who is getting what, from whom, when and how?

Chapter 24

Managing the programme

A perfect partnership may have been identified and developed, an innovative programme put together, but without effective implementation and project management the results can be disappointing and fail to achieve objectives. Several books have been written on the importance and process of effective project management and this chapter simply aims to highlight some of the key issues relating to Cause Related Marketing partnerships generally.

Nature of the activity

As with any successful marketing programme, following the inspiration of an imaginative and creative idea, the secret is in keeping the mechanic and the process simple and straightforward and managing the process thoroughly. From research carried out it is clear that enlightened self-interest is a key theme for Cause Related Marketing. The charity or cause and business are coming together in partnership for mutual benefit. If benefit can be extended to include the consumer and other stakeholders, research suggests that this is likely to have an even greater impact. This should therefore be borne in mind when developing the detail of the activity.

> I think it's a very good idea. I think that all companies, all main brands should give a bit to charity because then as everybody's got to eat food, everyone could contribute to charities.
>
> **Consumer quote from The Game Plan**[1]

> It's beneficial for both, they have come to an arrangement that makes sense for everyone.
>
> **Consumer quote from The Game Plan**[1]

The easier the Cause Related Marketing partnership or programme is to understand and participate in, the greater the number that are likely to participate. Cause Related Marketing is no different from any other marketing discipline in this respect. Naturally there are many ways to affect and demonstrate Cause Related Marketing but the principle of 'keep it simple' is appropriate.

Leverage

Leverage was mentioned at length in the asset audit section in Chapter 21, the point here being to identify the tools and assets potentially at one's disposal and at the disposal of the potential partner. Leveraging and integrating the partnership internally, across departments and functions and externally through each organization's networks, involving other suppliers, non-competitive organizations and their customers, can be to the benefit of everyone. This should be seriously considered not only in the planning, preparation and negotiation but also in all aspects of the programme including the management, implementation and communication. By encouraging ownership and interest in the programme across a number of internal organizational functions and through external networks and audiences, the potential benefits can multiply.

From a communications point of view all the tools should be considered right through the pre-, during and post-communications cycle. This can range from advertising, below-the-line, direct marketing, sponsorship, merchandising, sales promotion, spokespeople and ambassadors, PR, events and internally it can include employees including the sales force, internal media and events.

In addition to this one should consider the other resources at one's disposal, e.g. loaned, gifts in kind, financial contributions, premises and the leverage of the organization itself to attract other powerful supporters, all of which could provide added value and leverage in pursuit of mutual objectives. It can be interesting to ask other parts of the organization how a relationship could be further leveraged within their area to deliver against their objectives, thus engaging interest and potentially increasing resources and support.

To manage a programme effectively, it is important to be clear about the roles and responsibilities for all parties:

■ businesses;
■ charities or causes;
■ third parties, such as suppliers, distributors, partners, agencies and consultants.

Setting out a work plan and communicating regularly throughout the process will help to ensure that the partnership works effectively. At a basic level, it will be important to understand who has responsibility for the activities set out in the formal agreement. At the detailed project management level, the following questions should be considered:

- What are the work and timing plans for the programme?
- Who are the main points of contact?
- Who has decision-making authority?
- What is the decision-making process and time scale?
- Who has responsibility for different aspects of the process in what time frame?
- Who is being paid to carry out what tasks?
- Who is responsible for recording meetings and decisions and in what time frame?
- What is the approval and sign process and how long should it take?
- What are the success criteria and have the processes been put in place to measure them?

If due to unforeseen circumstances something does go wrong it is vital to be as professional in the management of these circumstances as it is to be professional in the management of the programme itself.

The stakeholder and media spotlight is never so intense as when it is focusing on difficulties. The formal agreement and the key principles should clearly define the course of action and attitude to be taken and this should be followed with professionalism and dignity.

Regular, open and honest communication is at the heart of excellent project management and forms a crucial part of effective Cause Related Marketing.

Note

1 The Game Plan (1997) Business in the Community qualitative consumer research into Cause Related Marketing conducted by Research International (UK) Ltd, quotes from focus groups and in-store interviews.

Communication

The importance of communication has been a core theme running throughout the course of this book, with reference ranging from being sure that the message is being communicated – whether it is about corporate social responsibility, corporate community investment or Cause Related Marketing – to ensuring that you communicate to all the stakeholders in the appropriate way, leveraging all communications tools and opportunities as appropriate. It is then vital to communicate the programme in the right way, with a balanced message and an appropriate tone and style.

Effective communication throughout all stages of the process is the key to effective Cause Related Marketing. Essentially what is invested in effort and resource is often directly related to what is achieved. It is important that the communication is balanced, and must not mislead stakeholders and partners. The investment in the communication must also be considered in relation to the funds being raised and the balance of costs and mutual benefit must be appropriate.

To be effective communication must be compelling and based on the key principles which apply throughout all stages of the communication process, which includes:

■ preparing the ground;
■ securing support from all stakeholders, both internal and external;
■ pre-launch publicity;
■ publicity while the campaign is running;
■ post-programme and post-partnership feedback and follow-up.

All of these elements are important for effective Cause Related Marketing partnerships and in some cases are subject to legal requirements and the British Codes of Advertising and Sales Promotion. Apart from the legal requirements and codes and the fact that communication must be legal, decent, honest and truthful, the key concepts that should form the foundations of the communication are:

- Communication must give balanced emphasis to the business and the cause.
- All partners should promote the benefits of the partnership.
- It must not mislead partners or the public; in particular, the benefits to all parties need to be clear.
- It needs to be compelling, sincere and not patronizing.
- The contribution of the consumers needs to be acknowledged.

Consumers support the idea of businesses partnering with charities or causes for mutual benefit and expect such partnerships and programmes to be communicated. With your partner you should consider the message, the content, the tone and style, the amount of communication and the media used.

Both businesses and charities should be clear that research shows that consumers support the idea of Cause Related Marketing (see Chapter 11). They are also supportive of the idea that the charity or cause promote the Cause Related Marketing relationship or initiative. As previously mentioned, consumers can be sceptical about the sincerity of a partnership. The more that can be done therefore to demonstrate and reinforce the sincerity and mutual benefit the better. It is clear that consumers are encouraged when they see the cause or charity endorsing the work and the benefits of the partnership.

Some of the stronger Cause Related Marketing programmes are those where the recipient of the benefit, be it awareness, money or equipment etc., plays a role in promoting the Cause Related Marketing programme; in effect, endorsing and supporting the programme and the business. This not only raises awareness but also gives the relationship, the activity and the business credibility.

The more the Cause Related Marketing programme is communicated using as many elements of the marketing mix as possible, highlighting the mutual benefit, the better. This is true whether from the business or the cause side of the relationship. The Cause Related Marketing programme works best if all elements are employed in the partnership.

The Game Plan research provides a great deal of further information on consumer perspectives on this, some of which is discussed further here.

Identifying the stakeholders and messages

A thorough communications strategy is the corner-stone to any effective partnership. There is a matrix of stakeholders and messages to convey and promote throughout a Cause Related Marketing partnership. Communication can make the difference between a successful, a mediocre or a disastrous programme. Stakeholders can include any number of groups including the chairman or chief executive, the board, employees, supporters, volunteers, and

beneficiaries, opinion formers, media, central and local government, partnership organizations, distributors, suppliers and buyers as well as customers.
Indeed customers can fall into a number of different categories ranging from
loyal customers to trialists.

The key point is to identify the stakeholders and communicate with them
appropriately, proactively and consistently over time. Messages and timing of
the messages may vary but all groups need to be considered all of the time. It
should also be remembered that unless otherwise agreed, communication is
the joint responsibility of both partners.

Reassuring stakeholders

The key principles of integrity, ethics, openness, honesty, transparency,
sincerity and mutual benefit are essential elements in all aspects of effective
communication. Research clearly highlights that consumers are sophisticated
and have high levels of expectation. Consumers need to be reassured that the
relationship is honest and sincere and that the benefits are balanced and
mutual.

The Game Plan research clearly identified for instance that customers could
have concerns if the communication of a programme was not handled well. To
reassure consumers and indeed employees, supporters and other stakeholders
it is important to demonstrate and build credibility into the programme,
reinforcing sincerity. This can be achieved effectively if the programme is
shown to be part of an existing policy of social responsibility and community
investment. It cannot be assumed of course that the target audience are at all
familiar with an organization's previous work, support, experience or
commitment to a particular area, so as much as a Cause Related Marketing
strategy should, where possible, be clearly aligned with a corporate social
responsibility and corporate community investment policy, at the same time
Cause Related Marketing should also be regarded as a key communications
tool for these policies themselves.

In addition, communicating examples from the organization's past support
of issues will help to build credibility for the partnership and help counter
potentially negative reactions. Demonstrating the affinity between the organizations is key and needs to be clearly projected. As such a programme needs to
be turnkey and straightforward for the organization involved, it should be
equally clear for stakeholder understanding. The KISS principle of 'Keep it
Simple, Stupid' needs to be fundamental to the communications strategy.

Communication is on many levels and is crucial before, during and after the
particular programme and throughout the strategy. It also needs to be
considered in the context of all the various stakeholders (see Figure 25.1).

Pre-launch communication

Clearly ensuring the wider community and stakeholders are familiar with the business's social responsibility and community activity will form a key part of the pre-launch communication platform as will building the stakeholders' awareness of the cause.

From the outset, it is also essential to have senior internal commitment to the strategy and programme. This will help deliver leadership, organizational commitment and sincerity and indeed potentially further support and resources. Clearly leadership from the top provides encouragement and influence through the organization and potentially along the supply and distribution chain. Before communicating messages externally it is vital to establish internal engagement and support. Having secured the senior level of the organization, the whole of the organization needs to feel part of the relationship if the organization and the partners are to fully benefit. Programmes need to be sold internally before they are sold externally. This is an essential pre-requisite for the success of the programme.

The importance of this should not be under-estimated. It is important for different areas of the organization to understand the plans and the relationship. In some cases identification of the potential partners may well come from an internal survey and therefore the potential strength of the internal support should really help build the potential impact of the programme. Internal communications should remain a key feature throughout the partnership informing, encouraging and celebrating the employees' and other supporters' efforts (see Figure 25.1).

Launch communication

The key point to stress at the launch phase is that the programme needs to be launched to all the stakeholder groups and not purely the consumers for instance. Whilst depending on the nature of the partnership the consumer might be the largest audience from a numerical point of view, other key influencers on the success of this programme will be employees, media and other opinion formers to name but a few.

The success of programmes like TESCO Computers for Schools (UK) or any of the Sears Roebuck or Target Stores programmes (USA) would not be nearly so impactful were it not for this vital and fundamental contribution of employees. That support could not be counted on were it not for their sense of ownership of the programme generated by the focused, targeted internal communication over time. Reinforcing and celebrating the role of each stakeholder in achieving the targets will be an important aspect of the communications package beyond the cause, mechanic, the benefits and the goal (see Figure 25.1).

Ongoing communication

It is interesting to note how the communications spend changes over the duration of a programme. Naturally the launch of the event typically consumes the largest share of attention and budget, but the ongoing drip feed of the messages should not be overlooked as an important contribution to the excitement and success of the particular programme or strategy.

Throughout the programme whilst the cause, the partnership, the programme and the targets are being communicated, the duration of the programme should be kept squarely in mind. Clarity on the exit strategy is essential from the beginning in order to manage expectations and in order to pace the crescendo of the communication.

Consumers are clear that programmes won't last for ever and corporate commitment is likely to be time limited. None of this is an issue with the consumer provided expectations and communication are managed well. Being honest and transparent about the nature and duration of the commitment is crucial (see Figure 25.1).

Post-programme

So often forgotten, but like the entry strategy the celebration and conclusion of the programme and exit strategy need to be equally well managed and communicated.

No programme succeeds without a whole range of inputs and supports, and each group should be acknowledged, celebrated and thanked for their commitment. This includes employees, consumers, suppliers, and distributors, in fact everyone who has been involved. Public acknowledgement of stakeholders contributions to the success of a campaign not only provides the partner organization another advertising and PR opportunity, but it is a further opportunity to strengthen the ties that bind (see Figure 25.1).

Communications tools

The number of ways in which a Cause Related Marketing message can be communicated to the audience of stakeholders is huge; sadly however there are few programmes that seem to leverage each opportunity, although some are much more thorough than others.

Clearly the more the message is communicated, the greater the understanding, the greater the number of opportunities to see and respond to the message whatever the call to action might be, the greater, broader and deeper the potential success of the programme.

Timing	Purpose Internal	Purpose External
Pre-launch	• Develop internal senior commitment. • Generate other internal engagement individually, departmentally and in terms of additional resources and budgets.	• To reinforce the history of commitment and activity in the wider community. • To diffuse any potential cynicism by ensuring historical commitment over time is understood. • To engage further support through, for instance, suppliers and distributor networks.
Launch	• Gain internal commitment and active support. • Reinforce the vital role of the internal stakeholders in reaching the target and making the partnership a success. • To generate energy and commitment to achieving the target.	• To define the target and the duration. • To engage all stakeholders in supporting the partnership and participation. • To generate energy and commitment to achieving the target.
Ongoing	• To continue to fuel the energy and commitment to the partnership and participation. ← To provide updates on the status of achievement against targets. → ← Acknowledging and thanking stakeholders for their support so far. → ← To remind stakeholders of the targets and therefore by inference the time-limited nature of the partnership. →	
Post-launch	← Celebrating and thanking all stakeholders, internal and external, for their support. → ← Acknowledging all the heroes. → ← Providing the tangible results of the partnerships. → ← Communicating what next in relation to the partnership: whether this is the finale; the beginning of the next phase; or the start of a new relationship. →	

Figure 25.1 Communications matrix

Advertising above and below the line, use of the range of new media, on-pack, on-shelf communication – indeed Cause Related Marketing could be communicated through every route of communication with each group of stakeholders that each organization has available to it. Without even attempting to be comprehensive if one just takes a brief look at some of the communication tools available when communicating with different stake-holder groups one begins to see just how vast the options are.

According to Business in the Community research, businesses indicated that Cause Related Marketing messages were being communicated through a whole mix of elements. Very few businesses however seem to use the full weight of the marketing mix including above the line advertising (see Figure 11.11).

It is important to ensure that appropriate and acceptable methods of communication are employed. Increasingly both marketing directors and community affairs directors are using more of the marketing mix to leverage their Cause Related Marketing strategies. PR, internal newsletters, sponsorship and print advertising are the most frequently used marketing vehicles for implementing and communicating Cause Related Marketing. In addition to this other popular methods used are on-pack, corporate brand, point-of-purchase, sales promotion and direct mail – all of which were judged important by consumers.

This poses an interesting question from the communications perspective. Whilst consumers clearly support Cause Related Marketing when done well, they are also adamant that they wish to see sincere commitment to a Cause Related Marketing partnership. Indeed through The Game Plan research, it was found that consumers were clear that if a business would normally advertise on television for a particular promotion, then they should do this for a Cause Related Marketing programme. Not to do so can lead to consumer suspicion and scepticism.

Further research indicated that consumers supported the idea of companies promoting Cause Related Marketing programmes in a more overt way. Almost three-quarters (74 per cent) of consumers felt that it was acceptable for a company to run advertisements about its support and work on behalf of a charity or cause[1].

> I mean they do an awful lot of television advertising don't they? I think if more people are made aware that might just spur them on to buy this instead of perhaps their normal regular brand.[2]

As has been mentioned in an earlier chapter, research amongst consumers clearly indicates that consumers endorse the use of the full range of communications tools and methods in bringing Cause Related Marketing partnerships to their attention. Indeed not to consider and use an equal weight of communication and support for a Cause Related Marketing programme compared to another form of promotion can lead to consumer scepticism, concern, even rejection. During the course of the research consumers questioned how and why different techniques were used. It was felt that business appeared to be reticent about promoting their link to a charity or cause.

The activities that consumers believe to be the most effective methods of communicating a company's involvement in a cause or issue are:

- television programmes;
- advertising on a product or pack;
- in-store materials such as posters and signs.

Most acceptable methods, from the consumer perspective, are celebrities donating time to promote a cause, high profile events or fundraising and promotions to raise funds for causes. Most likely to alienate consumers are publicizing cases of specific victims and paying celebrities to promote a cause or issue (see Figure 11.12).

The total communication package is therefore appropriate for a Cause Related Marketing strategy.

Least effective communication vehicles were:

- sales staff;
- charities' brochures.

Clearly a variety of techniques could be used to promote Cause Related Marketing programmes ranging from advertising, sales promotion, direct marketing sponsorship and PR etc. Consumers are increasingly marketing literate and are therefore aware of this and an question how and why different techniques were used. During the course of the research[3] consumers indicated that they felt that business appeared to be reticent about promoting their link to a charity or cause. This led to concerns that businesses are therefore missing an opportunity to really develop the partnership and its potential benefits both to the business and the cause. It also led to questions about the sincerity of commitment between the partners.

Clearly communicating Cause Related Marketing activities and the company's motives for becoming involved with a cause or issue to the consumer is vitally important. Communication serves not only to generate stakeholder support and excitement but also helps to address any lack of awareness of a company's activities in this area and also helps to avoid consumer cynicism about a company's motivation for becoming involved in social causes or issues. It is vital to ensure that appropriate and acceptable methods are employed.

If businesses are going to get involved with any marketing activity they must communicate it. As they say, if you didn't tell anyone you did it, you might as well as not have done it. Not surprisingly research evidence clearly indicates that there is greater awareness and participation in Cause Related Marketing where there is a high level of promotional support, particularly advertising support. This indicates that, as for any other type of marketing activity, the impact of Cause Related Marketing will be maximized if it is promoted appropriately, effectively and 'loudly'.

It must be said that consumers recognize that television advertising, although highly effective, is an expensive medium and that it could reduce the amount of money that a company was able to make available to a cause or charity. Consumers however acknowledge and applaud the way some businesses intersperse their regular advertising with a Cause Related Marketing treatment. This serves to reinforce the consumers' belief in the sincerity of the commitment between the partners and engendered further goodwill towards the business.

Impact of promotions

Consumers shop at speed and the decision as to which product to buy is usually a very quick process, particularly if the consumer is a habitual buyer of a specific brand. In this 'hit and run shopping' environment, key differentiators are essential to engage the consumer. Cause Related Marketing can be a key differentiator but to be a key differentiator whatever the mechanic, the promotion must be clear, visible, simple and take the minimum amount of time to understand.

In this way therefore, a Cause Related Marketing partnership is no different from any other marketing activity in such an environment. A comment by one participant in a focus group illustrates this point well:

> When you think shopping in a supermarket is likely to give you coronary anyway, you haven't got time to stand there and think, 'Let's see what it's all about.'[4]

This is clearly a comment on the communications techniques generally rather than on Cause Related Marketing specifically. There is no doubt that the learning and expertise developed in marketing generally also needs to be applied to Cause Related Marketing strategies, if their potential is to be realized.

In-store promotional material

Clearly an obvious area for communication, the balance has to be found between the maintenance of in-store environments and communicating the partnership message. Through research conducted by Research International (UK) Ltd for Business in the Community, shoppers pointed to poor on-pack signalling and an absence of any supporting promotional material at the point of sale.

Problems with the communication on-pack fell into a number of different categories. Often the copy describing the Cause Related Marketing programme was in very small print, such that regular purchasers of the product had not even noticed it.

Shoppers also commented that more space on packaging was devoted to other types of promotions such as money off and free gifts, whereas manufacturers seemed more reticent about the Cause Related Marketing link which tended to have little presence on the front of the product. As a result compared to the Cause Related Marketing examples, the other types of promotions were much more eye-catching.

Consumer suggestions for in-store communication

■ Put it on the front and advertise it better.
■ More eye-catching displays.
■ Posters in the aisle which prominently featured the promotion, perhaps the logo of the cause or charity.
■ A sign on the shelf, with the cause or charity's logo or brief indication of the charity/cause link.

Source: The Game Plan (1997), Business in the Community qualitative consumer research into Cause Related Marketing conducted by Research International (UK) Ltd

---

I think it (Cause Related Marketing example) is a good idea. With any company, really, to give part of their profits to a charity is a good idea. It can only be publicity for them which is a good idea.[5]

Promotional context

The increasingly marketing literate consumer is able to compare and contrast business policies and strategies to their promotion and communication. They can therefore make direct comparisons with the other promotions in the store environment. The Business in the Community research[4] concluded that consumers liked the idea of Cause Related Marketing promotions in contrast to the standard money-off and free product promotions.

> I prefer it (the idea of giving money to charity) to a book (promotion on another product). I'd rather the money goes to charity.[5]

One shopper articulated their preference for one of the Cause Related Marketing examples to other types of promotions well.

> A hundred times better than these things ... trying to help charity, extra commitment.[4]

To be effective, any marketing activity needs to be well and appropriately communicated if it is to be understood and trigger a reaction amongst the target market. Often this is not the case as Cause Related Marketing communication can be so small and poorly supported that the call to action is never heard, and the potential impact on the corporate reputation and brand is never released. As a result Cause Related Marketing in the UK is a relatively untapped marketing opportunity. Effective communication of the Cause Related Marketing programme is key. A compelling communication strategy which is well supported will maximize benefits for both the charity or cause and the business.

> They might be doing it but they're just not promoting it as well as they could do.[4]

The communications challenge is clear. Consumers endorse Cause Related Marketing. Consumers have said that Cause Related Marketing would influence their buying decisions when price and quality are equal and when they are aware of it (see Chapter 11). The opportunity therefore lies in the hand of businesses and charities or causes to develop programmes based on the key principles and to manage, implement and communicate them.

Promoting the link

A recurring criticism of Cause Related Marketing partnerships is that the link to the charity or cause should be made more visible. Consumers are motivated by seeing the logo of a charity or cause. Failure to do so could result in a less effective programme and/or consumer cynicism and accusation of exploitation. Balance, tone and positioning are crucial elements; as one consumer put it, the communication of the cause or charity and the partnership should be 'big, bold, easy to read, easy to comprehend'.[4]

> To get over the cynicism just find a way, be it through PR, be it through magazines, news stories, find a way, take a good example to put it in a good light.[4]

Get the balance, tone and positioning right and there is much to be gained for all parties. It brings the stakeholder on side and detracts from any potential cynicism.

> It feels for the company that they're not just conning me and using the whole concept to get me to buy it but they are actually themselves making an effort. Because 10 per cent (of the cost of the product) would reduce their profits. That would be enough for me to feel that it's not just me making an effort and choosing their product, but they themselves are genuinely committed and making an effort.
>
> **Focus group, Leeds**

> They both benefit really. They've got to. They are going to sell more product and the charity are going to benefit too.[4]

In summary therefore, having conducted the research, identified the right partner and having negotiated the terms of the partnership it is essential to plan the communication strategy taking into account the different stakeholders, the variety of messages and the need to keep the communication going throughout the duration of the relationship. Balance, tone and extent are crucial and can make or break the programme. Equal energy and thought needs to be given to the exit strategy as to the entrance, and at the close of the partnership, the partner involved should be mindful of the need to celebrate the efforts and contributions of all stakeholders. Get it right and in the words of one consumer:

> If you manage to get communication of a product and a charity together to really move the psyche of the nation or the psyche of a specific group you can do anything, you can get them to give their world goods.[4]

The 'media test'

I believe what I have termed the 'media test' is an absolutely crucial part of the process. There is no excuse not to conduct one. This process helps to test the validity of the partnership and test the application of the key principles of integrity, ethics, openness, honesty, transparency, sincerity, mutual respect, partnership and mutual benefit. To make the test as effective as possible, it is important to identify the worst case scenarios and think through the answers from your perspective and consider the reactions of the different stakeholders, both positive and negative. It is about putting oneself in the mindset of the most cynical investigative journalist, identifying the hard and controversial questions and answering them. For example if the company is the facilitator for the donation it is essential that the communication of the programme does not imply more.

Through the Game Plan research, consumers made it clear that they could suspect for instance that the product or service price had been increased to cover the cost of any donation. Communication should be in line with the law and advertising and sales promotion guidelines and be clear.

As part of this process the most basic questions should be asked, including:

- Is the balance of benefits appropriate?
- Are the goals achievable?
- Is the affinity clear?
- Are all parties happy with the final details; is it based on mutual benefit?

Apart from these surface level questions there are many others to consider too. For example:

- Is the partnership incongruous with the organization's policies and behaviour?
- Does the charity or cause buy your product or services; if not why not?
- Does the charity have offices or representation in the areas of your manufacturing plants or key sites or throughout the UK? If not, does it matter? If it does, what is the organization doing to support them?
- Does the organization have any affiliations that could prove awkward?
- Despite the partnership can the organization still advocate on issues that are sensitive to your organization?
- Does the organization practise the core values of your organization?
- What is the organization's record on your particular cause?
- Is the organization well managed, free from corruption, etc.?

The questions can and should go on; these are just examples but they indicate the value and importance of carrying out such a process.

This 'media test' is essential preparation for the launch of your partnership: it can also be seen as part of the risk assessment process. It will prove helpful in identifying potential faults with the partnership before it becomes public, allowing time to adapt the programme if necessary. It also provides the opportunity not only to test out the balance of the partnership, the message and the communication, but also to prepare the detailed briefing papers for all potential ambassadors and spokespeople.

The media test is critical and the parties involved are foolish if they don't carry one out.

Notes

1 The Winning Game (1996) Business in the Community quantitative Cause Related Marketing research conducted by Research International (UK) Ltd.
2 The Game Plan (1997) Business in the Community qualitative consumer Cause Related Marketing research conducted by Research International (UK) Ltd, quote from in-store interviewing, TESCO PLC, Pitsea.
3 The Game Plan (1997) Business in the Community qualitative consumer research into Cause Related Marketing conducted by Research International (UK) Ltd.
4 The Game Plan (1997) Business in the Community qualitative consumer research into Cause Related Marketing conducted by Research International (UK) Ltd, quoted from a focus group.
5 The Game Plan (1997) Business in the Community qualitative consumer research into Cause Related Marketing conducted by Research International (UK) Ltd, quoted from in-store interviewing.

Chapter 26

Monitoring, measurement and evaluation

The old adage 'half the money I spend on advertising is wasted, and the trouble is I don't know which half'[1] whilst an amusing argument, is not a good enough excuse not to try to measure the effectiveness of Cause Related Marketing. The importance of monitoring, measuring and evaluating programmes and partnerships is a clearly understood discipline and a requirement in effective business management generally. Cause Related Marketing is no different. The investment made at the planning and preparation phase in identifying the key objectives will provide the performance indicators against which the programme or partnership can be monitored, measured and evaluated.

Monitoring, measurement and evaluation are the only ways in which one can effectively judge whether or not a partnership or programme has been effective and therefore whether or not to continue to invest the time, effort and money. It is in the interest of all parties involved and resources should be allocated from the outset.

This process can be divided into three stages:

1. When testing out the idea of whether the Cause Related Marketing idea is worthwhile, whether it will bring benefits to your company, and whether there is a good 'fit' or affinity between the particular Cause Related Marketing activity planned and your company and its corporate goals.
2. When assessing the effects of a particular Cause Related Marketing initiative once it is implemented.
3. When assessing Cause Related Marketing activities **overall** in terms of image shift or customer service, and the overall benefits to your company of this.

Monitoring a programme or partnership is essential in order to anticipate issues, avert them and to develop or refine a programme or partnership to ensure it is finely tuned. Obviously, how a programme is monitored will depend on the nature of the programme. At its most basic, monitoring can be as simple as a regular conversation and discussion between the respective project managers. Openness, honesty and transparency will be invaluable in ensuring sensible monitoring of a partnership.

Alternatively monitoring the programme may include setting particular objectives as key measurement indicators which track over time the agreed objectives of the programme and as a part of the project management meetings are regularly reviewed, discussed and acted upon.

Depending therefore on the agreed performance indicators, you should for instance consider measuring:

- funds raised;
- effect on sales, volume and/or customer traffic;
- media coverage;
- effect on reputation, image, and/or awareness;
- effect on usage and/or attitude/favourability;
- customer satisfaction;
- employee satisfaction;
- other stakeholder satisfaction;
- impact on society.

Without measuring these aspects of Cause Related Marketing partnerships some of the intrinsic benefits of the programme will be overlooked. Monitoring the programme makes it possible to refine the details of the partnership, while measurement and evaluation provide the evidence for continued investment or otherwise. Effective data makes it possible to judge the success of a programme and is the vital basis for future support.

There has been concern that some organizations do not regard measurement as an important part of a partnership or process. This is either short sighted or perhaps based on the assumption that measurement has to be expensive and difficult.

This does not necessarily have to be the case. Consideration should be given to what the existing research processes are in each organization and how they might be used or adapted to include the Cause Related Marketing partnership. Existing tools may already include press and media monitoring and attitude and usage tracking studies focusing on the development of stakeholder opinions towards the organization, products, projects, brands or services. If these tools already exist, they should be utilized. If they do not, they should be considered as a valuable way of measuring the effectiveness and influence of the Cause Related Marketing partnership. Alternatively, measurement may include looking at existing sales data, adding questions to existing customer satisfaction, image, attitude, awareness and usage tracking studies. It may involve organizing a limited number of focus groups or involve including questions about the partnership as part of the call cycle (visits or telephone) or indeed telephone surveys. Customer service being at the core of most organizations has led to the development of customer care lines and other systems. These provide the opportunity to use these systems and methods to include questions regarding the partnership. The point is to identify existing processes as well as developing bespoke methods of measuring the effectiveness of the partnership against the objective set.

Measurement is core to the future potential and development of Cause Related Marketing. As with any other activity, without clearly setting and measuring performance against objectives, the decision on whether or not to continue a programme is very difficult to make. Business in the Community's Corporate Survey II investigated the levels to which objectives were set against Cause Related Marketing programmes as well as the preferred methods of measurement (see Figure 26.1).

■ 53 per cent of respondents overall, reported that they set clear objectives for any Cause Related Marketing activity they carry out.
■ Looking at a smaller sample of larger businesses creating comparative samples from 1998 to 1996, 73 per cent of respondents in 1998 compared to 51 per cent in 1996 indicated that they set clear objectives for Cause Related Marketing activity indicating an increasingly serious approach to Cause Related Marketing.

It would seem from this research that Cause Related Marketing is now under a lot more scrutiny from every aspect. The problems associated with measuring the long-term effects of programmes and activities are not exclusive to this subject. Accurately disaggregating the effects of marketing a brand is an age-old problem, only too familiar to advertisers and marketers. Cause Related Marketing seems to be increasingly considered as a marketing discipline, with a focus on the programme achieving commercial success and having a significant benefit on the bottom line.

Clearly, the methods used for measurement of Cause Related Marketing, as in other areas of marketing, often differ from the ideal methods of measurement. Looking at the methods actually used for measurement *vis à vis* those that are preferred it is possible that the success of Cause Related Marketing could be undervalued (see Figure 26.1).

Often customer retention is a key benefit for Cause Related Marketing, yet the methods that are actually used for assessing effectiveness are perhaps not sensitive to this measure. In terms of methods actually used for measurement, with the emphasis on sales output, these techniques will not be sensitive to the positive long-term effects that Cause Related Marketing can have on brand building which ultimately affect sales and the bottom line.

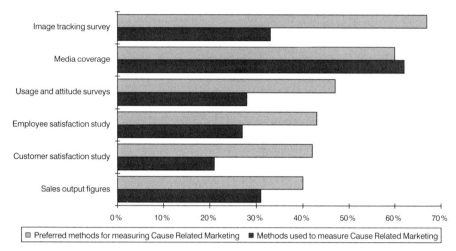

Figure 26.1 Methods of measuring Cause Related Marketing. *Base:* 97 marketing directors, 57 community affairs directors (methods used), 159 marketing directors (preferred method to use). *Source:* The Corporate Survey II, Business in the Community/Research International (UK) Ltd

The importance of measurement and evaluation is self-evident. Without effective data against which to judge the success of a programme, future funding and support will always be in jeopardy.

What is undoubted is that Cause Related Marketing is becoming too much a part of the marketing armoury to be left to its own devices. It will not be enough that it is seen broadly to be a 'good thing' and there will be increasing impetus from those holding the budgets to have proof of effectiveness. It is likely that researching Cause Related Marketing will become as normal as advertising pre-testing and evaluation and measuring of promotions.

Cause Related Marketing is a complex area. No two partnerships will ever be the same due to the difference in causes and businesses, the combination of mechanics used and tools leveraged, the stakeholder group that one hopes to influence and the objectives that the partnership hopes to meet.

Cause Related Marketing has enormous potential strengths in being able to make a significant impact on both business and cause objectives, thereby providing mutual benefit. It is about integrity, ethics, openness, honesty, transparency and mutual benefit. Cause Related Marketing does have weaknesses. Cause Related Marketing is not a panacea for all ills; it is not a fig leaf to cover up the inadequacies of an image, product or service. Cause Related Marketing requires long-term, senior management commitment and is not a cheap option.

Cause Related Marketing also has risks. Planned, implemented or communicated poorly Cause Related Marketing can backfire and damage the reputation

Table 26.1 Typical monitoring, measurement and evaluation techniques

Stage	Purpose	Typical questions	Type of research
Pre-programme	To check out and verify the nature of the proposed relationship	▪ What do particular stakeholder groups think of Cause Related Marketing overall? ▪ What is the 'fit' or affinity between the concept and the proposed partner? ▪ How does the proposed programme enhance/detract from the corporate reputation, etc.? ▪ What are the stakeholders' views on the proposed mechanic? ▪ Suggestions on the best way to implement the programme? ▪ What view do the stakeholders have on the proposed advertising and communications of the programme?	Qualitative research (focus groups)
During	To monitor ongoing effectiveness of the programme against objectives	▪ Is it meeting the PR objectives? For example, awareness/damage limitation, communication of key messages, etc. ▪ Awareness of the Cause Related Marketing programme? ▪ How much media coverage have we received as a result of our Cause Related Marketing activities? ▪ Has this coverage been mainly favourable or unfavourable? ▪ Which (new) audiences have been reached? ▪ Would this have been coverage that our organization would not have had otherwise? ▪ What messages about our company has it promulgated? ▪ What are stakeholder attitudes in the light of the coverage received? ▪ Effectiveness when measured against sales/volume? ▪ Targets: are redemption levels meeting, exceeding or failing to meet expectations?	PR evaluations Exit interviews/ service evaluation/ stakeholder surveys and opinion polls Sales/volume data

Stage	Purpose	Typical questions	Type of research
Longitudinal	To track the effects of a Cause Related Marketing programme over time	■ How strong is my brand vis à vis competitors? ■ What are the stakeholders' perceptions of the company? ■ What are the main image associations and are these good or bad? ■ How could my image be improved to improve the perceived rating of the company? ■ How have recent campaigns (Cause Related Marketing, promotions, advertising campaigns) positively or negatively affected our company image? ■ What, if anything, has been the image 'shift' since the last time the tracking was conducted? ■ How have you been made aware of our company over the past few months? ■ What particular campaigns come to mind? ■ Have you heard/seen anything of our recent Cause Related Marketing campaign? ■ What did you associate it with? ■ Has it affected your perception of the company favourably or unfavourably or not changed it? ■ If your perceptions have changed, how? Stakeholder service/loyalty measurement ■ Overall customer satisfaction ■ Overall customer loyalty ■ Reasons for satisfaction/dissatisfaction ■ The relative importance of different elements in contributing to a company's satisfaction score ■ Performance relative to competition	Research survey

Stage	Purpose	Typical questions	Type of research

Post programme	Continued tracking of the effectiveness of the campaign	■ How conscious are employees of our Cause Related Marketing initiatives?
		■ What do employees think of the initiatives?
		■ How are the stakeholders' perceptions of or feelings towards the company affected?
		■ How have stakeholders themselves participated?
		■ What difference has this made?
		■ How have stakeholders reacted to the initiative?
		■ What ideas do stakeholders (the staff) have for future Cause Related Marketing activities?
		■ How would stakeholders like to see the initiative develop, e.g.:
		  – At a local or at a national level?
		  – In relation to a particular charity area (children, health, arts etc.)?
		  – How could staff help or contribute more?
		■ Level of familiarity with your company?
		■ Level of favourability towards the company (pre and post the Cause Related Marketing initiative)?
		■ Degree of awareness of the Cause Related Marketing initiative itself?
		■ Where seen/heard of (press, TV, in store, on pack, word of mouth, etc.)?
		■ If participated in the activity (bought the product, sent off the coupons or whatever)
		■ Greater likelihood to buy product or service as a result of the Cause Related Marketing
		■ Perceived success in the way the initiative was communicated?
		■ Perceived success of the initiative?
		■ Image associations with the company (these tested pre and post to provide indications of image shift)?
		■ Overall perceptions of the company and feelings towards it?
			Specific Cause Related Marketing quantitative research

of all involved. Indeed more than that, if Cause Related Marketing is implemented badly, not only does it affect the partners directly involved, but it has a significant effect on all charities, causes and issues. One bad example will ruin the opportunity that Cause Related Marketing has to make, not only on the impact of the social issues of the day but also on the business. It is not in anyone's interest for this to happen.

Following the key principles, planned, implemented and communicated well, Cause Related Marketing will provide a win for charities and causes, a win for business and a win for the wider community.

Note

1 Viscount Leverhulme, quoted in Ogilvy, D. (1994) *Confessions of an Advertising Man*, NTC Contemporary Publishing Company.

Part Five

The Way
Forward

Chapter 27

The future of Cause Related Marketing

I think Cause Related Marketing will be the single most exciting aspect of marketing in the next ten years.

**Ruth McNeil, Deputy Managing Director,
Research International (UK) Ltd**

Business and the community

As the concepts of the stakeholder, neighbour of choice and licence to operate become more established in the business community's lexicon, managing corporate reputation, impact on society and relationships with the full spectrum of stakeholders will, I believe, become the overriding focus of marketing.

Relationships between businesses, the wider community, charities and causes have evolved. They have developed from the one relationship of pure philanthropy, to the many relationships of philanthropy. Strategic philanthropy is where the programme of giving is aligned to the objectives of the business, to also include community investment, one-off sales promotions, sponsorships and indeed the whole spectrum of Cause Related Marketing. As in commerce generally where there is more than one tool, technique or strategy to achieve business objectives, this is also the case in terms of business relationships with the wider community.

Business increasingly has a number of options or tools to use to support the community in which it operates and from which it benefits. Pure philanthropy and the Quaker approach of 'do well by doing good' has not been surpassed, rather it has been enhanced. Pure philanthropy forms a vital and essential part of the health of our society and will continue to do so but enhanced and leveraged by Cause Related Marketing, corporate community involvement and investment will mean that the potential impact of any contribution can be enhanced.

Cause Related Marketing has the added dimension of being able to directly deliver against the general business, marketing and philanthropic objectives of an organization. Relationships between business and the wider community are no longer one-dimensional but multi-dimensional.

Relationships are formed on many different levels using a variety of approaches. I suggest that Cause Related Marketing will become a more dominant feature. It is clearly visible and reflects the mood of society which demands corporate citizenship and corporate social responsibility. Reluctance from companies to communicate their corporate community investment is no longer viable. To accrue the benefit of the investment from what is currently going on but is unknown and unrecognized, and, moreover, to counter accusations of lack of investment, companies in the future will need to demonstrate and communicate their programmes to stakeholders. At the same time I believe companies will become much more comfortable about talking about their cause partnerships, in an appropriate way, as they appreciate not only the business benefit but the cause benefit too.

Clearly, if a cause or charity is able to 'advertise' their corporate supporters it helps them to attract additional support. Businesses, I believe, will increasingly appreciate the leverage they have and the positive impact that talking about their relationship has for the particular cause or charity. Consumers want to know, indeed are increasingly demanding about the level of information they expect to have. Consumers are in fact suspicious if they are aware of a charity/cause–business partnership and are not clear on the 'deal'. Demands for greater transparency by consumers and other stakeholder groups, whilst potentially painful for some organizations, will lead to increased benefits for those without skeletons in their cupboards as well as for the charities and causes themselves.

Cause Related Marketing can meet so many business needs at the same time as having the potential to make a significant positive impact in the community.

> Cause Related Marketing is an effective way of enhancing corporate image, differentiating product and increasing both sales and loyalty ... Cause Related Marketing will become a natural part of successful business; it is after all no more than enlightened self-interest. A company promotes its products or services in conjunction with a good cause, raising money for the cause while at the same time enlisting consumer loyalty and purchase for its own products or services. Cause Related Marketing is part of the overall issue of corporate social responsibility.

Sir Dominic Cadbury, Chairman, Cadbury Schweppes plc, Founder of the Business in the Community Cause Related Marketing Campaign

The strength of Cause Related Marketing over more traditional forms of marketing is that it can provide the emotional as well as the rational engagement of the consumer. It engages the consumer's heart as well as the mind and thereby has the potential to build a much stronger longer-lasting bond based on much more than price and quality.

It is becoming more acceptable to talk appropriately about what organizations do in relation to the community in which they operate as it is increasingly understood that demonstrating, articulating and communicating corporate values is an essential part of business. Stakeholders increasingly want to know what stands behind the brand, what the values and beliefs of the organization are and whether the organization's intentions are honourable. As the world gets 'smaller' due to the advances in information and communications technology, stakeholders not only feel they have the right to know about an organization but have the means to investigate it. Transparency is an increasing fact of life. The more sophisticated companies appreciate and acknowledge the need to behave in an open, honest and transparent way, and by so doing understand the benefits to enhancing and investing in their corporate reputation.

Demonstrating corporate reputation

Cause Related Marketing is an outward demonstration of an inner system of beliefs and values. Finding ways of demonstrating and communicating the brand or corporate essence will, I think, be a key aspect of the future. Cause Related Marketing is ideally placed in this context as one way of actively demonstrating these values. As the stakeholder demands for the understanding of these values increases, so too will the opportunities for Cause Related Marketing.

Internal collaboration

Cause Related Marketing will present new opportunities to business in the way in which it operates. It will encourage much greater internal co-operation and collaboration. Departments will increasingly realize that Cause Related Marketing can deliver against their objectives and that by co-operation and collaboration mutual benefits can be achieved across the business. As the importance of corporate reputation rises up the corporate agenda, teams will, I am sure, be encouraged to work across departments and with other teams to find the most appropriate strategies, and in so doing Cause Related Marketing will be increasingly recognized as a viable option delivering against several different divisions objectives and contributing to the overall objective of enhanced corporate reputation. This is a key component of successful business.

The overall corporate values, vision and mission will, I believe, begin to dictate the area from which the cause or charity partners are sought. Marketing, human resources, philanthropy and other areas of business will increasingly work together to deliver the one overarching message from an organization. With the increasing pressure on budgets and return on investment, individuals within organizations will be forced to be more creative in finding ways of getting the budget to work harder. Clearly if one department can achieve its ends by partnering or 'piggy backing' on a campaign or initiative led or funded by another part of the business, everyone benefits.

This cross-department collaboration is where the challenges and opportunities lie for both the business and the charity or cause. The greater the breadth of business support for a cause, the greater the sustainability of that relationship, as it is founded on many relationships. In the next few years I anticipate we will see the 7Ps increasingly coming together in support of a particular cause or issue, using all of these different tools in concert to achieve a greater impact on the cause or issue (see Chapter 6).

It is the responsibility of everyone to look for these opportunities, to find the strategic fit and to leverage the benefit. These opportunities may include partnerships linking a Cause Related Marketing programme and a human resources strategy to increase employee morale and linking a Cause Related Marketing programme and a corporate affairs strategy to develop relationships with key opinion formers. There are so many permutations for cross-departmental co-operation and collaboration in pursuit of shared and departmental goals, and by identifying and fostering them, the potential positive impact is increased. There is no doubt that internal collaboration has enormous benefits, not only for the organization itself in terms of achieving its goals, but also for any external partnership. As one marketing director of a FTSE 100 company said to me, Cause Related Marketing provides him with the opportunity to leverage the chairman's budget!

The perceptive player in a Cause Related Marketing relationship will deliberately identify these linkages. From the cause point of view helping the business partner identify these opportunities not only helps the business meet a greater number of objectives through the relationship but further cements the partnership between the charity and the business. By creating as great a number of connections across different parts of the business as possible *and* increasing the overall pot of resources and funds in support of the charity or cause objective, the charity or cause will establish a multi-faceted relationship, providing greater security, leverage, and sustainability.

Leveraging the supply chain

Clearly there are a number of dynamics at work in any given relationship, be they internal within the organization, between the primary partners or indeed beyond that and through the supply chain. Cause Related Marketing is no different and can also impact beyond the immediate primary partners. This potential leverage of the supply chain is well demonstrated in the retail environment.

With the relative 'power' of the retailer, there is increasing evidence both in the UK, USA and further afield that this retailer dominance in many relationships can lead to supplier support of the retailers' and cause objectives. Of course such an approach clearly strengthens the supplier relationship with that retailer, thereby meeting the supplier's objectives.

TESCO PLC: Mencap Charity of the Year Relationship

An early example of how this can be demonstrated is the TESCO PLC: Mencap Charity of the Year relationship in 1997. This is strictly a one year relationship. Mencap was selected as the Charity of the Year which essentially meant that proceeds from TESCO PLC fundraising, be it staff fundraising, in-store activity or event sponsorship would go to Mencap.

Both Mencap and TESCO PLC were experienced in Cause Related Marketing and had appreciated the benefits. What had until then been a purely fundraising relationship with TESCO PLC and Mencap became a fundraising-plus relationship.

The Charity of the Year relationship between TESCO PLC and Mencap was further leveraged and saw TESCO PLC supplier involvement including Cause Related Marketing promotions with Calypso orange drink, a Dennis the Menace cake, mineral water, Sellotape and Princes Foods.

The TESCO PLC: Mencap partnership was therefore supported locally with staff fundraising and events whilst being leveraged nationally through the supply chain. Other retailers in the UK and USA have achieved similar leverage for the causes with whom they partnered. I believe we will see a lot more of this and not just amongst retailers but service providers too. This is not exclusively a retailer driven opportunity.

Pillsbury Customer Community Partnerships Programme

In America, Pillsbury, part of DIAGEO run a 'Pillsbury Customer Community Partnerships' programme which illustrates a similar approach but where the manufacturer is in the lead. The Pillsbury Community Relations Team developed this programme to build Pillsbury's reputation as a good corporate citizen and to involve other parts of the company and their retail customers in their community work.

The programme works through the community relations team, the sales and the marketing people who together identify a suitable retail grocery customer; one that is interested in community work and is keen to form partnerships and promote Pillsbury's products over an agreed period of time. In return Pillsbury agree to make a donation on the retailer's behalf to a local youth-focused non-profit organization.

Mechanics

The retailer features and provides merchandising support for Pillsbury's products and highlights the partnership and the non-profit in newspaper advertisements and store displays. In return the retailer gets a volume-building merchandising programme and public recognition for its charitable donation.

Pillsbury develops the partnership and makes a cash donation to a non-profit in the name of the retailer. In return it gets merchandising support for its products, high sales and an enhanced image as a contributor to the community.

The non-profit helps promote the partnership and receives a donation from Pillsbury and public exposure for its work as a result of advertising, in-store support and public relations activities.

Consumers benefit as well because they are helping local youth-serving programmes, while saving money on Pillsbury products.

Pillsbury selected these organizations through which local support is channelled: Big Brothers/Big Sisters of America, Boys and Girls Clubs of America and Second Harvest's Kids' Cafe.

The retailer displays and provides point-of-sale support for the Pillsbury products and highlights the cause related and the non profit through print advertising and in-store material. In return, the retailer gets a volume building programme and public recognition for its charitable donation.

Pillsbury further cements its relationship with the retailer, gets merchandise support and profile for its products, sales and an enhanced image in the local community and makes a cost donation to the non profit partner in the retailer's name.

The non profit helps promote the partnership and clearly receives a cost donation as well as profile for its cause. The consumer also benefits as through the course of their daily lives they are helping local youth projects whilst saving money on Pillsbury products.

Customer Community Partnerships are not just 'win-win' they are 'win-win-win-win' because the retailer, Pillsbury, the non profit and consumers all benefit.

Grand Metropolitan – Report on Corporate Citizenship 1997

In another market, Visa in America had great success through the 'Read Me a Story' campaign in encouraging a host of merchant partners as did American Express in its Charge Against Hunger Campaign with Share Our Strength (see Chapter 17).

These extensions of the primary partnerships will grow and develop over the next few years. The benefits of these strategic alliances are obvious. As suppliers to major retailers, if the supplier is supporting the chosen cause of the retailer, crudely put, the supplier is more likely to build goodwill and strong relations with the retailer.

It is not always retailer led, however, as the New Covent Garden Soup Company's relationship with Crisis indicates (see Chapter 16). In this case the retailer liked the idea of supporting Crisis and therefore decided to match the funds raised by New Covent Garden Soup Company through its Cause Related Marketing promotion. Not only did the cause therefore receive double the funds, but New Covent Garden Soup Company's relation with the retailer developed and they earned a greater amount of shelf space for their products. Clear business and cause benefits resulted from this leverage.

Strategic partnerships

Partnerships will continue to develop between businesses and between businesses, charities and causes. Increasingly I think we will see these partnerships developing well beyond that. Strategic alliance is a buzz phrase and is usually used in the context of business-to-business relationships in pursuit of a commercial objective. Currently we are seeing these strategic alliances forming between businesses with charities or causes as appreciation of how these relationships can enhance corporate and brand reputation develops. Likewise we are also beginning to see strategic alliances between causes and charities themselves as charities too appreciate the benefits of working together to achieve greater impact and benefit.

Waterstone's and Crisis

The *Book of Stars*, a collection of original writing by celebrity authors was created through a collaboration between Random House and Waterstone's. This was on sale in Waterstone's stores with all profits donated to Crisis. To leverage the programme Crisis involved two more of its non-competing corporate supporters. Jigsaw Menswear stocked the book and displayed it in their store windows, and Majestic Wine supplied the wine for wine tasting in Waterstone's, with Waterstone's donating to Crisis the money saved on the cost of the wine.

Strategic alliances are therefore not confined to just the business sector and greater impact is achieved for all by the nature of leverage.

The Children's Miracle Network in the USA is a clear example of the value of the whole being greater than the sum of the parts, as is the Jeans for Genes day concept in the UK. The Children's Promise concept which was launched by Marks & Spencer in partnership with The New Millennium Experience Company in June 1998 in the UK is another example of strategic co-operation within the charity sector whereby seven charities have come together, each 'promising' to achieve a particular objective for the millennium under the umbrella of 'The Children's Promise'.

The aim is to persuade everyone in the UK to 'donate the value of their final hour's earnings of this millennium so that the children of the next have the basic right to a happy, healthy, safe and more fulfilling future'. Funds will be split between the seven charities in order to help them fund their individual objectives (see Table 27.1).

By coming together and focusing the message on 'children' in a year which will be crowded with initiatives, highly competitive and potentially cluttered, the intention is that through this strategic alliance the charities together are more likely to achieve publicity and funds by projecting themselves through

Table 27.1 Charities participating in 'The Children's Promise'

Name of charity	The charity promises...
Barnardo's	The best start in life and the best opportunities for children
BBC Children in Need	To help even more children in need through small children's charities and voluntary organizations
ChildLine	A telephone lifeline for children in trouble or danger
The Children's Society working with Aberlour Child Care Trust in Scotland and EXTERN in Northern Ireland	A safety net for runaways and young people at risk on the street
Comic Relief	A fairer, brighter, safer future for some of the world's poorest children
NCH Action for Children	A place to go for children in every community for help and support
NSPCC working with Children 1st in Scotland	To help rebuild the lives of abused children

one message. The whole is greater than the sum of the parts and gives a greater chance for each charity to achieve its fundraising objectives. In the near future I think we will also see examples of groups of businesses coming together working as one in partnership with a particular cause or charity or groups of charities to achieve objectives.

Research indicates that fundraising for Cause Related Marketing programmes, whilst increasingly coming from marketing budgets, is also supported by corporate community investment and corporate affairs budgets (see Figure 12.2).

The strategic partnerships within and across the business or charity sector however will lead to a more creative approach to funding with a multitude of budgets and resources potentially being identified, released and harnessed in pursuit of mutual objectives. This creative approach and quest for additional support should not be confined to the business or charity sectors. The government and non-governmental bodies like the UN, WHO, etc., both national and international, should also be considered as potential sources of support. This support could range from passive endorsement to active matched funding. In the UK and Europe, government and European Union funding can be available. It is often the case that, if commitment and support can be generated amongst business and the local community, the government or other body can match fund on the basis of certain ratios particular to the nature of the budget protocol or initiative.

Imagine a situation where the government priority is to increase literacy, and has funds to support it, and a business aims through a Cause Related Marketing programme to fund a way of providing books for schools. Creative partnering of these objectives and resources could lead to a much greater impact. As businesses, charities and causes realize the potential and begin to try to release it, I believe we will see greater research amongst all groups to identify where the objectives and funding between business, charities, causes and the government, intersect.

Global affinity

Taking these strategic partnerships to their logical conclusion we of course then have global affinities which are well demonstrated through programmes such as J&B Care for the Rare, a programme launched in 1993 which involved over 20 projects working closely with established conservation organizations around the world, and the Avon Crusade Against Breast Cancer. The Avon Crusade is a global Cause Related Marketing campaign that is delivered locally, nationally and internationally through a number of such partnerships (see Chapter 17, Case study V).

Cause Related Marketing has been considered by some as being the domain of the business and that charities are the passive recipient waiting to be selected. Clearly business does have the money and further resources, but the reason that a business is considering a link with a cause is because the cause or charity has something to offer of value to the business. The power of charities' brands are also increasingly understood by the charities themselves as well as businesses. Over time I believe we will increasingly find some charities taking the lead in these discussions.

> Some causes will gain the upper hand as their brands become stronger than the commercial brands they associate themselves with. After all, it is the causes' emotional bonds with their supporters that commercial brands want to tap into: the very fact that commercial brands feel the need to do this is an admission of their emotional (and perhaps moral) emptiness.

> **Alan Mitchell, Freelance Marketing Journalist**

It is already the case both in the UK and the USA that some non-profit organizations will not consider a partnership with a business unless it can guarantee to make a minimum contribution of £25,000. There is every chance that we will see charities asking businesses to pitch for relationships with them; indeed reports suggest that this is already the case in some markets.

For some time a number of charities have developed and have been developing their own product ranges under licence and this trend is increasing. In time we may well see interesting tensions and relationships developing between charities and the commercial brands themselves. Alan Mitchell encapsulates this thought:

> Causes will establish themselves as fully fledged 'passion' brands in their own right. Causes and companies will increasingly co-operate – and sometimes compete – in the same broad market, for share of customer trust and emotional attachment, and for share of purse . . . both sides approach to Cause Related Marketing will change. Occasions of conflict between cause brands and traditional brands will become more common as for example causes launch more 'own brand' products and services to raise revenue. On the other hand, successful Cause Related Marketing relationships will become more akin to traditional commercial strategic and brand alliances, with 'win-win' objectives expanding to include both sides' financial strategic, brand and marketing objectives.

Tax incentives

In the next few years in the UK, I am sure we will see consideration given to tax incentives and benefits for investing in the wider community. This would bring the UK market more in line with North America. Tax relief on funds invested in the community inevitably makes such activity more attractive from a business point of view, and as such will itself lead to even greater consideration of Cause Related Marketing.

In the UK in January 1999 the Rt. Hon. Tony Blair MP, Prime Minister, launched the 'Giving Age':

> We are warned often enough where society is heading – to an atomized, individualized, selfish, computer obsessed, lonely soulless hell. A society where rules and values count for nothing, respect for others dwindles, where money matters more than humanity. This is not what people want . . . In its place people yearn for a society that heals itself, a politics that reduces division, intolerance and inequality[1].

With this lead indicated from government where it is hoped that the millennium will be marked with an 'explosion in giving, acts of community' the environment for tax review and concession looks encouraging.

Against this backdrop, arguments for a much simpler and more encouraging tax approach which supports and rewards charity, community and social investment are likely to have a better reception.

> Government could encourage companies to disclose what business is doing, where and with what overall impact on communities affected. It could also consider tax incentives for good corporate citizenship.
>
> **David Grayson, CBE (1998)[2]**

Allowing companies to offset their donations in either cash or goods against their corporation tax bill and reductions in National Insurance contributions for employees that are seconded or volunteering should also receive a better reception, and, if adopted, are likely to see a greater incidence and consideration of all forms of business contribution to the wider community, including Cause Related Marketing. With marketing budgets some eight times the size of community affairs budgets[3] if marketing investment can be encouraged and has beneficial tax treatment, the potential of Cause Related Marketing both in providing much needed resources in to the community and as an effective marketing tool, the future is potentially very exciting.

As Tony Blair went on to say at the 1999 Annual Conference of the National Council of Voluntary Organizations:

> In the first half of this century, we learnt that the community cannot achieve its aims without the help of government providing essential services and a backdrop of security. In the second half of the century we learnt that government cannot achieve

its aims without the energy and commitment of others – voluntary organizations, business, and critically the wider public.

Reduction in government funding and its ability to support all society's needs is not a phenomenon unique to the UK. The USA, the former Soviet Union and indeed many governments around the world are reducing their support of society's basic requirements and are looking at the wider community, business, individuals and the voluntary sector to fill this void. In this environment, government and the consumers are increasingly looking to business to fill this vacuum (see Chapter 11).

As Jerry Wright, Senior Strategist at Unilever plc argues:

> Large corporations play an ever increasing role in the global economy and so have a greater impact on global society. People in their dual role as consumers and citizens will expect companies to use their power and influence wisely and to meet their needs more effectively.
>
> Cause Related Marketing is one part of the portfolio of ways that companies will respond to these demands – helping them to contribute to the development of the societies in which they operate, as well as enabling them to build long-term benefits for brands.

Consumer expectations

Consumer expectations of business have been growing and show no signs of abating. We underestimate the intelligence and perception of the consumer at our peril. The majority are now very brand literate; socially aware; news reading; they know what is going on. Consumers care not just about the tangible aspects of products and services but the labour used to produce them, the renewable resources used in its manufacture, how much profit is made and what happens to that profit. Research clearly supports this trend, indicating in some cases the potential for the vigilante consumer (see Chapter 13). An extreme example is the labelling of all fur coats sold in Beverly Hills. They may soon have to carry labels which state:

> Consumer notice: This product is made with fur from animals that may have been killed by electrocution, gassing, neck breaking, poisoning, clubbing, stomping or drowning and may have been trapped in steel-jaw, leg-hold traps.[4]

The Times, 4 February 1999

It has been reported[4] that half the local councils in Beverly Hills have approved the concept, with a final reading due in the summer of 1999.

The intangibles are also of core importance, as the earlier discussion on corporate reputation and values suggests. The service industry is growing and consumers are increasingly buying beyond the functional benefits of a product or service and increasingly focused on the values behind the corporate, brand, product or service. This trend will, I believe, develop further over the next few years. What was value added yesterday, is value expected today. What was perhaps regarded as a superior intellectual position in the past is taken as a given today. Taking a stand against child labour, testing on animals or polluting the environment and other such issues were at the leading edge of the business ethics agenda and practice a decade ago. Today in the world of social and environmental auditing these issues are increasingly regarded as a basic requirement of good business practice.

Couple this with the growing speed and accessibility of information technology readily available giving consumers a wealth of information at a touch of a button means that not only is the world 'getting smaller' but it is increasingly transparent. A mistake, be it an environmental disaster or an infringement of employment law on one side of the world, will be transmitted and known about on the other side of the world within moments. Compliance will not work as a defence in the 'global village' in which we now live. It will not be sufficient to be operating within the law of a community if other communities believe that law to be unjust. Today's environment demands compliance plus. Whether or not information is accurate, consumer perceptions can be influenced in the matter of seconds it takes the information to be shared around the world. And despite the suggestion that we are suffering from information overload, the consumer seems to have an insatiable appetite for news, good and bad.

As John Ballington, Corporate and Consumer Affairs Director at Lever Brothers Ltd, said:

> Bringing the consumer's agenda, their concerns, preferences, dreams and desires into the brand's agenda has always been the challenge for marketers. The new dimension is that social responsibility is increasingly part of the consumer's agenda and how enduring brands can fulfil this need, is the new challenge ... Cause Related Marketing will increasingly provide the tools for brands and businesses to get involved within a manageable transparent framework that provides a win/win logic. The future is bright for Cause Related Marketing.

Managing the organization's reputation, messages and impact on society is a vital marketing function. Being seen to demonstrate the values of the corporation or brand through practical action is increasingly important as part of the development and reinforcement of those values. Cause Related

Marketing is one of the most visible ways of doing just that. With the power and skills of marketing and communication, the impact of an organization's investment in a charity, cause or the wider community can be brought to life through Cause Related Marketing. Based on this, well planned, implemented and communicated Cause Related Marketing will grow because it can address so many of these issues effectively and provide a win for all.

Consolidation of markets means the world is getting tougher; competition is getting fiercer and actually gaining and sustaining competitive advantage in this environment is increasingly challenging. It requires managing all aspects of the business in projecting a consistent image and message.

Failure to do so on all fronts can result in the wrath of the vigilante consumer who is not just the 18–35 year old who demonstrates with placards and ties themselves to trees, but is also the over 55s, 53 per cent of whom supported law breaking if they felt that practices were unjust or wrong. In addition, 65 per cent of the 45–54 age group, who on average tend to have more spending power than other groups, claimed that they were more likely to stop doing business with a company as a form of protest[5]. It is also interesting to consider the importance of this age group to businesses and the wider community as the population ages. The Employers Forum on Age have projected that by 2026 the 55–64 age group will form the largest group in the working age population at 24 per cent, having increased by 3 million from 15 per cent in 1996.

Sally Shire, Head of Brand Management at Barclays Plc, believes that:

> Cause Related Marketing is approaching a cross-roads. One path will lead to Cause Related Marketing becoming an integrated part of a company's marketing mix. It will help companies express the 'personality' of their brands enabling them to forge closer relationships with their customers. However to achieve this, companies will also need to develop long-term relationships with their cause.
>
> Managed properly this could provide significant opportunities for charities and other non-profit organizations which will also be able to use Cause Related Marketing to build their brands and create relationships.
>
> The other path is much less rewarding for us all – companies, non profits, their causes and beneficiaries, and consumers. The second option is that Cause Related Marketing remains a marginal activity, understood and practised by a minority of companies and causes. It's our choice!

Thomas Cowper Johnson, Group Brand Manager for Norwich Union, had a similar view.

> I see two futures for Cause Related Marketing. One where marketers try to exploit Cause Related Marketing at a marginal level, creating sales promotions designed to make their consumers 'feel good'. This future has no future.

Alternatively marketers will see Cause Related Marketing as further evidence of a new set of consumer evolves. As a result, Cause Related Marketing will become central to their marketing strategies, shaping decisions about product, service and communications. In this future Cause Related Marketing will become the bedrock of the customer relationship.

Whilst the consumer is increasingly independent in their access to information, they are on the other hand increasingly expectant of a business to supply their every need. In so doing it is vital to therefore understand the motivations and emotional attachments consumers want to have with the products, services brands and companies with which they do business. Price and quality are still the key differentiators and they are increasingly taken for granted. If price and quality are equal then it is essential that the brand positioning is built on a series of values which are demonstrated in every aspect of the way the organization conducts its business. It is these emotional attributes that are and become the differentiators. Strong brands connect with the rational but also the emotional level, and, as has been seen from the research, a fundamental attribute of Cause Related Marketing is its ability to rationally as well as emotionally engage the consumer. For this reason Cause Related Marketing will grow.

John Stubbs, Chief Executive of The Marketing Council, considers:

> Cause Related Marketing allows the firm and its customers to share a deeper commitment to the community, on which they both depend. There is a new breed of demanding and discriminating consumers who favour marketing that transcends the frivolous and banal. For them Cause Related Marketing offers an extra reason to buy.

As was clearly highlighted in The Game Plan[6] consumers have less and less time to volunteer and are increasingly making purchasing decisions in a 'hit and run shopping' environment.

> In this day and age we all visit the supermarket and if you're given the chance to donate to charity through that . . . Possibly 20, 30, 40 years ago everyone went to church and you gave to charity through that, whereas people don't go to church, they go to the supermarket. Thinking it through, it's probably a good idea.[7]

In this environment key differentiators are essential to engage the consumer and Cause Related Marketing can be a key differentiator. Through Cause Related Marketing, by going about their daily business, consumers have the opportunity to make a difference.

According to Bob Thacker, Senior Vice President for Marketing, at Sears Roebuck:

> Cause Related Marketing provides an excellent alternative as by going about their regular shopping they are able to give something back and invest in their communities. Cause Related Marketing really does suit today's realities.

From a short-term point of view the opportunity is for organizations – be they business, charities or causes – to seize the day. Some organizations may look at Cause Related Marketing as a tactical opportunity; many will start from that point. The opportunity however and indeed the evidence suggests that provided these programmes are well constructed and that they do in fact deliver mutual benefit, what may start as a one-off tactical promotion, may turn into a long-term sustainable partnership. The TESCO Computers for Schools programme is a case in point (see Chapter 16). This began as a one-off Cause Related Marketing sales promotion, and is now in its eighth year having contributed the equivalent of one computer for every school in England, Scotland and Wales.

Championing a cause

It could be argued that TESCO PLC in the UK 'own' the area of IT in education. Education is a key concern for parents, the key consumers for TESCO PLC, and TESCO PLC are seen as the champions of a key part of this cause. This has been achieved through long-term sustainable investment and commitment and through growing the programme over time and developing the various Cause Related Marketing mechanics in line with teachers', pupils' and consumers' needs.

I believe we will increasingly see organizations championing particular causes so that in the consumers' mind company X is synonymous with cause or charity Y thereby using Cause Related Marketing to further build and reinforce key brand attributes.

There will I believe be far less 'promiscuity' of organizations jumping from one cause to another. After all if the planning and preparation have been carried out thoroughly, the organization should be very clear what cause is most appropriate for them. Having invested the time, effort and money in reaching that conclusion, increasingly we will see partnerships lasting and looking for the long-term return on that investment, developing the programme and relationships within the parameters of the identified cause or charity. Partnerships will become much deeper and therefore have a greater impact on the core values and enhancement of the corporate and the brands involved. This will also mean that the charities and causes will have far more reliable income and resource streams allowing much more long-term planning.

Developments and innovations

In the last few years there have been some interesting developments, extensions and innovations with regard to Cause Related Marketing in the UK. The simple sales promotion mechanic of a donation triggered by purchase is an effective staple approach and will continue as the market grows. However, there are many others which reflect the impact of the ICT (information and communications technology) revolution, the expectation of greater choice and personalization, the insistence on greater transparency and ethical conduct.

On-pack

There have also been examples in the UK of creative uses of resources. New Covent Garden Soup and its relationships with both the National Trust and Crisis saw the use of the product packaging, not only to communicate the Cause Related Marketing 'offer' which was to raise money for a National Trust project in one case and to raise funds through a telephone hotline for Crisis in the other, but also used the packaging to communicate the message of the cause (see Chapter 16). In the case of the National Trust partnership this included using the same amount of space to thank customers for their participation as was used for communicating the Cause Related Marketing partnership, completing the communications loop.

The National Missing Persons Help Line in their relationship with Iceland Frozen Food used the side of milk cartons to 'ask' consumers to help try and find missing people. This message went out on thousands of milk cartons per week and was seen in 770 stores – a simple but extremely innovative use of product packaging to engage the consumer's help and address a very real issue. It is not only about a donation triggered by purchase, although of course cash is so important. Awareness of the cause and calls to action can be equally important and effective.

New media

As new media develops so too do the potential opportunities to increase and communicate corporate and charity brand visions and values. New media also provides additional means to communicate a Cause Related Marketing partnership and the call to action to support it. Clearly with the growth and access to all types of new media including the Internet, the ways in which Cause Related Marketing partnerships can be leveraged and communicated will develop. Fundraising on the net is already a growing area as are corporate sponsored websites. As the technology and the medium grow so too will the opportunities.

We will see more Cause Related Marketing campaigns planned to incorporate a strong Internet element. Aside from the predicted growth of the net, there is an obvious reason for this: both the world-wide web and Cause Related Marketing programmes are about links.

Robert Gray, Freelance Marketing Journalist

First Direct's Anorak Amnesty with Shelter

First Direct, the pioneering telephone banking business in the UK, created a Cause Related Marketing partnership to launch to their website. Building on the concept that customers expect the unexpected from First Direct, an innovative partnership was developed with Shelter. Traditionally the Internet had been linked with computer buffs, or 'anoraks', but with the Internet fast becoming part of everyday life for more and more people, First Direct wanted to develop the premise that you don't need to be an 'anorak' to surf the web or indeed to visit their website.

The Anorak Amnesty, a national appeal supported by press, was launched as the First Direct website went live. The website detailed the 'amnesty', the work of the charity, linking to the Shelter website and encouraged visitors to the site to donate their old anoraks and other coats to Shelter. These would then be resold through Shelter's 84 national shops for between £4 and £30. Thousands of anoraks were donated including those from Hugh Grant, Elton John, Julian Clary, Helen Mirren, Tim Henman, Patsy Palmer and Mystic Meg which were auctioned on the Internet.

Technogiving

I am sure that as SMART card technology continues to develop and purchasing becomes more automated, we will see retailers and others fully utilizing and extending the capabilities of their electronic point-of-sale systems, etc. Donation direct from swipe cards and bar codes for instance will become the efficient way of managing the process of calculating and distributing any donation. The statement systems will also be used as a key communications tool to acknowledge and celebrate the contribution.

As consumers become increasingly comfortable shopping over the Internet, this has provided a new, interactive and additional source of Cause Related Marketing revenue which is being labelled as 'technogiving'. Companies such as Shop2Give, Charityweb, iGive and 4Charity host Internet shopping mall sites and make donations to causes when customers browse and shop on-line. Customers register as members of these sites and then nominate the cause they want to support.

In the case of iGive the charities supported can range from a large registered non-profit to a small community operation. By the beginning of 1999, 38,885 members had signed up, supporting 4300 causes, and they reported a total of $265,830 as already having been donated.

Concern however has been expressed over the effectiveness of these sites as a fundraising mechanism for charities. Problems have arisen for businesses hosting these types of sites in verifying the charities consumers nominate to receive their funds. Other problems have arisen in the distribution of funds, with charities having to wait, until for example a $10 threshold is met, before receiving any donations. In addition to this, criticisms have been made that these sites are using charities' names without approval and in the US state regulators and charity watchdogs are apparently suspicious that many of these sites are not accountable, with only a few – Greatergood, Shop2Give and 4Charity – saying that they have registered under state law to do Cause Related Marketing.

Ad share

In terms of new media, the 'HelpAd' concept illustrates the creativity that is being applied to fundraising and Cause Related Marketing. A concept initiated by Bob Doyle of Interfriendship and developed by the International Red Cross, HelpAd was launched into the marketplace in October 1996. Essentially a product allows HelpAd, a trading arm of the Red Cross, the right to sell space on its packaging to another company or product inside a HelpAd framed logo. HelpAd sell the opportunity to advertise on this space to a complimentary brand. HelpAd has now raised over £500,000 to help support Red Cross work at home and abroad.

A diverse range of brands have taken advantage of the HelpAd mechanism, for example, Hovis bread has hosted a number of advertisements on its packaging; including ones for a brand of butter and a brand of chocolate spread. The host brands are seen to be supportive of a good cause and benefit from positive consumer perception of the brand. The advertising brand has a unique opportunity to be positioned alongside the affinity product and encourages the likelihood of purchase, the consumers benefit from buying the product, knowing that their action supports a good cause and the Red Cross receives substantial funds and awareness.

This is a new medium which is increasingly establishing itself and I am sure we will see this and other innovations develop over time as individuals who appreciate the mutual benefits of Cause Related Marketing, look for creative ways to develop and leverage the opportunity.

Self-selection

Choice and customization have been key features of the 1990s. In Cause Related Marketing terms this has been reflected in the way some programmes have been designed. Most notably the affinity credit card market has provided examples of this approach in action (see Chapter 15).

As an example, the Co-operative Bank in the UK introduced the 'Customers Who Care Scheme' in 1994. It was planned to last one year but due to its success has continued ever since and by the end of 1998 had raised £1,335,022 for charities.

The scheme is straightforward and enables customers to support a variety of worthwhile causes. For every £100 spent using their Co-operative Bank visa Credit Card, £1.25p is donated to charity by the Bank. Each quarter consumers vote for one of four charities nominated by the Bank and the money raised is then divided in relation to the number of votes received for each.

> Perhaps the most attractive aspect of the scheme is that everyone wins. Large amounts of money are donated with no effort required. It doesn't cost our customers or causes a penny. And we of course, benefit from the increased usage of our credit cards.
>
> **Jim Sinclair, Group Marketing Manager, Co-operative Bank**[8]

There are other variations on this theme. This approach of using payment cards has also been developed by retailers in the USA and has been piloted in the UK. In these cases again through using a payment card, money is donated to a good cause and in some of these trials examples, the good cause is the local school as nominated by the individual customer.

The trend towards customer choice in selecting the good causes will, I am sure, develop over the next few years.

Options for the future

Cause Related Marketing in my opinion has three options.

First, this high road whereby Cause Related Marketing is seen and developed as a strategic marketing and fundraising tool through which the organization's core objectives, visions and values are connected, and as a result, long-term sustainable programmes are constructed based on integrity and mutual benefit.

Alternatively, Cause Related Marketing will be exploited by short-termist attitudes that see the opportunity only as a short-term, one-off, one-hit sales promotion which is one of a series of two- or three-month promotions which do little to reinforce the brand or corporate values. Whilst this approach can have positive short-term impacts it could expose the brand to potential accusations of band-wagoning, cynical exploitation and worse.

The third option is that an increasing number of organizations will begin to appreciate the strategic potential of Cause Related Marketing in its ability to deliver serious business objectives whilst at the same time making a positive impact on a particular cause or issue. As a first step, pilot programmes will be put in place but the aspiration is for the pilot programme to become the long-term sustainable partnership for that organization where they intend partnerships with the charity or cause to make a significant difference. The third option is therefore seeing Cause Related Marketing being tested as pilot programmes as part of an overall strategic vision to invest in the wider community and make a long-term sustainable difference. The future lies in using the power of the brands in partnership to change behaviour and address key social issues, making a positive impact on society. The future is about the full integration of the needs of the business with the needs of society, for the benefit of all.

The future of Cause Related Marketing lies in appropriate relationships with all stakeholders be they employees, consumers, suppliers, opinion formers, or the community in which the business operates and indeed the wider community. The relationships with the wider community which include charities and causes must be sustainable and founded on the key principles of integrity, transparency, sincerity, mutual respect, partnership and mutual benefit.

The future for Cause Related Marketing is about partnerships and not patrons; it's about strengthening the ties that bind.

Notes

1 The Rt Hon. Tony Blair MP, Prime Minister, launching The Giving Age at the Annual Conference of the National Council of Voluntary Organizations (January 1999).

2 Grayson, D. CBE (1998) Communities and Partnerships, A Business in the Community paper prepared for Committee of Inquiry: Into a new vision for business.

3 The Corporate Survey II (1998) Business in the Community quantitative Cause Related Marketing research conducted by Research International (UK) Ltd.

4 *The Times*, 4 February 1999, p. 14 "Fur flies out West as 'pelt posse' rides to animals' rescue"

5 The Vigilante Consumer and The New Honesty (1996), research by GGT.

6 The Game Plan (1997), Business in the Community qualitative consumer research into Cause Related Marketing conducted by Research International (UK) Ltd.
7 The Game Plan (1997), Business in the Community qualitative consumer research into Cause Related Marketing conducted by Research International (UK) Ltd.
8 In Touch Customer Newsletter, Spring 1996.

Many thanks are extended to Roger Beale and *The Financial Times* for their kind permission to use this cartoon.

Index